RETAIL MARKETING

Edited by
GARY AKEHURST
and
NICHOLAS ALEXANDER

FRANK CASS • LONDON

First published in Great Britain by
FRANK CASS & CO LTD
Newbury House, 900 Eastern Avenue
London IG2 7HH, England

and in the United States by
FRANK CASS
c/o ISBS
5804 N.E. Hassalo Street, Portland, Oregon 97213-3644

Library of Congress Cataloging-in-Publication Data
Applied for.

British Library Cataloguing in Publication Data
Applied for.

ISBN 0-7146-4175-8

This group of studies first appeared in *The Services Industries Journal*, 1984–95,
published by Frank Cass & Co. Ltd.

Printed in Great Britain by
Antony Rowe Ltd., Chippenham, Wilts

RETAIL MARKETING

Contents

Introduction   **Gary Akehurst and Nicholas Alexander**   vii

1 The Status of Marketing in the UK Service Industries   **Graham Hooley and Donald Cowell**   1

2 Problems Confronting UK Retailing Organisations   **Gordon E. Greenley and David Shipley**   13

3 An Empirical Overview of Marketing by Retailing Organisations   **Gordon E. Greenley and David Shipley**   25

4 The Status Quo of the Marketing Organisation in UK Retailing: A Neglected Phenomenon   **Nigel Piercy and Nicholas Alexander**   43

5 The Impact of New Technology on Services Marketing   **Nigel Piercy**   64

6 Customer Service in Retailing   **Leigh Sparks**   76

7 Retail Location at the Micro-Scale: Inventory and Prospect   **Stephen Brown**   96

8 The Retail Park: Customer Usage and Perceptions of a Retailing Innovation   **Stephen Brown**   131

9 Tenant Mix, Tenant Placement and Shopper Behaviour in a Planned Shopping Centre   **Stephen Brown**   144

10 Elements of a Franchise: The Experiences of Established Firms   **Jim Forward and Christina Fulop**   164

11 Retail Buying in the United Kingdom   **David Swindley**   184

12 A Comparison between Dutch and   **René G.J. Den Hertog**
    German Retail Price Setting   **and A. Roy Thurik**   196

13 Shopping Motives   **Francis Buttle and Marilyn Coates**   204

14 Shopping Motives Constructionist Perspective   **Francis Buttle**   215

Further Reading   235

Notes on Contributors   237

Introduction

This collection of articles, previously published in *The Service Industries Journal*, explores the emerging and diverse world of retail marketing. We have not set out to create a conceptual framework for the analysis of retail marketing functions and problems, as others, such as McGoldrich [1990] and Collins [1992] have done; rather we have concentrated on organisational aspects of retail marketing and certain aspects of the retail marketing mix such as customer care, retail location, buying and pricing together with an understanding of shopper motives. This book supplements existing texts and, we modestly hope, adds to the body of retail marketing knowledge while providing an introduction to this growing field of study.

This collection traces the development of retail marketing through the 1980s into the early 1990s. Many of the papers are classics, often taking up analysis and explanation in areas previously unexplored or documented, and therefore can fairly lay claim to having advanced our understanding of this emerging area of study labelled 'retail marketing'.

The marketing concept has been well defined by Jobber [1995] as 'companies achieving their profit and other objectives by satisfying (even delighting) customers' [Jobber, 1995:4; Houston, 1886]. But businesses must do more than this; they must go beyond merely satisfying customers, they must do better than their competitors not only in attracting new customers but also in retaining existing customers. Jobber, therefore, gives us a good working definition of the modern marketing concept – 'the achievement of corporate goals through meeting and exceeding customer needs better than competition' [Jobber, 1995: 5].

The market-driven company shows concern for the customer throughout the organisation, throughout all functions and departments. Such a company tries to understand how customers choose their purchases, identify the criteria they use, and tries to ensure that the marketing mix meets those criteria better than the competition. Investment in marketing research is therefore as important as innovation and striving for competitive advantage.

Understanding customers and developing an integrated marketing organisation is essential before the marketing mix is developed further. This mix traditionally has four main elements: product, price, promotion and place. For the retailer, these four elements may appear obvious – which range of products and services should be offered, where, at what price, and how these activities should be advertised, promoted and developed. Not only should the marketing mix meet and match customer needs, but the elements should form a coherent whole or theme, a consistent message should be communicated to the target audience and the mix should match corporate resources.

There has been an incredible growth in retailing since 1945, with a shift in the manufacturer–retailer relationship (engendered in part by increasing concentration), such that retailers now have considerable power in marketing consumer products [Gabor, 1977; Walters, 1979; Monopolies and Mergers Commission, 1981; Office of Fair Trading, 1985]. Changing and increasing concentration [Akehurst, 1983], the decline in numbers of shops but increasing numbers of multiple retailers together with the emergence of franchising in the late 1980s [Seaman, 1988] have all combined to make retail marketing of peculiar importance.

Whereas previously the channels of distribution were reasonably well specified, and the place and functions of the retailer well defined in terms of buying, stocking, promoting, displaying, selling, delivering and financing the transfer of goods to the end-user, we can now add further functions of design, production, branding and pricing. Many retailers have now undertaken the function of physical distribution and often have significant inputs into the design and production of products.

The retailing mix has been defined by Lazer and Kelley [1961] as 'the total package of goods and services that a store offers for sale to the public. The retail mix, then, is the composite of all effort which was programmed by management and which embodies the adjustment of the retail store to its market environment'. Definitions, of course, are one thing, reality may be another. Managerial decisions need to be made concerning the mix, which has both tangible and intangible components; it is part product, part service and in the case of retailing there is a distribution element. This concept of a composite package of tangibles and intangibles is an accepted part of services management literature.

McGoldrich [1990: 7] introduces a useful discussion of the retail marketing mix elements such as product range, product image, consumer franchise or loyalty, shelf price, shelving, distribution and advertising. There is insufficient space to introduce a detailed discussion of these specifically retailing elements and refinements but the reader could do no better than to refer to McGoldrich's book [McGoldrich, 1990].

The development of a marketing function and implementation of the modern marketing concept within retail businesses has been a relatively new development which gathered pace during the 1980s. Piercy, in particular, has analysed the development of the implementation of the marketing concept, and made recommendations as to how the marketing function should be organised in retail businesses [Piercy, 1987a; 1987b; 1988]. Piercy shows and explains the different emphases within the different types of marketing department, from the 'high-integration' marketing department, where responsibility is taken for all marketing strategies, plans and tasks, through to the 'merchandising-oriented' marketing department (where the traditional buy-ing/merchandising activities are foremost) through to the 'services-oriented' department (where the functions of marketing research and advertising are carried out but with less involvement in other marketing functions).

The development of personal transport, and in particular the car, has increased the catchment areas of stores and, as a consequence, the intensity of competition over a wider spatial area. Above all, the car enables one-stop shopping. This places at a premium the need for each retail business to have up-to-date marketing intelligence feeding into a well-developed marketing information system, which in turn informs managerial decision-making both at the tactical and strategic levels.

As competition has intensified so different retail formats have been devised. Retail formats based on price, convenience and service have been tried using different combinations of these essential elements, so that we have seen for example, low-price-low-service outlets at one end of the format con-tinuum and high-price-high-service at the other.

Along with different formats we have witnessed different sizes of stores, with superstores (generally considered to be over 25,000 sq ft) and hyper-markets (over 50,000 sq ft). We have also seen the development of shopping centres, especially since the mid-1970s when the development of the out-of-town shopping centre gathered momentum. Schiller [1987] has identified three waves of out-of-town development: food led by the superstore groups; bulky goods retailing (carpets, DIY, furniture, large electrical goods, and gar-den centres); and clothing and other comparison shopping. Schiller goes on to describe the four main types of out-of-town shopping centre – *speciality cen-tres* (small, independent shops), *district centres* (offering a mix of goods with an 'anchoring' superstore), *retail parks* (started as groupings of retail ware-houses) and *regional centres*, such as the Metro Centre, Gateshead, near Newcastle.

The changing motives, habits and preferences of consumers are widely documented [see, for instance, McGoldrich, 1990: 69]. Tauber [1972], for example, focused attention on why people shop, that is, concentrating on shopping as an activity rather than the fulfilment of the basic need to purchase goods for survival. Personal motives include diversion from the daily routine, self-gratification to alleviate boredom or loneliness, physical exercise and sensory stimulation. Added to these personal motives are social motives, of social experiences or interaction, status and pleasure from shopping around for bargains.

While each customer has different needs and motives it would be very dif-ficult to adjust the business marketing mix to an individual customer. Therefore, retail marketers endeavour to identify reasonably homogeneous groups or segments of consumers to target. There has thus been a search to develop systematic approaches to market segmentation, targeting and hence positioning. We need to understand the needs of viable market segments in order to select the most appropriate target segments. In turn, selection of target segments includes evaluation of several criteria listed by Mason and Mayer [1987]; these criteria include size and future growth potential of the segment, investment required, strength of present and expected competition, and profit potential.

Following selection and evaluation of the most appropriate target markets, the retail business must position the retail mix in order 'to serve the target customers most effectively and profitably' [McGoldrich, 1990: 112]. This positioning must be favourably perceived by the target customers. Walters [1989] shows positioning as the cumulative effect of four functional strategies: merchandise strategy, format strategy, customer service strategy and customer communications strategy.

In the first essay in this collection, Graham Hooley and Donald Cowell describe the status of marketing in UK service industries based on a sample of 320 service oriented companies. The study had been commissioned by the Institute of Marketing as part of a major investigation into the status, practice and performance of marketing in British industry. At the time the authors were writing [1985], marketing in service companies lagged behind product companies; in particular, there was a marked difference in inclination to plan for the future.

The second paper by Gordon Greenley and David Shipley is a report of a survey carried out in the late 1980s on the nature, prevalence and importance of major problems facing retailers, including those of the competitive environment, customer environment, other external environment problems, labour force, general management and manufacturer–retailer relations.

The third chapter, again written by Gordon Greenley and David Shipley, investigates the way British retailing organisations use marketing. Not surprisingly they found room for improvements to be made. Three findings stand out as particularly significant: first, the most highly rated source of marketing information was considered by retail respondents to be management judgement (well before marketing research and test marketing); second, executive judgement was given far more importance than customer requests, sales assistants' suggestions and marketing research as influences on the composition of the product mix; and third, attractive prices were the most highly rated promotional device.

Nigel Piercy and Nicholas Alexander describe and analyse the role of the marketing department in retailing organisations. They report the findings of a survey of 70 of the largest retailing companies in the UK. This study describes marketing activities, reporting structures and the marketing information function. It goes on to consider the degree to which these retail businesses perceived the elements of marketing strategy in the distribution channel to be under their control rather than that of the supplier.

Nigel Piercy discusses the nature and significance of new technology in services marketing. In a seminal paper Piercy argues that the strategic nature of pending changes in information technology (the time of writing was 1984) was such that organisations faced an urgent need to formulate marketing/ information technology strategies. Experience in the eleven years since this study was published has diminished neither the importance of Piercy's findings nor indeed their relevance in today's retail organisations.

Leigh Sparks reviews aspects of customer service in retailing. Examples of US service are used in an effort to show how changed service orientations could improve customer relations.

Three articles by Stephen Brown explore aspects of the 'place' element in the retail marketing mix. The first article takes as its starting point micro location, that is, location within planned shopping centres and unplanned shopping districts. Normally, the literature on retail location has concentrated on national, regional and urban levels. The second article examines customer usage and perceptions in a retail park. Looking at the perceived advantages and disadvantages of shopping in a retail park he advances the idea that these may help to explain the evolution of retailing innovations. Stephen Brown's third article concentrates on tenant mix, tenant placement and shopper behaviour in a planned shopping centre. The major customer-attracting role of the magnet stores is well illustrated, as are the benefits to be gained by locating compatible outlets in close proximity.

Jim Forward and Christina Fulop examine alternative operational methods used by British franchisers. The experiences of well-established companies which have chosen to introduce franchising as a means to expand are particularly interesting.

David Swindley undertook a much-needed survey of what retail buyers actually do, how they interact with other functions in the retail business and the characteristics needed by successful buyers. To date this survey remains the single most important source of information about retail buyers.

René Den Hertog and A. Roy Thurik examine retail price setting using an econometric approach. Such an approach supplements other pricing studies and illustrates the power of econometrics when applied to retailing; sadly, econometric studies of retail pricing remain rare.

The final two articles, by Francis Buttle, with the first co-written with Marilyn Coates, examine shopper motives in a novel and interesting way. We still need to understand in greater detail the needs and motives of shoppers but the work of Buttle reminds us of the importance of this area.

REFERENCES

Akehurst, G.P., 1983, 'Concentration in Retail Distribution: Measurement and Significance', *The Service Industries Journal*, Vol. 3 No. 2.

Collins, A.C., 1992, *Competitive Retail Marketing: Strategies for Winning and Keeping Customers*, London: McGraw-Hill.

Gabor, A., 1977, *Pricing, Principles and Practices*, London: Heinemann.

Houston, F.S., 1986, 'The Marketing Concept: What It Is and What It Is Not', *Journal of Marketing*, Vol. 50.

Jobber, D., 1995, *Principles and Practice of Marketing*, London: McGraw-Hill.

Lazer, W. and E.J. Kelley, 1961, 'The Retailing Mix: Planning and Management', *Journal of Retailing*, Vol. 37, No. 1.

McGoldrich, P.J., 1990, *Retail Marketing*, London: McGraw-Hill.

Mason, J.B. and M.L. Mayer, 1987, *Modern Retailing: Theory and Practice*, Plano, Texas: Business Publications.

Monopolies and Mergers Commission, 1981, *Discounts to Retailers*, London: HMSO.

Office of Fair Trading, 1985, *Competition and Retailing*, London: Office of Fair Trading.

Piercy, N., 1984, 'Is Marketing Moving From the Manufacturer to the Retailer?', *Retail and Distribution Management*, Vol. 12, No. 5.

Piercy, N., 1987a, 'Marketing in UK Retailing, Part 1', *Retail and Distribution Management*, Vol. 15, No. 2.

Piercy, N., 1987b, 'Marketing in UK Retailing, Part 2', *Retail and Distribution Management*, Vol. 15, No. 3.

Schiller, R., 1987, 'Out of Town Exodus', in E. McFadyen (ed.), *The Changing Face of British Retailing*, London: Newman Books.

Seaman, R., 1988, 'Franchising: The New Marketing Tool of British Business', *MBA Review*, October.

Tauber, E.M., 1972, 'Why Do People Shop?', *Journal of Marketing*, Vol. 36, No. 4.

Walters, D., 1979, 'Manufacturer-Retailer Relationships', *European Journal of Marketing*, Vol. 13, No. 7.

Walters, D., 1989, *Strategic Retailing Management*, London: Prentice Hall.

1

The Status of Marketing in the UK Service Industries

by

Graham Hooley and Donald Cowell

This article describes the status of marketing in the UK service industries based on a sample of 320 service companies. It draws comparisons between service marketing companies and product marketing companies in terms of marketing orientation and marketing practice. Some significant differences are found between the two types of companies and it is suggested that there is scope for increased marketing professionalism in many service industries; and a greater sensitivity to market needs is required as markets become more competitive.

INTRODUCTION

Since the Second World War the UK has become a service economy: that is, in terms of output and in terms of employment, services have become the largest sector of the economy. Yet this particular transformation has been largely uncharted and largely neglected by many groups, including writers on marketing. Symptomatic of this neglect of the burgeoning service sector in marketing is our relative ignorance of the current status of marketing performance and marketing practice in our service industries. We have known from what patchy evidence exists that:

- the dominantly intangible nature of service products may pose particular marketing problems for managers in the service sector.
- some traditional 'professional' organisations are opposed to the idea of marketing on ethical or other grounds.
- many service organisations are small and in direct contact with their customers and may not need to espouse marketing practices adopted by larger goods-producing organisations.
- many service organisations are in the 'public sector', where there is still generally limited use of marketing ideas.
- marketing practitioners in the service sector are often critical of the utility of published marketing work for their particular industries.

It is, however, difficult to generalise across such a large sector whether organisations in it are or are not market-oriented in ideas and practice.

What has been lacking until now has been major empirical evidence of the status of marketing in the service sector. A number of reported studies have examined the status of marketing in particular service organisations or in a similar group of services. In North America, for example, the status of marketing in banking [Stall, 1978] the Canadian postal service [Barnhill, 1974] and United States utilities has been examined [Warshaw: 1962 and 1976]. Also there are at least two reported Studies of Marketing practices in United States service industries [Johnson, 1964 and George and Barksdale, 1974]. The latter piece of work in particular focused upon similarities and differences between marketing activities in services and manufacturing. No such study, however, has been available in the UK until now. Earlier studies of the status of marketing in UK industry had not analysed the service sector separately [e.g: B.I.M. 1970]. The first to do so in any systematic way was *Marketing in the UK: A survey of current practice and performance* [1984] published by the Institute of Marketing. This article is based on evidence collected in that study which deals specifically with UK service industries.

METHODOLOGY

The study reported below was commissioned by the Institute of Marketing as a part of a major investigation into the current status, practice and performance of marketing in British industry. The full findings have been published elsewhere [see Hooley, West and Lynch, 1984]. This paper focuses on the service marketing companies investigated during the study and compares them with their product marketing counterparts.

The full methodology of the study has also been reported elsewhere [see Hooley, West and Lynch 1984; Hooley and West, 1984]. Briefly, the mailing lists of *Marketing*, a weekly magazine for marketing management, were used to draw a sample of senior marketing executives from a wide spectrum of industries. A mailed questionnaire was despatched to 12,744 such senior managers. After four weeks, 1,775 replies (14 per cent) had been received. One hundred in-depth personal interviews were also conducted with a sample of executives drawn at random from the original 12,744 to estimate non-response bias in the mailed survey. It was found that the mailed survey had elicited a higher proportion of replies from the more marketing-oriented companies and hence marginally overstated the acceptance and role of marketing in British industry. For the purposes of this paper, however, comparing service marketing and product marketing respondents, this bias affects absolute data only, and not comparative figures.

In all, 544 service companies replied to the postal questionnaire. Of these, 238 were the providers of specialist marketing services such as marketing research, advertising agencies and marketing consultants (see Table 1). Because of the presence of this large, atypical group of service companies they have been excluded from the tables and discussions that

TABLE 1
BREAKDOWN OF SERVICE COMPANIES IN THE SAMPLE

	Number	Percentage
Market research agencies	40	7.2
Advertising Agencies	102	18.3
Marketing Consultants	92	16.5
Packaging and design consultants	21	3.8
Training Consultants	20	3.6
P.R. Consultants	32	5.7
Sales Promotion Consultants	56	10.0
Total Specialist	238	42.6
Other Service Companies	320	57.3

Note: The service companies listed above are not in mutually exclusive groups. Thus the
number shown against each type of company does not equal the total figure.

follow. Hence, for our current purposes, 320 service marketing companies are compared with 1202 product marketing companies.

THE RESEARCH FINDINGS

The findings from the research fall into three main categories:

1. the current marketing environment facing service companies;
2. the marketing approach of service marketing companies;
3. the strategic planning tools and techniques employed by service companies.

The Current Marketing Environment

As might be expected, Table 2 demonstrates that the service marketing
companies have suffered relatively less than their product marketing
counterparts during the recent economic recession. 65 per cent of product
marketing companies reported little or no effect from the recession
compared with 70 per cent of service marketing companies. The reason

for this is that the service companies are more likely than their product counterparts to be operating primarily in new or growth markets (42 per cent of service companies but only 28 per cent of product companies). (See Table 3.)

TABLE 2
EFFECTS OF THE RECESSION

Effects	All Companies	Product Companies	Service Companies	Service Company Deviation from Product Companies
	(1514)	(1196)	(318)	
No or small effect	65.7%	64.6%	69.8%	+ 8%
Major or disastrous effect	34.3%	35.4%	30.2%	- 15%

chi-square = 2.77. Significant at .10 level

TABLE 3
THE LONG-TERM NATURE OF THE MAJOR MARKETS SERVED

Nature of Market	All Companies	Product Companies	Service Companies	Service Company Deviation from Product Companies
	(1491)	(1179)	(312)	
New, emerging	3.6%	3.4%	4.2%	+ 24%
Growth	27.2%	24.5%	37.5%	+ 53%
Mature and stable	47.1%	49.1%	39.7%	- 19%
Decline	22.1%	23.0%	18.6%	- 19%

Chi-square = 22.45. Significant at .001 level.

This is not to say, however, that the service companies have not been affected by the recession. Many have been hit, and many are operating in mature, or even declining, markets. Typically, however, they see more hope for the future than their product marketing counterparts. (See Table 4.)

TABLE 4

FUTURE PROSPECTS FOR THE COMPANY

Prospects	All Companies	Product Companies	Service Companies	Service Company Deviation from Product Companies
	(1451)	(1151)	(300)	
Bright and healthy	33.8%	32.1%	40.3%	+ 26%
Some hope for future	40.0%	40.9%	36.7%	- 10%
A long uphill battle	26.1%	26.9%	23.0%	- 14%

Chi-square = 7.20. Significant at .05 level.

The Marketing Approach of Service Marketing Companies

There was no statistically significant difference in the *claimed* marketing approach of service and product marketing companies (see Table 5). However, when the *practice* of marketing was examined differences did become clear. A lower level of marketing research activity of the service companies was detected (see Table 6). While the majority (62 per cent) of product marketing companies claimed to conduct marketing research, only 56 per cent of service companies did so.

In addition, Table 7 shows that the service companies are more likely than their product counterparts still to utilise cost plus pricing methods and less likely to charge 'what the market will bear'.

As would be expected, the major emphasis of service companies in gaining new business is much more likely to centre on the ability of their personnel (sales force) and the service and support they give to customers than for product marketers (see Table 8). There is correspondingly less emphasis on the product or service itself. Table 9 shows that service marketers place less emphasis than product marketing companies on product differentiation and total market size. They do, however, place

TABLE 5
MARKETING APPROACH OF THE COMPANY

Approach	All Companies	Product Companies	Service Companies	Service Company Deviation from Product Companies
	(1470)	(1160)	(310)	
Product Orientation	13.8%	13.9%	13.5%	- 3%
Selling Orientation	26.7%	26.3%	28.4%	+ 8%
Marketing Orientation	59.5%	59.8%	58.1%	- 3%

Chi-square = 0.55. Not significant

TABLE 6
THE USE OF MARKETING RESEARCH

User	All Companies	Product Companies	Service Companies	Service Company Deviation from Product Companies
	(1505)	(1188)	(317)	
Yes	60.8%	62.1%	55.8%	- 10%
No	39.2%	37.9%	44.2%	+ 16%

Chi-square = 3.89. Significant at .05 level.

greater importance on the competition and utilising their capacity to the full. This latter aspect (capacity utilisation) is significant when one remembers the perishable nature of services. Unlike products, services cannot be stock-piled for sale later, and unused capacity or resources are lost to the company.

Table 10 shows the methods used to evaluate and control marketing effort among the service and product companies. The only statistically significant difference between the two groups was the relatively greater

TABLE 7

PRICING METHOD EMPLOYED

Method	All Companies	Product Companies	Service Companies	Service Company Deviation from Product Companies
	(1411)	(1116)	(295)	
What the market will bear	46.6%	48.0%	41.0%	- 15%
Cost plus	14.3%	13.4%	18.0%	+ 34%
Competitive pricing	39.1%	38.5%	41.0%	+ 6%

Chi-square = 6.15. Significant at .05 level.

TABLE 8

MAJOR EMPHASIS IN WINNING NEW BUSINESS

	All Companies	Product Companies	Service Companies	't' Value	Significance Level
	(1522)	(1202)	(320)		
Product performance	49.4%	51.9%	40.0%	3.78	.001
Product Design	14.3%	14.7%	12.5%	1.00	n.s.
Sales force	8.7%	7.0%	15.3%	4.67	.001
After sales service	4.1%	3.0%	8.1%	4.10	.001
Advertising and promotion	6.6%	6.2%	7.8%	1.03	n.s.
Pricing	18.7%	19.1%	17.2%	0.77	n.s.

TABLE 9
PRIME IMPORTANCE OF FACTORS WHEN MAKING MARKETING PLANS

Factors in Marketing Plans	All Companies	Product Companies	Service Companies	't' Value	Significance Level
	(1522)	(1202)	(320)		
Total market size	33.3%	34.4%	29.4%	1.69	.10
Company market share	14.6%	14.7%	14.1%	0.27	n.s.
Competition	15.6%	14.5%	20.0%	2.41	.05
Product differentiation	8.7%	9.8%	4.4%	3.05	.01
Contribution margins	16.8%	17.4%	14.4%	1.28	n.s.
Scale and experience	22.2%	2.2%	2.2%	0.00	n.s.
Capacity utilisation	4.9%	3.8%	8.8%	3.70	.001
Market growth rate	11.4%	11.6%	10.6%	0.50	n.s.

emphasis service marketing companies place on visibility – i.e., achieving higher levels of awareness. This in turn may well be a result of operating primarily in few emerging markets where visibility can be paramount.

Strategic Planning Tools and Techniques

The service companies are generally less sophisticated in their strategic planning than their product marketing counterparts. Table 11 shows a lower incidence of planning among service companies. The extent and type of planning conducted in service companies is lower than among product companies. In particular, the service companies tend to restrict

TABLE 10

MAIN METHOD OF EVALUATING MARKETING PERFORMANCE

Evaluation of Marketing Effort	All Companies	Product Companies	Service Companies	't' Value	Significance Level
	(1522)	(1202)	(320)		
Overall profit	52.7%	53.2%	50.9%	0.73	n.s.
Return on investment	15.2%	15.4%	14.7%	0.31	n.s.
Total sales volume	21.3%	21.5%	20.3%	0.47	n.s.
Market share	10.5%	10.1%	11.9%	0.93	n.s.
Awareness levels	2.4%	1.9%	4.4%	2.58	.01
Share of segments	3.5%	3.7%	2.8%	0.78	n.s.

their planning to shorter (one year) time horizons. This may, however, be a function of the dynamic nature of the markets in which they operate making long-range planning particularly difficult. Table 12 shows a lower level of usage of all strategic planning tools covered in the study among service companies with the single exception of a marginally greater (though statistically non-significant) use of market simulations.

While it may be argued that some of the techniques (such as, for example, the experience curve) are not particularly applicable in the service sector, all are used to some extent, but to a lower extent than among product marketers. In short, the extent of planning and its level of sophistication encountered in the service marketing companies lags some way behind that encountered among their product marketing counterparts.

CONCLUSIONS

This study has sought to draw a comparison between service marketing companies and product marketing companies in terms of marketing orientation and practice. As far as we are aware it is the first UK attempt to do so. Clearly all surveys have their imperfections and this one is no

TABLE 11
EXTENT OF FORMAL STRATEGIC PLANNING

Strategic Planning	All Companies	Product Companies	Service Companies	Service Company Deviation from Product Companies
	(1468)	(1160)	(308)	
Little or none	6.5%	5.9%	8.8%	+ 49%
Annual budgeting	21.7%	21.1%	24.0%	+ 14%
Annual marketing plan	20.6%	20.0%	22.7%	+ 14%
Annual marketing plan and long range plan	51.2%	52.9%	44.5%	- 16%

Chi-square = 8.18. Significant at .05 level.

exception. For example, the actual number of respondents to the mailed questionnaire was low. Even though our results include the comments from over 300 service companies, the overall response level indicates that caution must be exercised in placing too much emphasis on the findings.

Nevertheless there are a number of points of interest:

- Marked differences were observed, in this sample, in the effects of the recession on the service companies compared with the product companies. Service companies were less affected by the recession which can be related to the finding that service industries perceived themselves to be more often in new, emerging or growth markets than mature, stable or declining markets.
- In spite of this, marketing in service companies lags some way behind that in product companies. Indeed in some cases marketing is 'the forgotten function' on which Johnson [1964] commented in his work with United States Companies some 20 years ago; while many companies in the sample paid *lip service* to adopting marketing ideas, the evidence on marketing *practice* was less convincing. In particular service companies were:

- less sensitive to environmental and market factors
- less likely to undertake marketing research
- less inclined to plan far into the future
- less receptive to the use of strategic planning tools

TABLE 12
USE OF STRATEGIC PLANNING TOOLS

Planning Tools	All Companies	Product Companies	Service Companies	't' Value	Significance Level
	(1522)	(1202)	(320)		
S.W.O.T. (Strengths, Weaknesses, Opportunities, Threats) analysis	48.2%	50.7%	38.7%	3.82	.001
(P.L.C.) Product Life Cycle concept	34.0%	36.8%	23.4%	4.50	.001
Experience curve	17.7%	18.2%	15.9%	0.96	n.s.
Growth-Share matrix	10.3%	11.3%	6.6%	2.46	.05
Marketing audit	17.4%	17.6%	16.6%	0.42	n.s.
Simulations	7.7%	7.6%	8.1%	0.30	n.s.
Test marketing	26.9%	28.5%	20.6%	2.83	.01

Some of these findings are compatible with work a decade ago in the United States [George and Barksdale, 1974] which also concluded, for example, that service firms there were less likely to use marketing research. On the other hand, there appeared to be no significant differences in their study between service and manufacturing firms in their approaches to goals, policies, audits and overall plans for their offerings. They did, however, suggest that service firms were less market-orientated than manufacturing firms.

The survey shows that there is undoubted scope for many service organisations to take a much more professional marketing approach than they do at present. As their markets become increasingly competitive and inevitably mature, so a greater sensitivity to market needs will be required and an increased willingness to embrace more fully a true marketing perspective, not only in theory but also in practice.

REFERENCES

Barnhill, J.A., 1974, 'Developing Marketing Orientation in a Postal Service', Optimum No.3, pp.36–47.

B.I.M. Survey, 1970, *Marketing Organisation in British Industry*, British Institute of Management, London.

George, W.R. and W.C. Barksdale, 1974, 'Marketing Activities in the Service Industries', *Journal of Marketing*, Vol.38, Oct. pp.65–70.

Hooley, G.J. and C.J. West, 1984, 'The Untapped Markets for Marketing Research', *Journal of the Market Research Society*, Vol.26, No.4. pp.335–52.

Hooley, G.J., C.J. West and J.E. Lynch, 1984, *Marketing in the UK: A Survey of Current Practice and Performance*, Institute of Marketing, London.

Johnson, E.M., 1964, *An Introduction to the Problems of Service Marketing Management*, The Bureau of Economic and Business Research, University of Delaware.

Stall, R.B., 1978, 'Marketing in a Service Industry', *Atlanta Economic Review*, Vol.28, No.3, pp.15–18.

Warshaw, M.R., 1962 and 1976, 'Effective marketing – key to public utility growth', *University of Michigan Business Review*, November, pp.16–20; and the later follow-up studies, 'Re-appraising Public Utility Marketing', *University of Michigan Business Review*, May, pp.18–22.

This chapter first appeared in *The Service Industries Journal*, Vol.5, No.3 (1985).

2
Problems Confronting UK Retailing Organisations

by

Gordon E. Greenley and David Shipley

This article examines recent survey findings of a range of problems facing British retailers of convenience and shopping products. Perspective is provided in a discussion of phenomena and trends currently affecting the retailing environment. The retailer-problems described are set in six categories relating to the environment: customer; competitor; workforce; supplier; general management; and other external factors. It is conjectured that, as well as the other alternatives referred to, market or customer specialisation is an appropriate strategy for minimising or removing many of the problems identified.

In accordance with the marketing concept, the general problem of retailing is how to create the right match between product offerings and customer needs while simultaneously meeting profit requirements. For retailers adoption of the marketing concept is an immediate problem [Berman and Evans, 1986; Arnold, Capella and Smith, 1983], even more than for any other kind of business institution [Fram, 1965]. This is because the retailer's daily contact with consumers means that although he is the first channel member to gain from consumer satisfaction, he is also the first to experience the consequences of consumer dissatisfaction [Lewison and DeLozier, 1982]. Solving the general problem of retailing requires the reconciliation of two further problems. These are the consumer's problem of the right choice and the retailer's problem of the right blend. In turn, then, and at the risk of over-simplification, solution of the retailer's problem is his provision of the product, price, place, time, quantity and appeal that is right in terms of his own profit requirements and the consumer's choices concerning what to buy, for how much, where, when, in what amount and from whom. The difficulty of solving this problem satisfactorily is increasing due to the growing turbulence and hostility of the retailing environment. Therefore, in planning their future retailing marketing strategies, firms need to identify and understand any major problems confronting them.

The foregoing route to customer satisfaction and retailer profitability is well known by both academics [Bates, 1979] and contemporary successful retailing practitioners [Conran, 1985]. However, knowing which route to take in practice can be problematic, as many retailers are aware. Indeed, our findings illustrate that there are numerous obstacles obscuring and/or blocking the attainment of satisfactory performance. The problems identified in this article take form in three sets existing in the retailer's external and internal environments. Their effects can forestall the retailer's objective in three different ways. The first group of problems constrains the match between retailer's blend and consumer's choice to an imperfect one, as for example, when product deficiencies arise further back in the distribution channel. The second set of problems reduces any close match to a temporary one as, for instance, when the price balance is disturbed by cost inflation. The third group of influences can mean that even a sustained close match becomes ineffective, as when competitors provide an even better fit to customer preferences.

This article is presented in five sections. The first gives a background to the UK retailing environment. The second gives the methodology of the survey, the results are presented in the third section, and comments are made in the fourth. The last section provides a summary.

THE UK RETAILING ENVIRONMENT

A brief review of developments in the UK retailing environment reveals some important opportunities as well as some major impediments to solving the general retailing problem.

During recent years the UK retailing environment has become more hostile, transient and uncertain as significant demographic, social and economic changes have occurred. Consumers' product tastes, shopping habits and preferred shopping locations continue to evolve as the population ages, family sizes shrink, female employment grows, car and home ownership levels expand and real income increases, while disparities between north and south as well as the employed and unemployed widen [Morrell, 1985; Saunders, 1985]. Slow or no growth in retail sales and the requirement to raise volumes to spread high fixed-cost formations have heightened competitive intensity [Knee and Walters, 1985]. High and persistent rates of inflation and interest have served only to exacerbate the situation.

Retailing itself has evolved through a sustained metamorphosis over the last decade or two. Store sizes and the number of out-of-town locations have multiplied while ownership concentration has tightened markedly [Akehurst, 1983, Burns, 1983]. On this latter issue, the share of total retail sales appropriated by the large multiple chains has grown from 39 per cent in 1961, through 52 per cent in 1979 to an estimated 60 per cent in 1985 [Richards and Smiddy, 1985]. Meanwhile, of course, many small and independent shops have disappeared [Bamfield, 1980], perhaps as many as over 40,000 in total [Davies et al., 1984].

These trends toward bigness and local fewness are resulting in competitive uncertainty and other problems characteristic of oligopoly. They are also necessitating more management levels, more complex decision-making processes and more sophisticated information [Knee and Walters, 1985].

Richards and Smiddy [1985] contend that UK retailing generally (markets and companies) has reached maturity and that there is a surfeit of stores. They cite a number of symptoms: an epidemic of take-overs and mergers; stagnation and decline in gross margin trends; falling returns on investment; greater price competition and advertising expenditures; reduced creation of new retailing capacity; etc.

Some individual companies have grown and prospered through this period through careful segmentation or positioning, by encouraging bigger customer spends, by acquisition or by product and/or inter-national diversification. Also, many retailers have enjoyed short-term profit gains from the recent boom in consumer spending. However, given the environmental conditions outlined above, the future is likely to be extremely complex for all retailers and it is starkly daunting for many of them.

Against this background, the principal purpose of this article is to present and examine the nature, prevalence and importance of major problems facing retailers. We believe, however, that most of the problems and associated discussions have a much wider application.

METHODOLOGY

The data presented in the following section are extracted from a broader study in which the authors are seeking to provide some empirical insights into the use of formal marketing procedures by UK retailing organisations. Data collection was achieved by means of a postal survey questionnaire dealing with a range of questions on marketing practices. The sampling frame was taken as the Retail Directory [1985] and the sample was chosen so as to exclude very small retailers, among whom lack of specialist managers was considered likely to limit the use of a systematic marketing approach. Also excluded were retailers of services, such as banking, insurance, holi-days and travel. Hence, the sample surveyed was comprised of retailers of physical goods, including department stores and all other retailers having more than five outlets.

A total of 1,650 questionnaires were dispatched in May 1985. These were directed by name to the senior executive responsible for market-ing or, where this identity was not available, they were sent personally to the managing director. As it was recognised that marketing practices were likely to differ between retailers of shopping and convenience products, the respondents were asked to consider the questions in relation to either category of goods, indicating their choice.

The questionnaire was pre-tested to facilitate the removal of ambiguities and other problems. The final document was designed to avoid unnecessary use of technical terms and respondents were given instructions about how to answer the questions. Also included in the questionnaire was an explanatory letter and offers of both anonymity and a copy of the findings. There were 15 questions, many of which contained multiple parts.

A total of 282 responses was obtained, giving an overall response rate of 17 per cent, of which 260 questionnaires were usable, yielding a net rate of 15.8 per cent. This was viewed as acceptable considering the lengthy questionnaire and the financial constraint which precluded a second mailing or any other method of contacting the sample. The response appeared geographically representative and a profile of the respondent organisations is displayed in Table 1.

THE RESULTS

The respondents were asked to rate on a five-point scale the importance to their companies of each of a number of possible problems. The five numbers on the scale were associated with degrees of problem importance ranging through nil, low, moderate, high and utmost. Multivariate techniques were used to analyse the data but these provided no meaningful associations. Accordingly, Table 2 presents results in terms of the prevalence and importance of problems among the respondents generally and by retailers of respectively, convenience and shopping products. Prevalence concerns the proportions of respondents citing particular problems while importance refers to the mean importance attributed by those same proportions of the samples. The results for the two subsets of firms are generally very similar so that findings are discussed mainly in terms of the combined sample. Several disparities are, however, emphasised.

A striking feature of Table 2 is the very high cited incidence of all 24 problems. The frequencies might be skewed upwards by the nature of the questions asked or because, like human behaviour more generally, retail managers may be tempted to exaggerate factors that limit their achievements. There is no way of knowing whether this occurred, however, and conversely, some respondents may well have played-down their problems to demonstrate their ability to overcome adversity. Prior awareness of these potential biases led to steps being taken to avoid them. The factors presented as possible problems were chosen on the expectation that they would be confirmed as actual problems. This expectation was based first, on our experience, secondly, on academic discussions with others and thirdly, on a literature search. Particular note was taken of environmental developments and particular factors were chosen because they had recently been identified as problems for other types of businesses, such as industrial distributors [Narus et al., 1984] and manufacturers [Shipley, 1985a]. Other variables were included because it was envisaged that there would be some overlap of

TABLE 1
PROFILE OF RESPONDENT ORGANISATIONS

	Convenience Goods N = 104 %	Shopping Goods N = 156 %
Position of Respondents		
Managing Director	34	34
Director	22	18
Marketing Director	6	9
General Manager	10	7
Store Manager	18	4
Marketing Manager	5	12
Others	6	16
Annual Sales Turnover (£ million)		
Under 5	28	45
5 to 24	19	19
25 to 99	14	13
100 to 499	11	6
500 to 999	2	3
1,000 to 2,999	14	1
Over 3,000	1	2
No response	11	11
Type of Store		
Department store	6	31
Supermarket	23	1
Hypermarket	6	0
Multiple-shop	41	49
Variety store	5	7
Convenience store	4	0
Co-operative store	13	0
Others	2	12
Number of Stores		
1 only	7	21
2 to 5	11	21
6 to 9	12	13
10 to 19	7	7
20 to 49	14	10
50 to 99	12	10
100 to 199	10	10
Over 200	27	9

factors among retailers' problems and factors known to be among retailers' vendor selection criteria [Brown and Purwar, 1980; Shipley, 1985b] and among variables known to affect channel members' motivation [Rosenbloom, 1978; Sibley and Teas, 1979].

There were then, reasons to expect the factors listed in Table 2 to be retailer problems. What was not anticipated, however, was their very wide prevalence and their substantial importance which together indicate a high degree of adversity and/or weakness facing and characterising British retail management.

TABLE 2
NATURE, PREVALENCE AND IMPORTANCE OF RETAILERS' PROBLEMS

	ALL RESPONDENTS N = ?CO			CONVENIENCE GOODS N = 104			SHOPPING GOODS N = 156		
	Prevalence %	Mean Import-ance	Rank by Mean	Prevalence %	Mean Import-ance	Rank by Mean	Prevalence %	Mean Import-ance	Rank by Mean
COMPETITIVE ENVIRONMENT									
Intense price competition among retailers	87.2	3.49	2	94.1	3.69	1	82.8	3.28	4
Too many competitors	89.0	3.21	7	98.02	3.27	7	83.1	3.14	6
Overall marketing strength of competitors	89.06	3.1	8	94.1	3.24	8	85.8	2.29	10
Weaknesses in your firm's overall marketing activity	83.9	2.96	11	87.1	3.01	12	81.8	2.9	12
CUSTOMER ENVIRONMENT									
Difficulty in attracting new customers	92.02	3.10	8	98.02	3.13	9	88.3	3.06	8
Decreases in customer demand	80.1	2.84	13	91.1	2.97	13	72.9	2.7	17
Insufficient knowledge of customer demand	82.03	2.7	18	86.1	2.71	18	79.3	2.68	18
Insufficient customer loyalty	83.9	2.68	19	88.1	2.72	17	81.3	2.63	19
OTHER EXTERNAL ENVIRONMENT									
Rising Costs	95.3	3.6	1	98.0	3.6	2	93.6	3.6	1
High interest rates	88.2	3.32	5	86.1	3.28	6	89.6	3.35	3
Government requirements, regulations, etc.	84.4	3.05	10	86.1	3.07	10	83.2	3.03	9
LABOUR FORCE									
High costs of labour	90.9	3.43	3	93.1	3.59	3	89.6	3.27	5
Obtaining good sales assistants	93.4	3.39	4	93.1	3.36	5	93.6	3.41	2
Low employee productivity	89.02	2.79	16	90.0	2.8	14	88.3	2.79	14

Table 2 (cont.)

	ALL RESPONDENTS N = 260			CONVENIENCE GOODS N = 104			SHOPPING GOODS N = 156		
	Prevalence %	Mean Import- ance	Rank by Mean	Prevalence %	Mean Import- ance	Rank by Mean	Prevalence %	Mean Import- ance	Rank by Mean
GENERAL MANAGEMENT									
Stock control difficulties	92.09	3.29	6	92.1	3.47	4	92.1	3.1	7
Difficulty in finding new products	78.7	2.80	15	85.1	2.77	15	74.5	2.83	13
MANUFACTURER-RELATIONS									
Manufacters prices are too high and their discounts are too low	73.4	2.9	12	83.16	3.05	11	73.4	2.74	15
Inadequate delivery by manufacturers	81.7	2.84	13	83.16	2.76	16	80.8	2.91	11
Inadequate manufacturers product return and other after-sales services	75.68	2.71	17	79.2	2.70	20	73.3	2.73	16
Inadequate manufacturers training of your staff	63.3	2.62	20	69.3	2.71	18	59.3	2.53	21
Inadequate credit offered by manufacturers	76.2	2.58	21	80.2	2.62	21	73.5	2.53	21
Inadequate personal contact and communications with manufacturers	75.3	2.51	22	81.2	2.56	22	71.4	2.45	23
Inadequate promotional support by manufacturers	78.2	2.4	23	86.1	2.22	24	73.1	2.58	20
Fears concerning continuity of business with manufacturers	60.6	2.38	24	58.4	2.37	23	62.2	2.38	24

In addition to assessing the problems listed in Table 2, the respondents were asked to specify 'other' problems. Easily the most common of the resulting 'write-in' problems were concerned with high and/or rising rents and/or rates. Other fairly common 'write-ins' included difficulties of finding suitable locations, thefts by staff or customers, labour problems, and harsh competitive conditions.

The problems identified in Table 2 and in the 'write-in' comments can be grouped into six categories, some of which contain common elements. It is emphasised that these groups and the variables within them reinforce each other and thereby substantially heighten the degree of retailers' overall difficulty.

Competitive Environment Problems

These problems were found to be widespread and very important. Indeed four of the first eleven ranked problems are intense price competition, too many competitors, overall marketing strength of rivals and weaknesses in the retailer's own marketing programme. 'Write-in' comments on this theme included 'our large competitors get bulk discounts' and 'we can't match our competitors' advertising spending'. All of the competitive problems scored considerably higher among the convenience than the shopping goods retailers. We attribute this to the more abundant opportunities for achieving real product and service differentials with shopping products and to consumers being less price-sensitive than in the case of convenience items.

Customer Environment Problems

These common and important problems were characterised by decreases in demand, difficulty in attracting new customers, insufficient customer loyalty and insufficient knowledge of demand. Again the lower sets of scores were assigned by the retailers of shopping goods. This may be due to the markets for food, cosmetics, newspapers etc., being more fully mature than those for shopping products where sellers can better enjoy the effects of fashion, rising real income, increasing home ownership, etc.

Other External Environment Problems

These problems included the most widespread and important problems. They include rising costs, high interest rates, government regulations and the 'write-in' citations of high rents, high local rates and scarce good store locations. The results concerning these factors were more similar as among the two sub-sets of retailers. The reader may find this surprising in the particular case of high interest rates. In theory this should be a greater problem for shopping goods sellers since, while both types of firms may face interest charges on borrowings and on extended credit from suppliers, only shopping products are sold on medium- and long-term credit to consumers. In practice, however, UK consumers have recently been buying heavily on credit despite the high interest rates prevailing. Our view is that consumers have come to expect price inflation and so find it expedient to buy sooner than later or that high interest rates have obtained for so long that consumer demand for shopping goods has become less sensitive to high interest rates.

Labour Force Problems

High labour costs and obtaining good sales assistants received very high scores and low employee productivity is also very widespread. 'Write-in' remarks were confined to convenience resellers and included 'dishonest staff', 'fast staff turnover' and 'staff training problems'. Labour problems when they exist are, of course, bound to be serious in an industry where sales depend heavily on the attitudes and abilities of sales staff [Smith, 1983; Woodside and Davenport, 1976]. Moreover, retailing is one of the few remaining labour-intensive industries [Stern and El-Ansanary, 1982] and unit labour costs in UK retailing escalated at an average annual rate of 16.5 per cent from 1973 to 1979 and at 8.5 per cent thereafter to 1985 [Morrell, 1985].

General Management Problems

The wide prevalence and importance of this group is typified here as stock control difficulties, weaknesses in marketing, difficulty in finding new products and inadequate knowledge of demand. There were also 'write-in' comments concerning theft control, keeping catalogues current and provision of enough parking space.

Manufacturer–Relations Problems

This group includes manufacturers' inadequate provision of prices, delivery, product return and after-sales services, help with staff training, credit, communications with retailers, promotional support and assurance of continued business relationships. These factors have been found to be important determinants of retailers' source selection [Brown and Purwar, 1980; McGoldrick and Douglas, 1983; Shipley, 1985b]. Receiving such factors is obviously highly valued by channel members [Sibley and Teas, 1979]. Hence, in our view the low relative and high absolute prevalence and importance of these cited manufacturer–relations problems serves to emphasise retailers' extent of concern about factors in the other groups of problems.

COMMENTS

The previous section depicts retailers operating in a tight and mature market with strong upward pressure on costs and marketing expenditures, along with simultaneous downward pressure on prices. These problems are seen to be exacerbated by important and common workforce and general management problems, while government regulations seem to be making matters worse with suppliers doing too little to make matters better.

As this is the first set of findings drawn from the broader survey of retail marketing, we consider it inappropriate to provide detailed recommendations at this early stage. Instead, we confine our comments to two major observations. The first is a reiteration of the obvious but important principle that success in retailing is extremely unlikely in the absence of a close, competitive and profitable match between retailers' offerings and consumers' requirements.

Our second observation concerns a strategy that has been utilised by a number of UK retailing companies, such as Body Shop International, Habitat, Mothercare, Kwiksave and Harrods. This strategy is based on the principle of specialisation, being consistent with solving the general problem of retailing. Moreover, it is apt to discuss it here since it does offer advantages which can help to overcome many of the problems identified in this article.

Specialisation, as seen by Knee and Walters [1985], involves establishing a recognisable, well-differentiated image that is congruent with the needs of a clearly-defined market segment of appropriate size. Obvious risks of a specialisation strategy include the danger of misjudging the precise needs of the segment, excessive concentration of invested capital and the risk of becoming too rigid to adapt to opportunities and threats as they arise.

Specialisation does, however, provide substantial benefits. We constrain our comments to those that are advantageous to firms facing the kinds of problems found among the current respondents, which can be summarised as follows:

- building customer demand and loyalty by providing a coherent product mix aimed at clearly defined segments
- creating competitive advantage as protection against competitive strategies
- improving cost savings, especially in relation to transport, warehousing, selling and buying discounts
- allowing specialism of personnel in order to enhance the quality of service offered to customers
- strengthening negotiations with suppliers for more favourable conditions of supply.

It is not our intention to offer the concept of specialisation as a solution for all types of problems or for all types of retail organisations. We merely observe that this can be a successful strategy in many cases and that it can reduce many of the major problems reported in this article. Nevertheless, other strategies such as those based on repositioning, cost leadership, integration, product or market proliferation and diversification could also be equally beneficial for particular firms and circumstances. Indeed, much of the endeavour in our general survey has been directed towards gaining an understanding of which and why particular strategies are successful.

CONCLUSIONS

A large number of widespread and important problems are found to exist among a sample of UK retailers. These problems are grouped into the six categories named as customer problems, competitive problems, other environment problems, work-force problems, general management problems and manufacturer-relations problems. Little difference obtains in the prevalence and severity of these groups of problems between convenience and shopping products retailers. The little difference that does exist shows that shopping products sellers exhibit a slightly lower intensity of problems. We attribute this mainly to differences in the scope for securing competitive edge and customer preference through genuine product and service differentiation.

Overall the results have provided an understanding of the range of problems perceived by UK retailing organisations, within the retailing environment as outlined in the first section. We envisage that these results are of use to retailers since they provide them with an understanding of retailing environmental adversity and aid the formulation of more appropriate and effective strategies.

REFERENCES

Akehurst, G., 1983, 'Concentration in Retail Distribution: Measurement and Significance', *Service Industries Journal*, Vol. 3, No. 2.
Arnold, D.R., L.M. Capella and G.D. Smith, 1983, *Strategic Retail Management*, London: Addison-Wesley.
Bamfield, J.P., 1980, 'The Changing Face of British Retailing', *National Westminster Bank Quarterly Review*, May.
Bates, A.D., 1979, *Retailing and its Environment*, New York: D. Van Nostrand.
Berman, B. and J.R. Evans, 1986, *Retail Management: A Strategic Approach*, New York: Macmillan.
Brown, J.R. and P.C. Purwar, 'A Cross-Channel Comparison of Retail Supplier Selection Factors', in Bagozzi, R.P. (ed.), *Marketing in the Eighties*, Chicago: American Marketing Association.
Burns, J., 1983, 'A Synoptic View of the Food Industry', in Burns J., J. McInnery and A. Swinbank (eds.), *The Food Industry, Economics and Policies*, London: Heinemann.
Conran, T., 1985, 'The Retail Image', in Healey and Baker, *Retail Report 1985*, London: Healey and Baker.
Davies, K., C. Gilligan and C. Sutton, 1984, 'The Changing Competitive Structure of British Grocery Retailing', *The Quarterly Review of Marketing*, Vol. 10, No. 1.
Fram, E.H., 1985, 'Application of the Marketing Concept to Retailing', *Journal of Retailing*, Vol. 41.
Knee, D. and D. Walters, 1985, *Strategy in Retailing: Theory and Application*, Oxford: Philip Allan.
Lewison, D.M. and M.W. DeLozier, 1982, *Retailing: Principles and Practices*, Columbus: Merrill.
McGoldrick, P.J. and R.A. Douglas, 1983, 'Factors Influencing the Choice of a Supplier by Grocery Distributors', *European Journal of Marketing*, Vol. 17, No. 5.
Morrell, J., 1985, 'Social Change: Its Impact on Retailing', in Healey and Baker, *Retail Report 1985*, London: Healey and Baker.
Narus, J.A., N.M. Reddy and G.C. Pinchak, 1984, 'Key Problems Facing Industrial Distributors', *Industrial Marketing Management*, Vol. 13, No. 2.

Retail Directory 1985, London: Newman Books.

Richards, J. and P. Smeddy, 1985, 'The Retail Market – The Non-Property View', in Healey and Baker, *Retail Report 1985*, London: Healey and Baker.

Rosenbloom, B., 1978, 'Motivating Independent Distribution Channel Members', *Industrial Marketing Management*, Vol. 7.

Saunders, K., 1985, 'Developments in Retailing Techniques', in Healey and Baker, *Retail Report 1985*, London: Healey and Baker.

Shipley, D.D., 1985a, 'Constraints on Marketing Performance', *Management Research News*, Vol. 8, No. 2.

Shipley, D.D., 1985b, 'Reseller's Supplier Selection Criteria for Different Consumer Products', *European Journal of Marketing*, Vol. 19, No. 7.

Sibley, S.D. and K.R. Teas, 1979, 'The Manufacturers' Agent in Industrial Distribution', *Industrial Marketing Management*, Vol. 8.

Smith, H., unpublished thesis reported in Livesey, F., 1983, *Economics for Business Decisions*, Estover, Plymouth: Macdonald and Evans.

Woodside, A.G. and J.W. Davenport, 1976, 'Effects of Price and Salesmen Expertise on Customer Purchasing Behaviour', *Journal of Business*, Vol. 49.

This chapter first appeared in *The Service Industries Journal*, Vol.7, No.2 (1987).

3

An Empirical Overview of Marketing by Retailing Organisations

by

Gordon E. Greenley and David D. Shipley

Research into the way British companies utilise marketing has been largely restricted to manufacturing companies. Although the literature shows an accelerating interest in the marketing of services per se, surprisingly little research has been done to investigate the way British retailing organisations use marketing. This article presents and discusses the results of a recent survey that was designed to investigate the use of marketing by a sample of British retailers. The overall result is that while a large majority of the retailers studied claim that marketing is of major importance, analysis of their marketing behaviour suggests scope for improvement. These results are preceded by a discussion of the British retailing environment at the time of the survey.

A review of the marketing management literature shows that, like the majority of researches into the use of marketing, it is heavily biased toward manufacturing firms, with relatively scant attention focusing on retailers. This, no doubt, is owing to historical causes in that writers have tended to treat retailers merely as distribution outlets for producers. As suggested in numerous piecemeal 'success stories', however, many retailers are far from being mechanical 'slave outlets' for manufacturers, and are instead first-rate exponents of marketing management as it is prescribed (for other institutions) in the literature. What is patently lacking in the literature, however, is an extensive empirical assessment of how marketing is practised by retailing firms generally. Such a study is essential if appropriate recommendations are to be offered to these organisations now when they are particularly needed owing to the profound on-going restructuring of the retail sector.

In response to this major need for information, the authors designed a far-reaching study of the use of marketing by British retailers. This article offers an early overview of the findings. The overall result is that although a large majority of the retailers studied claim that marketing is of major importance to their success, analysis of their marketing behaviour suggests that there is much scope for improvement.

Unlike the planned series of papers that is to follow it, this paper offers no normative prescriptions. The first section presents the background to the study while the methodology is described briefly in the second section. The results are set out and discussed in the next section, before being summarised and assessed in the last.

BACKGROUND TO THE STUDY

We begin by providing a background to the empirical study, allowing the research results to be considered in context. First, we outline various major features of the prevailing British retailing environment. Secondly, we briefly discuss some major aspects of retail marketing that are prominent in the literature.

The British Retailing Environment

Many of the current features of British retailing are familiar to the members of the general public who have observed physical changes in shops since the war. The reduction in the number of 'corner shops', the development of self-service, the growth of supermarkets and the spread of nationwide chain stores are obvious day-to-day observations. However, the overall impact of these changes has been systematically recorded in the literature, providing a base for empirical studies.

Dawson [1979] has appraised the magnitude of the effect of these changes, not only in Britain, but across the Western world. He considers the impact on society to be profound. While retail outlets have remained the major channel for manufacturers of consumer goods to distribute their products, they have achieved greater prominence as the major source for the public to obtain the many goods and services required to satisfy the complex range of needs and wants experienced in modern Western societies. Shopping as a human activity appears to have become more complex than the mere acquisition of goods. Early research by Tauber [1972] identified eleven shopping motives, ranging from housewife role-playing, through self-gratification, to peer group attraction and social encounters. Similar research by Buttle and Coates [1984] also showed that shopping is based on many motives, of which the acquisition of goods is but one.

Major changes in the retailing sector have been cited by Akehurst [1983], Burns [1983], Davies and Kirby [1984], Davies and Gilligan [1985] and Richards and Smiddy [1985]. These changes have been classified as; increased concentration, intensified competition, growth of own labels and generics, improved productivity, increased retailer power, and industry maturity.

Increased Concentration: Davies and Kirby [1984] cite the decline in shops in Britain as being from about 583,000 outlets in 1950 to around

354,000 in 1980, representing a reduction of 40 per cent. This has obviously led to a smaller number of larger stores, while the retailing organisations have become larger and have obtained higher market shares. For example, by 1980, as shown by Burns [1983], the top ten grocery firms held over 40 per cent of sales in Great Britain. Although the 1970s saw the metamorphosis to larger retail outlets, development was slow compared with the rest of Europe. This was hampered by government policies and adverse attitudes of local authorities [Sumner and Davies 1978 and Cassells 1980].

Intensified Competition: The general picture is a movement to an oligopoly-type market structure. Rushton [1982], for example, has suggested that the large food retailing organisations typify this type of competition. Although objectives relating to increasing market share and its retention have affected competitive conditions, other considerations are of equal importance. Larger stores mean larger overheads per store, which need to be recovered from high sales volume per store. This has led to price competition among retailers, as well as consequential pressure for quantity discounts being applied to producers. Moreover, both intensified competition and largeness of organisations have led to changes in management structures, causing writers such as Knee and Walters [1985] to comment on the complexities of decision-making in these organisations.

Growth of Own Labels and Generics: By 1980 many large retailers, including the majority of supermarkets, had their own brands, selling in competition with manufacturers' brands. Although they were sold partly through price competition, evidence recently reported in the trade press indicates that some customers may be concerned about a perceived lack of fairness on the part of manufacturers that is not attributed to retailers. Consequently, such perceptions may well contribute to the sale of own labels and generics.

Improved Productivity: Livesey and Hall [1981] conclude that retailing has become an industry of high productivity in the British economy. Dawson and Kirby [1977] found that, particularly in grocery retailing, sales per employee have increased as store sizes have grown. Although such measures do not include sales generated as a ratio of store overheads, they do at least point to some improvements across the industry.

Increased Retailer Power: Given some of these trends, it is not surprising to find that all the writers mentioned above make some reference to the power that retailers have been able to exert over manufacturers. Whereas producers used to be able to dictate the manufacturer-retailer relationship, the large and growing size of retailers has enabled them to reverse the relative degrees of power. Two further developments have contributed to the power shift. First, there has been a rapid decline in the use of wholesalers, as illustrated by Hall [1979], so that most large retailers deal direct with the manufacturers. Second, although perhaps a nebulous claim at the present time, advances in information technology within distribution channels are likely, as argued by Piercy [1983], to give advantages to retailers but not to manufacturers.

Industry Maturity: The final point considered here is the contention of Richards and Smiddy [1985] that British retailing has moved into the maturity stage of its industry life-cycle. Those two writers point to several symptoms of this, including a surfeit of stores, an epidemic of take-overs and mergers, decline in gross margins, falling returns on investment, greater emphasis on price competition and increased advertising expenditure. However, although we raise this contention, we take the view that there is currently insufficient evidence to support such a claim fully.

The Nature of Retail Marketing

In this section we address three major features of retail marketing that have been given considerable attention within the literature. These provide part of the background against which the research results need to be considered.

First, as already mentioned, shopping has become a complex human activity, going far beyond the mere acquisition of goods, with the research by Tauber [1972] indicating eleven shopping motives. In accordance with this, we specify the retail product offering as consisting of four levels. These are:

- physical products produced by manufacturers, which them-selves can be classified into core, tangible and augmented product levels[1]
- the physical nature of the store, including its appearance, internal organisation and physical presentation
- the services performed by the staff which are necessary for the acquisition and consumption of physical products
- the total tangible, intangible and atmospheric environment that is made available for the gratification of all shopping motives.

Within these levels there is obviously a mixture of product and service marketing. However, as much of the former is conducted by manufacturers, retail marketing is very concerned with service marketing, with some added product marketing enhancing that of manufacturers. This combination of product and service has been well discussed within the literature, in relation to the debate on the nature of service marketing. For example, Kotler [1982] points out that services are often associated with physical products, while Shostack [1977] gives a classification of company offerings on a continuum from a pure tangible good to a pure service. Therefore, this first feature of retail marketing is that it not only needs to be concerned with the buyer behaviour associated with physical products, but also needs to tackle fully the complexities resulting from the necessity to provide the four levels of the retail product offering.

The second feature is the nature of marketing activities that are likely to be needed by retailers. Major marketing management texts suggest that the concept of the marketing mix is as applicable to retailers as it is to manufacturers. For example, Kotler [1984], Assael [1985] and Murphy and Ennis [1985]. Similarly, Piercy [1983] has suggested a simple paradigm consisting of a marketing strategy, a marketing mix programme and marketing information. This could be adopted in principle by any type of organisation seeking to orientate its activities to the requirements of the customers it serves. Davies, Gilligan and Sutton [1984] have provided some tentative observations on how grocery retailers appear to have, in general, developed marketing strategies and marketing mix programmes. For the former their observations are based on the work of Porter [1980]. Here they claim that cost reductions have been pursued to give a cost leadership element to strategy, differentiation strategies have been achieved through image, innovation and quality, while a focus element to strategy is also claimed, through buyer groups or geographical selection. The marketing mix observations of Davies et al. [1984] are that it has tended towards three elements; being selective price reductions, adding value to products, and placing greater reliance on advertising.

The third feature of marketing the retail product offering is the planning of marketing into the future, as opposed to performing ad hoc marketing activities. Moyer [1983] has suggested that retailing has traditionally been concerned with the tactics of selling and merchandising, rather than the strategic issues of marketing. Similarly, Walters [1979] has suggested that retailers tend to practise a reactive management style, as opposed to one that features systematic strategic planning. However, he goes on to emphasise that this is despite the existence of strategic issues that retailing organisations need to address, in common with other organisations. Davies and Gilligan [1985] provide some additional tentative observations on the use of strategic planning by grocery retailers. One of those observations is that perhaps only the top three or four organisations use strategic planning at the level of sophistication prescribed in the literature.

METHODOLOGY

In designing the empirical study we considered it to be inappropriate to establish hypotheses, given the low level of previous empirical evidence and the current state of knowledge. Instead, we developed a range of objectives for the study, the attainment of which would provide an assessment of the practice of marketing by retailers. This range provided the basis for the formulation of a questionnaire, which was subsequently sent to a sample of British retail organisations.

The sampling frame was the Retail Directory [1985]. The sample was selected by including all retail organisations with more than five outlets, plus department stores. Excluded from the sample were organisations marketing services, such as banks, insurance companies and travel agents, so that the selected retail organisations all offer physical goods manufactured by other organisations. The sample excluded very small firms on the grounds that these might lack sufficient marketing management expertise necessary for the implementation of a systematic and structured marketing approach.

A structured questionnaire was mailed to 1,650 British retailing organisations. These were personally directed to the chief executive responsible for marketing or, where this identity was not available, personally to the Managing Director. As it was recognised that major marketing differences were likely between shopping and convenience goods, the respondents were asked to respond in relation to either group of products, indicating their choice. All respondents were asked to confine their comments to the store or stores for which they had marketing responsibility.

The overall aim of the survey was to examine marketing orientation through investigations of the utilisation of the elements of the marketing mix. Additionally we investigated perceptions of the overall importance of marketing and the sources of information used in marketing decision-making. Each question was of a similar type. Each included a number of relevant factors and the respondents were asked to indicate the relative degree of importance of each of the factors to that particular investigation. Importance was measured on a 1 to 5 scale representing levels of importance ranging through nil, low, moderate, high and utmost. For each question the factors were presented in a randomly determined order, although the order of the questions themselves was based on a logical progression to avoid respondent fatigue or confusion.

A total of 282 responses was obtained, giving an overall response rate of 17 per cent, of which 264 were usable, yielding a net response rate of 15.8 per cent. The profile of respondent organisations is given in Tables 1 and 2. Several features of this profile are worth noting. First, nearly 60 per cent of the responses were from directors, although almost all respondents can be considered to be at a senior level. Second, the distribution of respondent organisations by size, based on the measures of annual sales turnover and number of stores, appears to show little significant difference from the population from which it was drawn. Third, a reasonable distribution of respondents by type of store was obtained. Finally, the split by convenience and shopping goods was considered to be acceptable to give a balance of likely differences necessary for the marketing of the two different product classifications.

THE RESULTS

The results are presented in six sections. First, we report respondents' views on the overall importance of the marketing function, while section two addresses the relative importance attaching to individual elements of the marketing mix. The third section concerns sources of marketing information and sections four to six refer to marketing decisions about the mix elements of products, prices and promotions.

Declared Importance of Marketing

Here the respondents were asked to rate on the five-point scale ranging from nil to utmost the importance of marketing to the success of their company. The response is shown in Table 3. Significantly, nearly 30 per cent of the sample perceive marketing as being of utmost importance while 73 per cent cited it as having high or utmost importance and this might be interpreted favourably. However, some 30 per cent of the respondents assigned only moderate, low or nil importance to marketing and this will be regarded as disappointing by the current audience. We would point out that a truly marketing orientation among all the respondents and their firms would, of course, have resulted in a 100 per cent allocation of the term utmost to the importance of marketing.

Marketing Mix Factors

For this enquiry we listed various factors relating to the marketing mix and asked respondents to rate them on the five-point scale of importance. A notable feature of the resonse, shown in Table 4, is that almost all of the variables achieved high means. Of the 16 variables, six have a mean higher than 4 (high importance), three more exceed 3.5 (moderate to high importance) while only one mean was below 3.

Company/store image achieved the highest mean and this is consistent with retailers needing to find an effective marketing strategy given the trends of tightening concentration and increasing competition. Although the development of own labels and generics has allowed retailers to develop some competitive differential, lack of differentiation of manufacturer brands at the point of sale necessitates continued store differentiation.

The other variables with means higher than 4 are quality of sales assistants, product quality, product range, product display and store layout. We equate this group with components of the retail product, as discussed in the first section. Sales assistants are obviously of central importance in the execution of all the service elements of the retail product, quality and range relate to the importance of manufacturers' physical products, whereas display and layout relate to the importance of the physical nature of the store. We might also consider superior products over competitors and product uniqueness to be part of the retail product. However, these variables were given lower means and this was perhaps predictable since they are likely to be more influenced by manufacturers, leading retailers to see them as less critical features of their own mix formulations.

TABLE 1
PROFILE OF RESPONDENT ORGANISATIONS

	Absolute Frequency	Relative Frequency (%)
Annual Sales Turnover (£m)		
Under 5	104	39.4
5 to 24	49	18.6
25 to 99	31	11.8
100 to 499	26	9.8
500 to 999	6	2.5
1,000 to 2,999	12	4.5
Over 3,000	8	3.0
No response	28	10.6
	264	100
Number of Stores		
1 only	39	14.7
2 to 5	44	16.7
6 to 9	34	12.9
10 to 19	18	6.8
20 to 49	30	11.4
50 to 99	29	11.0
100 to 199	26	9.8
Over 200	44	16.7
	264	100

Although Table 4 shows price to be less important than image or features of the retail product it is nevertheless important in absolute terms. This accords with the view expressed earlier whereby price competitiveness is a major theme of retail marketing strategy. Price is, of course, always likely to be important since it is a principal determinant of consumer demand and for retailers it is the only mix ingredient that directly generates revenue – all others being cost creation variables that support price.

Excluding after-sales service and credit terms, the remaining variables can be seen as the promotional activities of retailers. Apart from sales promotions, all these factors received a mean score slightly in excess of moderate importance. Hence, the results suggest that, although promotions feature in marketing mix programmes, they are

TABLE 2

PROFILE OF RESPONDENT ORGANISATIONS

	Absolute Frequency	Relative Frequency (%)
Position of Respondents		
Managing Director	87	33.0
Director	39	14.8
Marketing Director	27	10.2
General Manager	25	9.5
Store Manager	24	9.1
Marketing Manager	28	10.6
Other Title	34	12.8
	264	100.0
Type of Store		
Department store	56	21.2
Supermarket	27	10.3
Hypermarket	6	2.3
Multiple-shop	116	43.9
Variety store	13	4.9
Convenience store	3	1.1
Co-operative store	14	5.3
Mail order	8	3.0
Other type	21	8.0
	264	100.0
Product Classification		
Convenience goods	107	40.5
Shopping goods	157	59.5
	264	100.0

generally perceived to be less important than the previously discussed variables. Finally, after-sales service and customer credit are services that retailers could use to pursue competitive differentials over other retailers. Therefore it is perhaps surprising that they were not found to be higher in the rankings. We anticipate that further analysis will reveal considerable variation of the importance given to some of these mix

TABLE 3

DECLARED IMPORTANCE OF MARKETING FOR SUCCESSFUL
COMPANY PERFORMANCE

Degree of Importance		Absolute Frequency	Relative Frequency (%)
No response		7	2.7
Nil	1	1	0.4
Low	2	15	5.7
Moderate	3	48	18.2
High	4	114	43.1
Utmost	5	79	29.9
		N = 264	100

TABLE 4

MEAN IMPORTANCE OF MARKETING MIX FACTORS

Factor	Mean Importance	SD
Company/store image	4.40	0.71
Quality of sales assistants	4.37	0.76
Product quality	4.34	0.73
Product range	4.23	0.68
Product display	4.02	0.79
Store layout	4.01	0.73
Price	3.81	0.90
Sales promotions	3.62	1.00
Superior products over competitors	3.61	1.05
After sales service	3.37	1.29
Advertising	3.35	1.11
Labelling	3.33	0.98
Brand/Trade marks	3.33	1.06
Packaging	3.23	1.04
Product uniqueness	3.04	1.21
Customer credit terms	2.39	1.23

elements by retailers of, respectively, shopping and convenience products.

Sources of Information

The respondents were asked to rate each of several information sources using the five-point scale of importance in relation to their marketing decision-making. Analysis of the response shown in Table 5 indicates that objective information collection is not a feature of retailers' marketing management practices. Management contributions (executive judgement) was given high importance while customer and sales assistants' contributions as well as marketing research and test marketing received less than moderate importance. Although the high score attached to awareness of competitors' activities appears apt, there is otherwise clearly much scope for improving the quality of the information sources, and thereby the information itself, which underlie retailers' marketing decisions. These findings suggest an absence among many retailers of the high levels of reliable strategic and marketing planning discussed in the literature.

Product Decision-Making

In researching retailers' product decision-making in the context of the retail product we pursued two lines of enquiry. One question asked about the importance of factors that influence product mix decisions while the other question was concerned with the importance of the services provided for customers. The two sets of responses are set out in Tables 6 and 7.

As in the previous section, the most important influence on the marketing mix decision is management judgement, while marketing research received less than moderate importance. Moreover, other variables that should be associated with a marketing orientation toward product mix management are customer requests, competitors' products and sales assistants' suggestions, but these received only moderate importance. These results confirm the suspicions of a general low level of strategic and marketing planning referred to above. Another notable aspect of Table 6 is that both manufacturers' and wholesalers' suggestions are given moderate importance. We attribute this to the increased power of retailers which leads them to downgrade the importance of the judgement of external organisations that are further removed from the market than are retailers themselves.

Table 7 shows friendly and effficient sales assistants are of major importance in the customer service ratings, with a mean score of 4.49, the highest in the entire study. This was perhaps predictable given the high service element of the retail product allied to the inseparability of services *per se* and those who perform them, as discussed by writers such as Cowell [1984]. It is somewhat perverse, however, that although the respondents attach major importance to the role of sales assistants in the service mix, they pay them, as noted earlier, far less regard as sources of marketing information and as contributors of suggestions concerning product mix decisions.

Other factors in Table 7 having more than moderate importance are wide product choice, easy to find products, quick service, little queuing, plenty of space and adequate car parking. All except the first of these relate to the store itself which is patently of considerable importance to retailers of all types since it directly affects customers' shopping efficiency. The remaining variables were given less than moderate importance on average across the sample. We suggest, however, that the importance of these factors varies substantially across retailers by product type. For example, credit is probably highly important among sellers of electrical appliances, with music being

TABLE 5
MEAN IMPORTANCE OF SOURCES OF INFORMATION FOR MARKETING DECISION-MAKING

Source	Mean Importance	SD
Management contributions	4.01	0.70
Awareness of competitors' activities	3.72	0.84
Customers' contributions	3.11	0.88
Sales assistants' suggestions	2.98	0.89
Manufacturers' contributions	2.92	0.99
Marketing research	2.74	1.25
Test marketing results	2.73	1.22

TABLE 6
MEAN IMPORTANCE OF FACTORS IN PRODUCT MIX DECISION-MAKING

Factor	Mean Importance	SD
Management judgement	4.31	0.65
Customer requests	3.28	0.95
Competitors' products	3.14	0.85
Manufacturers' advertising	2.99	1.09
Sales assistants' suggestions	2.93	0.89
Marketing research results	2.90	1.19
Manufacturers' representatives' suggestions	2.78	0.97
Wholesalers' suggestions	2.38	0.98

TABLE 7
MEAN IMPORTANCE OF CUSTOMER SERVICES

Factor	Mean Importance	SD
Efficient & friendly sales assistants	4.49	0.67
Wide choice of products	3.90	0.88
Easy to find products	3.72	0.85
Quick service	3.69	0.96
Little queuing	3.57	0.97
Plenty of space	3.24	0.88
Adequate car parking	3.14	1.38
Late night opening	2.72	1.25
Credit facilities	2.54	1.28
Delivery service	2.32	1.32
Seating for customers	2.12	1.06
Background music	2.04	1.05

emphasised more by retailers of fashion clothes. Finally, late-night opening may be interesting in light of the current changes in legally permitted retail opening hours. The relevant response here suggests that retailers view this as having only near-moderate customer-service benefits, although again this may well vary across retailer types. Forthcoming articles in this series will address such variations.

Pricing Decisions

The respondents were asked to rate each of several potential influences on their price decisions. The results set out in Table 8 show that all but the last variable achieved mean scores indicating above moderate importance. The two most highly rated factors are value to customers and customer acceptance. This is clearly consistent with a marketing orientation, as is the high score attaching to competitors' prices. We ascribe the low importance accorded manufacturers' recommendations to the increased power of retailers, while the much higher score given to mark-up on costs needs no explanation for readers of this journal. Finally, the remaining factors are pricing objectives, these being targets concerning profits, volume, price stability and market share. All of these were given substantial importance and all are common pricing objectives (see, for example, Shipley [1986]). The setting of objectives and monitoring of performance to achieve relevant objectives is, of course, standard practice in the systematic planning of any business function and it is likely to lead to improved efficiency (see, for example, Greenley [1986]). However, although these particular results do indicate some adherence to systematic planning by some retailers, some of the findings presented earlier run counter to this conclusion.

Promotions Decisions

In researching retailers' promotions and advertising decisions, we asked the respondents two questions. The first requested them to rate the importance of each variable in a list of promotional methods while the second asked them to indicate the importance of a range of influences on their advertising decisions. The respective responses are displayed in Tables 9 and 10.

The results concerning the importance of promotional methods shown in Table 9 confirm the ratings given earlier to sales promotions (3.62) and advertising (3.35) in Table 4 which showed these to be less highly rated than other mix elements. Attractive pricing is the most important promotional tool, closely followed by product displays, in-store promotions, press advertising and window displays. All the other variables were given moderate importance or less and some, such as trading stamps and cinema advertising, received very low scores indeed. A general influence is that factors associated with the internal organisation of the store such as product display and in-store promotions are more important than external media advertising. Again, however, we expect to find that the importance of the various promotional devices varies substantially among the retailers in different product groups.

The results given in Table 10 show customer requirements and target

TABLE 8
MEAN IMPORTANCE OF FACTORS IN PRICE DECISION-MAKING

Factor	Mean Importance	SD
Value to customers	4.21	0.77
Customer acceptance	3.96	0.73
Target profits	3.85	1.09
Competitors' prices	3.79	0.91
Markup on purchase costs	3.72	0.85
Target sales volume	3.34	1.02
Price stability	3.23	0.93
Target market share	3.06	1.16
Manufacturers' recommended price	2.64	1.12

TABLE 9
MEAN IMPORTANCE OF PROMOTIONAL METHODS

Factor	Mean Importance	SD
Attractive prices	3.89	0.97
Product displays	3.85	0.91
In-store promotions	3.68	0.98
Press advertising	3.53	1.19
Window displays	3.52	1.30
Packaging	3.05	1.08
Labelling	3.01	1.08
Posters	2.89	1.16
Television advertising	2.51	1.48
Competitions	2.23	1.01
Money-off vouchers	2.16	1.04
Radio advertising	2.10	1.11
Collectable items	2.03	1.21
Free samples	1.82	0.89
Trading stamps	1.24	0.80
Cinema advertising	1.18	0.50

TABLE 10
MEAN IMPORTANCE OF FACTORS IN ADVERTISING DECISION-MAKING

Factor	Mean Importance	SD
Customer requirements	3.75	0.99
Target profits	3.75	1.08
Target sales volume	3.66	1.08
Budget constraints	3.42	1.03
Manufacturers' advertising	2.98	1.08
Target market share	2.96	1.26
Competitors' advertising	2.91	1.10

profits to be jointly the most important factors underpinning retailers'
advertising decisions while target volume and budget constraints also
attain above moderate importance, followed quite closely by all the
other factors. The prominence of customer needs in advertising

planning is an important indicator of a marketing-orientated drive to provide information as well as, or instead of, merely persuasion. Setting targets for advertising suggests some systematic planning, although once more this is tempered by the earlier contradictory results. The moderate importance attaching to manufacturers' advertising merits some discussion. Producers' advertising has major pull-through effects on consumers which provide benefits for retailers. Indeed, Shipley [1985] has reported that producers' pull-through advertising and sales promotions activities are treated as major supplier selection criteria by many retailers of convenience goods and even by some sellers of shopping products. In this light, the cited importance of manufacturers' advertising by the current respondents may be considered rather low.

SUMMARY AND REMARKS

This article presents an early overview of results from a major empirical study of how marketing is used by British retailers. The principal findings are summarised as follows:

- as few as 30 per cent of the high-level respondents comprising the sample view marketing as being of utmost importance to their firms' success, although 73 per cent give it high importance or more
- company/store image was cited as the most important marketing mix component, followed by a group of variables representing the retail product, then by price and finally by promotional factors
- the most highly-rated source of marketing information was management judgement while marketing research and test marketing received the lowest ratings
- executive judgement was given far more importance than customer requests, sales assistants suggestions and marketing research as influence on the composition of the product mix
- efficient and friendly sales assistants was cited as the principal customer service variable followed by a wide choice of products and then by physical characteristics of the store which affect customers' shopping efficiency
- value to customers and customer acceptance were the most prominent influences in price decision-making while common formal pricing objectives are also specified
- attractive prices was the most highly-rated promotional device followed closely by promotional variables within the store which were generally treated as more important than media advertising
- customer requirements and profit targets are the principal factors affecting advertising decisions although there are several additional important variables.

Overall, these results provide an equivocal view of the efficacy of the marketing practices of retailers. On the one hand, a large proportion of the respondents attach high importance to the marketing function and in some cases to customer requirements. However, a formal systematic implementation of the marketing concept would result in the utmost importance being attached to these factors. Moreover, despite the high importance accorded the marketing function, the findings relating to marketing procedures do not support an application of this level of commitment. For example, while image was found to be of primary importance in the marketing mix, promotional mix variables to project image were found to be of relatively limited importance.

Similarly, while a group of factors representing the retail product were also of high importance within the marketing mix, little evidence of a systematic marketing approach to product decisions was found, with executive judgement being very prominent in both information collection and decisions on product offerings. Although sales assistants were seen to be the most important customer service (in line with services marketing theory), the results also demonstrate relatively little use of sales assistants' knowledge when forming marketing decisions, despite their continuing direct exposure to buyer behaviour.

Also confusing is that, although customer considerations were accorded principal importance in price determination, there is no clear indication of how these retailers learn about customer requirements, bearing in mind their limited use of formal information gathering methods. What is encouraging about the price component, however, is that it seems not to be the only, nor even the predominant, competitive weapon, despite the intensely competitive conditions currently affecting the retail sector.

Finally, we steer clear of conclusions at this early stage in our researches. We believe, nevertheless, that this paper is of use to both practitioners and academics alike.

NOTES

The authors wish to acknowledge the computing assistance given to them by Ralph Bailey in the preparation of this article.

1. For those readers, not familiar with these concepts, the core product is the major benefit of the product offering which is aimed at the central consumer need. The tangible product includes product features, product quality, packaging, brand name and styling, all of which enhance appeal relative to competitive products. Here image-building for competitive differential is important but augmentation can also include after-sales service, warranties, installation, delivery, credit facilities, and price-discounting.

REFERENCES

Akehurst, G., 1983, 'Concentration in Retail Distribution: Movement and Significance', *The Service Industries Journal*, Vol.3, No.2, 161–79.

Assael, H. 1985, *Marketing Management: Strategy and Action*, Boston: Kent Publishing.

Burns, J., 1983, 'A Synoptic View of the Food Industry', in J. Burns, J. McInnerney and A. Swinbank (eds.), *The Food Industry, Economics and Policies*, London: Heinemann.

Buttle, F. and M. Coates, 1984, 'Shopping Motives', *The Service Industries Journal*, Vol.4, No.1, 71–81.

Cassells, S.C., 1980, 'Retail Competition and Planning', *Retail and Distribution Management*, Vol.8, No.6, 32–7.

Cowell, D.W., 1984, *The Marketing of Services*, London: Heinemann.

Davies, K. and C. Gilligan, 1985, 'Changing Retailing Structures: the Implications for Marketing Education', *Business Education*, Vol.6, No.1, 22–9.

Davies, K., C. Gilligan and C. Sutton, 1984, 'The Changing Competitive Structure of British Grocery Retailing', *Quarterly Review of Marketing*, Vol.10, No.1, 1–9.

Davies, R.L. and D.A. Kirby, 1984, 'Current Trends in Distribution Research', *Management Bibliographies and Reviews*, Vol.10, No.1/2, 68–92.

Dawson, J.A., 1979, 'Retail Trends in the EEC', in Davies, R.L. (ed.), *Retail Planning in the European Community*, Farnborough: Saxon House.

Dawson, J.A. and D.A. Kirby, 1977, 'Shop Size and Productivity in British Retailing', *European Journal of Marketing*, Vol.11, No.4, 262–71.

Greenley, G.E., 1986, *The Strategic and Operational Planning of Marketing*, Maidenhead: McGraw-Hill.

Hall, M., 1979, 'The Place of the Wholesaler in Distribution', *Retail Distribution Management*, Vol.7, No.5, 49–51.

Knee, D. and D. Walters, 1985, *Strategy in Retailing: Theory and Appliation*, Oxford: Philip Allan.

Kotler, P., 1982, *Principles of Marketing*, Englewood Cliffs: Prentice-Hall.

Kotler, P., 1984, *Marketing Management: Analysis, Planning and Control*, Englewood Cliffs: Prentice-Hall.

Livesey, F. and R.J. Hall, 1981, *Retailing: Developments and Prospects to 1985*, London: Staniland Hall.

Moyer, M.S., 1983, 'Marketing Planning in Retailing: Making the Basics Work, *Proceedings of the Annual Conference of the Marketing Education Group*, Cranfield School of Management.

Murphy, P.E. and B.M. Enis, 1985, *Marketing*, Glenview: Scott, Foresman & Co.

Piercy, N., 1983, 'Retailer Information Power', *Marketing Intelligence and Planning*, Vol. 1, No. 2, 40–55.

Piercy, N., 1983, 'Retailer Marketing – Information Strategies', *European Journal of Marketing*, Vol. 17, No. 6, 5–15.

Porter, M.E., 1980, *Competitive Strategy*, New York: The Free Press.

Retail Directory, 1985, London: Newman Books.

Richards, J. and P. Smiddy, 1985, 'The Retail Market – the Non-Property View', in Healey and Baker (eds.), *Retail Report 1985*, London: Healey and Baker.

Rushton, A., 1982, 'The Balance of Power in a Marketing Channel, Profitable Co-operation of Manufacturers and Retailers, *ESOMAR Conference*, Brussels: ESOMAR.

Shipley, D.D., 1985, 'Resellers Supplier Selection Criteria for Different Consumer Products', *European Journal of Marketing*, Vol. 19, No. 7, 26–36.

Shipley, D.D., 1986, 'Dimensions of Flexible Price Management', *Quarterly Review of Marketing*, Vol. 11, No. 3, 1–7.

Shostack, G.L., 1977, 'Breaking Free from Product Marketing', *Journal of Marketing*, Vol. 41, No. 2, 73–80.

Sumner, J. and K. Davies, 1978, 'Hypermarkets and Superstores: What do the Planning

Authorities Really Think?', *Retail and Distribution Management*, Vol. 6, No. 4, 8–15.

Tauber, E.M., 1972, 'Why do people shop?', *Journal of Marketing*, Vol. 36, No. 4, 46–9.

Walters, D., 1979, 'Plotting Retailing Strategy', *Proceedings of the PTRC Summer Annual Meeting*, University of Warwick.

This chapter first appeared in *The Service Industries Journal*, Vol.8, No.1 (1988).

4

The Status Quo of the Marketing Organisation in UK Retailing: A Neglected Phenomenon

by

Nigel Piercy and Nicholas Alexander

Generally the function of marketing in many different types of organisations has been widely recognised in recent years, and accordingly various studies have described the development of the marketing department in both the manufacturing and service industries. However, surprisingly little attention has been devoted to delineating or describing the role of the marketing department in retailing organisations, in spite of evidence of increasing employment of marketing personnel to implement proactive retailer marketing strategies, and correspondingly large increases in marketing expenditures by retailers. This article seeks to redress the balance by reporting the findings of a survey of the operation of marketing departments by 70 of the largest retailing organisations in the UK.

INTRODUCTION

The importance attached to marketing as an organisational function is well known, and is reflected at various levels in the management literature. While much of this writing is concerned with philosophies of marketing-orientation, one tangible aspect of the implementation of marketing in companies is the formal organisational arrangements which pertain to the appointment of a Chief Marketing Executive (CME) and the location and establishment of a marketing department.

There are those who suggest that we should be concerned not with the 'trappings' of the organisational arrangements for marketing, but rather with the 'substance' of managerial attitudes and orientation to the marketplace [Ames, 1970]. However, accepting that marketing organisation is only one aspect of the implementation of the marketing concept, we have followed the precedent, set by various analysts [Hise, 1965; Weigand, 1961], of studying the formal organisation of marketing, following the logic, provided by one of the early seminal studies in this field, that:

> the marketing concept is perceived as the integration just below top management of those activities oriented primarily to customers . . . In particular organizational terms this means that the chief marketing officer (regardless of his title) has authority over selling advertising and market research. [Carson, 1968]

It is this approach which has been adopted explicitly or implicitly in the various studies of marketing organisation which are available.

When we turn to these earlier studies, however, it is apparent that a significant gap exists. There are a number of studies of the CME and the Marketing Department in manufacturing [e.g., BIM 1970; Hayhurst and Wills 1972; Piercy, 1986]. Similarly, there are some works concerned with the role of marketing in particular service industries, e.g., in banking [Stall, 1978], in postal services [Barnhill, 1974], in public utilities [Warshaw, 1976], and in public transport [Hovell, 1976]. Indeed, there have also been more general surveys of the role of marketing in the service sector, both in the USA [George and Barksdale, 1974; Upah, 1980], and in the UK [Hooley and Cowell, 1985].

However, in these various service industry studies – explicitly in the former group, and implicitly in the latter group – the role of marketing in the retailing of consumer products has been excluded from consideration. While some attention has been given to such general questions as developing a strategic marketing approach to services retailing [Bessom and Jackson, 1985], or the difference between retailing services and products [Judd, 1968], the authors have been unable to find any study of the emergence of marketing as a formally organised function in retailing.

Most recently, Greenley and Shipley [1987; 1988] have attempted to delineate the role of marketing in retailing but have focused on the ranking of marketing problems and activities in retailer marketing, rather than the organisational and strategic issues which preoccupy us here. This last work does, however, serve to reinforce the legitimacy of retailer marketing as an area for study, compared with the openly dismissive approach of some earlier researchers [Pugh, 1970].

This lacuna is all the more surprising in view of the evidence that retailers in the UK and the USA are increasingly involved in developing and implementing proactive customer-focused marketing strategies [e.g., Doyle and Cooke, 1979; Bensmore and Kaufman, 1985; Greenley and Shipley, 1988], which has been reflected in the major increases in retailer expenditure on marketing activities like advertising [*Retail Business*, 1986; Greenley and Shipley, 1987]. Indeed, at the purely observational level, retailing is an area of substantial growth in the employment of specialist marketing personnel.

Our interest in exploring this gap in knowledge is an extension of earlier studies of the marketing organisational forms adopted by manufacturing firms. In these earlier studies it was found that the operation of the marketing department varied in a systematic way and that it was possible to model four prototypical marketing department forms [Piercy, 1986]. The significance of this work lies in two areas. First, it provides an empirical basis for examining the development of the marketing organisation in a particular company [Piercy, 1987b], and secondly, it provides insight into the link between the structure and organisational processes surrounding the marketing department and decisional outcomes such as resource allocations and the strategies adopted by firms [Piercy, 1987a; 1987c]. However, one of the areas not covered by that earlier work was the impact of the channel of distribution on the organisational form taken by the marketing department. In fact, that earlier work led to the hypothesis formulated elsewhere [Piercy, 1987c] that the power of retailers to control marketing strategy in the channel of distribution (through their relative size and concentration, position in relation to the consumer, and technology-based information advantages) is directly related to the emergence of retailer marketing departments.

As a precursor to a full testing of this hypothesis and the attempt to replicate the manufacturer marketing department process and structure model in retailing, it was decided to undertake an exploratory study of the existence and form of marketing departments in retailing companies. It is the results of this exploratory study which are discussed below. These present findings are important in providing a bench-mark, and for the future research directions they suggest.

It is of some interest to note that other researchers have also focused on retailer marketing, in parallel but independent studies completed at approximately the same time as the work reported here [Greenley and Shipley, 1987; 1988]. Since these papers have appeared in recent issues of this *Journal* they provide an interesting point of comparison.

A SURVEY OF LARGE UK RETAILERS

In view of the suggestion that marketing is becoming an institutionalised function in retail companies in the UK, and that there has been little attempt to develop a base of knowledge or understanding of how this operates, a study has been made of the marketing function and its organisation in major UK retailing firms.

The descriptive *objectives* of the study start from a base of largely attempting to replicate similar studies of manufacturing firms [e.g., Hayhurst and Wills, 1972; Hooley, *et al.* 1984; Piercy, 1986]:

- to establish that marketing departments exist in retailing companies, and their standing in the organisation;
- where marketing departments do exist in retailing organisations, to examine their operation in terms of responsibilities;
- to examine, as an example of a critical marketing activity, the involvement of retailers in formal marketing information functions;

- to relate these organisational issues to the control by retailers of marketing strategy in the channel of distribution.

The *methodology* was to conduct a small number of pilot interviews with senior retail executives in a number of different types of retailing companies, leading to a pre-tested postal questionnaire mailed to retail firms, followed by a small number of telephone interviews of Chief Marketing Executives and Chief Executives, in a sample of the largest retail organisations in the UK. For the survey, 277 retailing companies were approached and some 25 per cent provided full responses. In fact, these 70 respondents represent of the order of 15 per cent of the retail work-force and 16 per cent of total retail sales turnover in the UK. The sample is approximately one-third food retailers, 54 per cent clothing and other non-food retailing, and the remainder are variety stores and service retailers, such as TV rental and the like. Further methodological details are provided in the Appendix.

RESULTS

Marketing Departments in Retailing Organisations

The following points were established about the nature of the marketing department in large-scale retailing.

(a) The Departmentation of Marketing

TABLE 1

DEPARTMENTATION OF MARKETING

	Yes %	No %
Is there a Marketing Department	96	4
		(N=70)

Table 1 shows that virtually all the responding companies did in fact, have a marketing department. However, in terms of the representativeness of the sample it seems probable that the response is biased (possibly heavily) towards those comapnies which do have a marketing department, i.e., it is likely that those retail companies with no marketing department simply did not reply. Taking the limiting case, we can say that 25 per cent of the UK's largest retailers are known to have marketing departments, and it may (but only may) be substantially more.

It is clear, however, that what follows can at best be representative only of large retailers *with* marketing departments, not large retailers in general.

(b) The Age of Retailer Marketing Departments

Table 2 shows the length of time that the responding companies have operated a marketing department, suggesting that the majority of the

TABLE 2

AGE OF MARKETING DEPARTMENTS

	%
Less than 1 year	17
1 – 5 years	38
6– 10 years	25
More than 10 years	20
	(N = 60)

TABLE 3

SIZE OF RETAILER MARKETING DEPARTMENTS

No. of Employees in Marketing Department	%
Less than 5	37
6 – 10	31
11– 20	18
More than 20	14
	(N = 65)

TABLE 4

TREND IN MARKETING DEPARTMENT SIZE

The number of people employed in the Marketing Department is:	%
Decreasing	3
Stable	36
Increasing	61
	(N = 67)

TABLE 5

STATUS OF THE CHIEF MARKETING EXECUTIVE

The status of the CME compared with other department heads is:	%
Lower	3
Equal	68
Higher	29
	(N = 66)

departments were established in the 1980s and very few have been around for ten years or more. If this is compared with the Hayhurst and Wills [1972] and BIM [1970] surveys, the formalised marketing function appears to have arrived significantly later in retailing than in manufacturing, and it is likely that the marketing function is in an earlier stage of its life cycle in retailing [Piercy, 1985].

(c) *Employment and Marketing Department Size*

Table 3 demonstrates that two-thirds of the marketing departments are relatively small, i.e., less than ten employees. However, Table 4 does show it is also the case that in two-thirds of the responding companies the level of employment in marketing was increasing.

(d) *Status of the Marketing Department*

Table 5 shows respondents' rankings of the status of the head of the marketing department compared to the other departmental chief executives. This suggests that the chief marketing executive (CME) is most frequently on a par with other department heads (two-thirds of the companies) although interestingly in nearly a third of the companies the CME has attained a higher status.

(e) *Power of the Marketing Department*

More explicitly, respondents were asked to list the major departments in their companies and to indicate the power ranking they would give to each such department.

Table 6 summarises the proportion of 'votes' for the most powerful department gained by each of the departments cited by respondents and the proportion of companies seeing each type of department as the most

TABLE 6

THE MOST POWERFUL DEPARTMENT

	% of 1st Positions	% of Companies
Marketing	22	44
Finance	19	40
Buying	16	31
Personnel	7	15
Property	8	17
Other	27	54
	(N=96)	(N=48)

TABLE 7

BOARD REPRESENTATION OF THE MARKETING DEPARTMENT

Number of 'representatives' of the Marketing Department on the Board	%
0	12
1	82
2	6
	(N=65)

powerful. While in both measures the marketing department was frequently seen as the most powerful department (followed by Finance and Buying), it is the case only in a minority of the companies in the sample that the marketing department is seen as the most powerful department.

(f) Board Representation

Table 7 shows the degree to which marketing departments had 'representatives' on the Board of Directors, and suggests that the normal pattern is for the marketing department to have one 'representative' (i.e. the CME) on the board. It would seem then that normally the marketing department has representation on a par with the other functional interests in the firm, although it is notable that 12 per cent have no such representation at all.

(g) Marketing Orientation

In assessing the 'philosophy' or 'orientation' that respondents saw operating in their organisations, they were asked to indicate which of three statements [adapted from Hooley et al., 1984] came closest to describing their company's approach to doing business. The first of these reflected an undifferentiated approach to buying and re-selling, which is taken as a 'merchandising orientation'. The second approach involved an emphasis on promotion to ensure sales, and is taken as 'sales orientation'; and the third statement describes market analysis and adaptation to consumer needs, which is taken as 'marketing orientation'.

Even in these relatively crude terms, it is clear from Table 8 that few of these major retailers saw themselves as passive re-sellers of goods, i.e., simply merchandisers. Approximately one-third of the companies saw their approach to doing business as 'sales-oriented', while two-thirds saw themselves as 'marketing-oriented'. It should be borne in mind that this

TABLE 8

MARKETING ORIENTATION IN RETAILING

The Company's marketing approach	%
We buy from what is available and sell to whoever will buy (MERCHANDISING ORIENTATION)	6
We place a major emphasis on advertising and promotion to ensure sales (SALES ORIENTATION)	29
We place a major emphasis on prior analysis of the market and consumer needs, adapting our product-mix to meet them, if necessary (MARKETING ORIENTATION	65
	(N = 65)

sample is heavily weighted towards those companies *with* marketing departments, so it should be expected that most would recognise and claim to follow the dictates of the marketing concept, but none the less this does indicate a high degree of penetration of the marketing paradigm in a sector which has not previously been analysed in these terms.

(h) *Discussion*

A number of points may be summarised as a profile of marketing departments in large retailing organisations:

- in this sample, almost *all* firms had marketing departments (which limits the representativeness of the findings to large retailers *with* marketing departments), although indicating a relatively high penetration of major retailers;
- while most of the retailer marketing departments are small (fewer than ten employees) in the majority of the companies, marketing department size is increasing;
- in spite of its recency, the retailer marketing department enjoys equal status with other departments (and in one-third of the companies it has attained higher status);
- the marketing departments studied normally enjoy Board representation on a par with other departments, although this is not the case in a significant minority of companies;
- among the companies studied there is a claim in the majority of cases that they are marketing-oriented (as opposed to merchandising or sales-oriented), although it might well be expected that a sample of the type here would generally make such a claim.

At this stage it would seem that evidence has been found of a relatively high degree of penetration of the formalised marketing department in major retailing organisations, in terms of the existence of such a department and its growth, status, and representation.

There is no available earlier empirical bench-mark against which this can be compared, but we can conclude that marketing has clearly arrived in a sample of some of the largest companies in UK retailing (thus rendering obsolete the explicit or implicit assumption for these companies, at least, that marketing is in any way restricted to being a manufacturer function) and providing us with some justification in seeking to identify the nature of retailer marketing-operation.

CHIEF MARKETING EXECUTIVES IN UK RETAILING

Attention focused secondly, on the CME as the key figure in implementing marketing in a company.

(a) *Job Titles*

Table 9 shows a summary of the actual job titles reported (to an open-ended question rather than the normal checklist) and on the face of things contains few surprises – in three-quarters of the companies the CME is Marketing Manager or Director. The most revealing factor is what is by implication omitted – that none of the companies reveal the finding in some of the pilot interviews that the chief buyer or the merchandising director is, as such, the head of 'marketing'. In this sample, at least, it is clear that the head of marketing has a distinct identification, at least in terms of job title.

TABLE 9

CME JOB TITLES IN RETAILING

Job Titles	%
Marketing Director	60
Marketing Manager	15
Marketing Controller	15
Advertising Manager	1
Other	9
	(N=67)

TABLE 10

CME REPORTING LEVEL

CME reports to:	%
Managing Director/Chief Executive	73
Chairman	3
Group Sales/Marketing Director	9
Other	15
	(N=67)

(b) *Reporting Level*

The organisational level of the CME is shown by the line reporting levels shown in Table 10, which suggests that in three-quarters of the companies the CME reports to the chief executive level. The only major exception to this is where the respondent was operating in a subsidiary or division and reported to the local general manager. In only 15 per cent of the cases did the CME report to a level below the chief executive, i.e., where the CME was more junior in the hierarchy.

(c) *Chief Marketing Executive Responsibilities*

Table 11 shows the responses to the question, 'what degree of responsiblity has the head of the marketing department for decisions in the areas listed?'
    In relatively few cases were these areas of decision-making considered to

TABLE 11

CME RESPONSIBILITIES

	CME has full and sole responsibility %	Average Responsibility Score (5 = Full and sole, 1 = No responsibility)
Marketing Research	66	4.5
Marketing Staff Selection	62	4.5
Advertising	51	4.3
Marketing Planning	49	4.4
Sales Promotion	47	4.2
Marketing Training	46	4.1
New Product Launches	22	3.3
Negotiation with suppliers	21	2.5
Price setting	47	2.8
Own-brand decisions	19	2.8
In-store merchandising	17	3.2
Product selection & buying	15	2.7
Selling operations	10	2.4
Sales forcasting	10	2.8
Diversification Studies	9	2.8
Corporate planning/ Strategic planning	5	3.3
Stock levels	5	2.0
Investment appraisal	3	2.2
Selection of store sites	2	2.0
	(N = 64)	

be inappropriate, and generally where this was the response this seemed quite reasonable and easily explained – e.g., own-brand decision are not applicable if there are no own-brands, decision-making responsibility for the selection of store sites is not held if there are no new sites being considered, and so on.

In three areas, namely advertising, marketing research and marketing staff selection, the majority of marketing departments covered by the survey had full and sole responsibility. The majority (66 per cent) said they had full responsibility for marketing research, followed by 62 per cent with full responsibility for marketing staff selection and 51 per cent for advertising. These may, of course, be considered as core marketing service functions. It was perhaps a little surprising to find marketing planning being in the sole hands of the marketing departments in only 49 per cent of cases, though a further 40 per cent had major responsibilities in this area.

Staff selection for the marketing department is generally in the hands of the departments concerned: 96 per cent had major or full responsibility. A similar finding for marketing training was that 80 per cent had full or major control.

In the areas where a marketing department might clearly be expected to possess a certain degree of autonomy, the majority tended to do so, i.e., staffing of the department and marketing planning, market research, promotion and advertising and training. In these areas, nine out of every ten departments had substantial control over these functions (i.e., scored above the mid-point of the five-point scale used, with a mean greater than four).

A majority of departments had full or major control in new product launches and corporate or strategic planning (in the sense they scored above the mid-point of the scale). This displays a considerable involvement by the marketing departments of major retail companies in these areas, although this was rarely a full or sole responsibility of the CME.

In all the other decision areas CME responsibilities were scored below the mid-point of the scale suggesting a limited role compared with other executives in the company.

The picture which emerges is one of the retailer marketing department with quite considerable responsibility, though typically shared with others, within the areas of market research and planning, as well as sales promotion, and corporate and strategic planning, coupled with the internal organisational aspects of the department; but typically a far more limited degree of influence as far as the products themselves and store location are concerned, and perhaps most significantly even less in relation to the 'hard-edge' areas of the selling or merchandising functions.

(d) *Discussion*

The findings relating to the CME in retailing suggest the following points:

- the CME is normally a marketing manager or director (rather than buying or merchandising manager);
- the CME normally reports directly to the managing director, though in a significant minority of cases this is not the case;
- the CME's responsibility analysis suggests that (apart from marketing staff selection and training) the typical retailer CME is directly responsible only for advertising, sales promotion and marketing research. The involvement of the CME in the other areas of the marketing mix – product policy, pricing, stock levels, and so on – is typically far less. The CME appears only rarely to have direct control over strategic decision-making in such areas as investment appraisal, store site selection, sales forecasting for the company, and corporate/ strategic planning.

While it is normally the case that the retailer CME has the status of an identified job title and a reporting line to the managing director, it would appear that responsibilities for the key areas of marketing are normally shared with others. High levels of CME responsibility are usually restricted to advertising, promotion and marketing research, and do not extend to the other areas of the marketing mix, or to corporate strategy. In some cases it may be that we should accept that the marketing department has arrived in name but is relatively limited in its present impact on the retailer decision-making structure.

MARKETING INFORMATION IN RETAILING

It has been argued that the most critical activity in marketing is actually the processing of information from the marketing environment, particularly in the context of retailer power in the manufacturer/retailer relationship [Piercy, 1984]. A number of key points in this area, which have not previously been studied in the UK retailing sector, were isolated in the survey.

(a) *Marketing Research Organisation*

Table 12 suggests that formally organised marketing research (MR) units are found in less than half this sample of large retailing organisations, and in less than half of these cases was the MR unit located in the marketing department, reporting to the CME. It is important to note the majority of MR organisations were located in departments such as planning/research,

TABLE 12

MARKETING RESEARCH DEPARTMENTS

		Yes	No
Is there a formal marketing research unit?	No	32	37
		46%	54%

TABLE 13

AGE OF MARKETING RESEARCH DEPARMENTS

Age of MR Unit	%
Less than 1 year	46
2 – 5 years	33
6 – 10 years	18
More than 10 years	3
	(N=33)

TABLE 14

SIZE OF MARKETING RESEARCH DEPARMENTS

Number of MR Employees	%
1 – 2	45
3 – 5	40
More than 5	15
	(N=33)

performance analysis, or corporate planning, and reported to the heads of those departments, or directly to the chief executive.

(b) *Age of the Marketing Research Organisation*

Table 13 shows that the majority of the MR units which are formally organised, nearly 90 per cent are new to the companies concerned, i.e., they were established in the 1980s, indeed almost half are less than one year old.

(c) *Size of the MR Organisation*

As would be expected, in the vast majority of cases these units were small, as shown in Table 14. These figures are similar to the situation found regarding the age and size of the marketing departments themselves.

(d) *Types of MR Conducted in Retailing*

Retail firms in the survey were asked to indicate the frequency of their use of different types of marketing research, whether conducted by a formal MR unit or by others, with the results shown in Table 15.

TABLE 15

TYPES OF MARKETING RESEARCH IN RETAILING

| | Level of Use | | |
	Frequently	Sometimes	Never
	%	%	%
Market share analysis	63	31	6
Store audits	61	23	16
Pricing studies	54	36	10
Identification of customer characteristics	56	40	4
Competitor analysis	56	41	3
Market characteristics	51	42	7
Market potential for new stores	50	33	17
Consumer attitudes	50	42	8
Evaluation of store selling effectiveness	46	34	20
Studies of advertising effectiveness	43	41	16
New product/brand acceptance/ potential	37	42	21
Research into business trends	35	60	5
Market potential for existing stores	31	48	21
Advertising media research	31	48	21
Product test marketing	29	50	21
Studies of in-store layout effectiveness	27	44	29
Advertising copy research	13	48	39
Other types of marketing research	30	65	5
(N=61)			

In one sense, there was evidence of wide use of MR, in that all the listed forms of MR were reported by at least some of the firms. However, in terms of the types of MR conducted at least 'sometimes', the only really common MR is basic studies of markets and customers and business trends. At the other extreme, relatively large numbers of respondents 'never' conducted MR work in such areas as in-store lay-out studies or advertising research. It would be a mistake to read too much into the relatively crude data in Table 15, but the impression is one of very mixed approaches to MR in these companies, and this is reinforced by examining MR budgets (see below).

TABLE 16

ANNUAL MARKETING RESEARCH EXPENDITURE

	%
(a) In-house MR Expenditure	
0– £10,000	36
£10,000 – £50,000	42
More than £50,000	21
	(N=33)
(b) MR Agency Expenditure	
0– £10,000	36
£10,000 – £50,000	32
More than £50,000	32
	(N=41)
(c) Total MR Expenditure	
0– £20,000	34
£20,000 – £100,000	33
More than £100,000	33
	(N=30)

(e) *MR Expenditure*

In terms of the allocation of financial resources to MR, 33 companies identified their in-house expenditure as shown in Table 16. The range of annual expenditures is of some note, i.e., from zero in six cases to more than £100,000 p.a. in three cases.

As shown in Table 16 (b) agency MR expenditure was reported by 47 companies. The range of expenditure was again substantial – six stated zero, ten were spending less than £10,000 p.a., but four were spending more than £200,000 p.a.

More companies identified agency MR expenditure than in-house expenditure (although this may reflect the difficulty of costing activities internal to the company, particularly where there is no separate MR organisation). However, agency expenditures were larger than identified in-house spends.

Looking at Table 16 (c) perhaps the most striking finding is the variation betwen those companies spending little or no money on MR, and those with very large total budgets – the top expenditure was £400,000 and four of the companies were spending more than a quarter of a million pounds a year.

This raises some interesting questions for further study, particularly regarding the pay-off from such expenditures and the impact on retailer/manufacturer relationships.

(d) *Discussion*

From the data above, a number of tentative conclusions can be advanced about the marketing information function in these major UK retailers. The following points appear reasonably substantiated:

- Some half of the sample of the largest retail organisations in the UK had formally organised marketing research (MR) units of one kind or another.
- These units are almost all recently established, i.e., they are products of the 1980s and many are post-1985, suggesting that, as with the marketing department itself, the marketing information function has arrived later in retailing than in manufacturing in the UK.
- However, while MR units share recency with marketing departments, they frequently differ in their organisational location, since the majority of the MR units are *not* located in the marketing department but in departments such as corporate planning, performance analysis and planning/research.
- Most of these MR units are restricted in size to one to three members of staff.
- There is evidence of a wide range of MR activities in these retailing companies in the sense that all the listed MR types were in use. However, this use of MR emphasised market, competitor and customer analysis, and little coverage of such central issues as advertising effectiveness and product testing. There appears to be considerable diversity in the sample in the use of MR, reflected both in the types of MR used and the resources allocated to this activity.
- Total MR budgets in the companies varied from zero in some cases to nearly half a million pounds a year in others.
- In the area of new information technology there was relatively little evidence of the use of scanning data for market research applications, although this was planned for the future in a number of cases.

It should be noted that Greenley and Shipley [1988] found that MR was littled used by retailers, who relied more commonly on subjective management judgement of the marketplace. The greater variability in our findings reflects the nature of the sample, since we were dealing with larger firms, who are more likely to have adopted and formalised such work.

THE STRATEGIC MARKETING POWER OF RETAILERS

In addition to the structural issues, internal to the retailer organisation, discussed above, the survey made some attempt to evaluate the channel relationship with suppliers in two ways.

(a) *The Locus of Strategic Marketing Decision Making*

A section of the questionnaire was devoted to the relationship between suppliers and the retailer, and in particular, the division of marketing responsibilities and decision-making. The aim of the questions was to ascertain the perceived balance, within the distribution channel, of responsibility for strategic marketing decisions. The questions covered the major marketing mix variables: pricing, merchandising, product launches, development and branding, transport, advertising and promotions, and market research.

The model implied by this scale reflects a changing balance between retailer and manufacturer power in the following way:

Locus of strategic marketing decision	Retailer Power	Manufacturer Power
Manufacturer alone	Low	High
Manufacturer, but consults retailer		
Joint decision	Medium	Medium
Retailer, but consults manufacturer		
Retailer alone	High	Low

Clearly, interpretation must be cautious since the data are subjective and perceptual and we might anticipate that they contain some respondent bias.

In six of the eleven areas of strategic marketing decision-making, the most common reply was that it was the retailer's decision (solely or in consultation with the supplier). In only two cases, namely branding and brand images, and package design, was the supplier typically described as having total control.

The areas where the retailer had most power were clearly in setting price levels (including price-cutting) and in-store merchandising. In these areas, more than 90 per cent of companies considered decisions either totally within the control of the retailer, or as the retailer's decision in consultation with the supplier. In only two cases, namely branding and brand images, and package design, was the supplier described as having total control. Transport and stockholding was also seen to fall primarily within the preserve of the retailer.

Advertising, sales promotions, market research, and the launch of new products tended to show the same degree of high retailer responsibility.

However, the development of new products, branding and package design were perceived as largely in the hands of the supplier and not the retailer.

Table 17 shows the overall balance revealed by the questions concerning commercial decisions. If 'joint' decisions are seen as the fulcrum within the model, on only three issues did the weight of perceived influence exerted by the suppliers outweigh that of the retailers, and these areas are essentially manufacturing issues.

TABLE 17

BALANCE OF POWER IN MARKETING DECISION-MAKING

	The supplier has greater control	Joint control	The retailer has greater control
	%	%	%
In-store merchandising	0	3	97
Price cutting	0	6	94
Price levels	2	5	93
Transport and stockholding	6	15	79
Sales promotion	5	23	72
New product launches	17	13	70
Advertising products to consumers	17	14	69
Market research	12	19	69
Branding and brand images	50	5	45
Packaging design	48	7	45
Development of new products	41	26	33

TABLE 18

PERCEIVED RELATIONSHIP WITH SUPPLIERS

		%
1.	Conflict	2
2.	Competition	2
3.	Co-operation	65
4.	Consultation	27
5.	Joint decision-making	5
		(N=63)

(b) *Channel Relationships*

Secondly, the retailers in the study were asked to describe their general relationships with suppliers on a descriptive scale with the labels: Conflict, Competition, Co-operation, Consultation and Joint Decision-making. The responses to this question are shown in Table 18, where it can be seen that two-thirds of the respondents saw their channel relationship as 'co-operative', while most of the remainder saw the supplier relationship as 'consultative'. Very few of the respondents perceived channel relationships as conflictual or competitive, though equally very few, acknowledged the existence of joint decision-making.

On the face of things this suggests that the vast majority of these large-scale retailers see their relationships with suppliers as co-operative/consultative. However, if we compare this perception with the fact shown in Table 16, that these firms see most of the marketing mix variables as under retailer control, then our interpretation of what co-operative/ consultative relationships involves may be somewhat different – not least if we speculate what the suppliers' responses might have been to the same question.

It is interesting to compare this with the Greenley and Shipley [1987] finding that manufacturer-relations problems were seen as relatively unimportant by retailers.

The implication may be that the manufacturer relationship is not seen as conflictual or competitive by retailers – or indeed very important compared with other problems [Greenley and Shipley, 1987] – because major retailers of this type have already gained control over most of the major areas of strategic marketing decision-making. In the sense that overt conflict is likely to lessen when the battle is over, the interpretation of these figures may be one of reluctant co-operation by manufacturers who have only limited choices or strategic freedom in dealing with the major retailers in the UK. The present data do not permit more than speculation in this area.

(c) *Discussion*

The following tentative conclusions regarding supplier relationships are advanced:

- In the majority of marketing mix decision areas, the retailer is perceived as exercising greater control, i.e., the locus of strategic responsibility is perceived by these retailers to be closer to the retailer than the manufacturer in these strategic marketing decision areas.
- These retailer companies, perhaps not surprisingly, perceive channel relationships as co-operative/consultative rather than conflictual, although this must be interpreted in the context of the fact that they would seem to be controlling most of the significant elements of marketing strategy. The most interesting comparison to which we plan to proceed in the next stage of the research is that between retailer and manufacturer perceptions of these issues in the same channel of distribution.

CONCLUSIONS

It would be a mistake to claim too much for a relatively limited set of descriptive data, but the modest objective set for this part of the research has been met, and our interest in the emergence of the retailer marketing department would seem to have been justified.

We showed, first, that a significant number of large-scale retailers in the UK do operate marketing departments, which is compatible with the findings by Greenley and Shipley [1988] that marketing activities are becoming more important in modern retailing. These are generally recent innovations and are small, though typically growing and enjoying higher status and prestige than the simple departmental site would justify.

However, secondly, taking the CME as the key point of focus, while normally reporting directly to the managing director, the CMEs' responsibilities are typically restricted to advertising, promotion and marketing research, and do not extend into the area of strategic marketing or strategic planning.

Thirdly, we examined the marketing information function, as an area central to the functioning of marketing. Here, a significant proportion of the sample did operate marketing research (MR) units, although they were also small and recent in introduction. There was evidence of very high levels of MR expenditure in some companies, and the case of a wide range of MR activities. The major finding, however, was one of diversity in practice, and we are led to suggest that using this indicator some retailers are considerably more 'marketing-oriented' than are others.

Finally, we considered the degree to which these retail firms perceived the elements of marketing strategy in the channel of distribution to be under their control rather than that of the supplier.

It does appear that our sample of retailers with marketing departments do typically see marketing strategies as under their control, rather than that of the manufacturer. Interestingly, relationships with suppliers are seen as essentially consultative/co-operative, possibly suggesting that in these instances manufacturers have become acquiescent in channels characterised by retailer-led marketing.

With the objectives of delineation and description achieved, we believe that we have demonstrated the importance of the retailer Marketing Department as a phenomenon of the 1980s.

We conclude for the present only that we have established some justification for taking the retailer marketing department as an important focus for study, where a better, empirically-informed understanding will improve our insight into the operation of marketing in the channel of distribution

Our attention turns next to the extension of these studies into a more detailed analysis of the positioning of the retailer marketing department, and to test the hypotheses that the strengthening of the retailer marketing organisation is related to the weakening of the corresponding manufacturers' marketing organisations, and that the retailer marketing department exists as a tool to implement the pro-active marketing strategies adopted by retailers.

APPENDIX

Survey Methodology

The survey used a postal questionnaire, which had been piloted in six personal interviews conducted with senior retailing executives. The model for the operationalisation of the variables was the research instrument used in the earlier studies of manufacturer marketing organisations [Piercy,

1986]. In a small number of cases, the questionnaire was completed through a telephone interview rather than respondent self-completion.

The survey was carried out in the period January–April 1986 with the initial mail-out followed by a postal reminder and then a telephone reminder. The sampling units were Chief Marketing Executives. The sample was made up of the 277 largest retailing organisations in the UK, identified using a number of directory sources. A total of 70 usable responses were collected giving a response rate of 25.3 per cent.

The product market classification of the sampling frame and the sample

TABLE A.1

PRODUCT-MARKET CLASSIFICATION

	Sampling Frame %	Sample %
Grocery	26	32
Clothing	18	20
Others	59	48
	(N=277)	(N=70)

Chi-Square = 5.6 with 5 d.f.

is shown in Table A.1, and the differences are not considered significant. The sample is regarded in this respect as reasonably representative of large-scale retailers in the UK. In fact, the 70 companies included in the sample in total represent 15 per cent of total retail sales and 16 per cent of total retail employment in the UK.

The questionnaire is available from the author to those who may be interested in the possibility of collaborating in replicative or comparative studies.

REFERENCES

Ames, B.C., 1970, 'Trappings Versus Substance in Industrial Marketing', *Harvard Business Review,* July/August.

Barnhill, J.A., 1974, 'Developing Marketing Orientation in a Postal Service, *Optimum*, No.3.

Bensmore, M.L. and S. Kaufman, 1985, 'How Leading Retailers Stay on Top', *Business,* April/June.

BIM, 1970, *Marketing Organisation in British Industry,* London: British Institute of Management.

Carson, D., 1968, 'Marketing Organization in British Manufacturing Firms', *Journal of Marketing,* Vol.32, April.

Doyle, P. and D. Cook, 1979, 'Marketing Strategies, Financial Structure and Innovation in UK Retailing', *Management Decision,* Vol.17, No.2.

George, W.R. and H.C. Barksdale, 1974, 'Marketing Activities in the Service Industries', *Journal of Marketing,* 35, Fall.

Greenley, G.E. and D.D. Shipley, 1987, 'Problems Confronting UK Retailing Organisations', *Service Industries Journal,* Vol.7, No.3.

Greenley, G.E. and D.D. Shipley, 1988, 'An Empirical Overview of Marketing by Retailing Organisations', *Service Industries Journal,* Vol.8, No.1.

Hayhurst, R. and G.S.C. Wills, 1972, *Organisational Design for Marketing Futures*, London: Allen & Unwin.

Hise, R.T., 1965, 'Have Manufacturing Firms Adopted the Marketing Concept?', *Journal of Marketing*, Vol.29, July.

Hooley, G. and D. Cowell, 1985, 'The Status of Marketing in the UK Service Industries', *Service Industries Journal*.

Hooley, G.J., C.J. West and J.E. Lynch, 1984, *Marketing in the UK - A Survey of Current Practice and Performance*, Maidenhead Institute of Marketing.

Hovell, P.J., 1976, 'Some Organisational Problems Facing the Marketing Function in Metropolitan Passenger Transport Executives', in R.J. Lawrence (ed.) *Marketing as a Non-American Activity*, proceedings: Marketing Education Group Conference.

Judd, R.C., 1968, 'Similarities or Differences in Product and Service Retailing', *Journal of Retailing*, Vol.43, No.4.

Piercy, N., 1984, 'Retailer Marketing - Informational Strategies', *European Journal of Marketing*, Vo.17, No.6.

Piercy, N., 1985, *Marketing Organisation: An Analysis of Information Processing, Power and Politics*, London: Allen & Unwin.

Piercy, N., 1986, 'The Role and Function of the Chief Marketing Executive and the Marketing Department', *Journal of Marketing Management*, Vol.1, No.3.

Piercy, N., 1987a, 'Advertising Budgeting: Process and Structure as Explanatory Variables', *Journal of Advertising*, Vol.16, No.2.

Piercy, N., 1987b, 'Marketing and Business Success', *University of Wales Business and Economics Review*, Vol.1, No.1.

Piercy, N., 1987c, 'The Marketing Budgeting Process: Marketing Management Implications', *Journal of Marketing*, October.

Pugh, D., 1970, 'The Structure of the Marketing Specialisms in their Context', *British Journal of Marketing*, Summer.

Stall, R.B., 1978, 'Marketing in a Service Industry', *Atlanta Economic Review*, Vol.28 No.3.

Upah, G.D., 1980, 'Mass Marketing in Service Retailing: A Review and Synthesis of Major Methods', *Journal of Retailing*, Vol.56 (Autumn).

Warshaw, M.R., 1976, 'Re-appraising Public Utility Marketing', *University of Michigan Business Review*, May.

Weigand, R.E., 1961, 'Changes in the Marketing Organization in Selected Industries, 1950–1959', unpublished Ph.D thesis, University of Illinois.

This chapter first appeared in *The Service Industries Journal*, Vol.8, No.2 (1988).

5

The Impact of New Technology on Services Marketing

by

Nigel Piercy

New information processing technology has already had a clear impact on the operational aspects of service organisations of all kinds, but what is only now becoming apparent is its fundamental impact on marketing systems. This last impact is of particular note in the service sector. Discussed in this paper are: the nature of new technology in marketing, the significance to information–communication systems, and the power created by the control of informational resources. This analysis is illustrated from the retailing sector and extended to other service organisations. The conclusion advanced is that the informational change currently faced is of a strategic nature and that organisations face an urgent need to formulate marketing/ information technology strategies.

SERVICES MARKETING

The academic debate as to whether services are the same as products, and thus whether services marketing is a comparable activity to product marketing, continues [e.g. Middleton, 1983], with some distinction attempted between 'service products' and 'product service' [Christopher, *et al.*, 1980], and stances being taken at almost all possible points on the available spectrum.

In fact, this argument is set aside for present purposes on the grounds that its resolution does not seem to be apparent or, indeed, particularly useful. For instance, taking the criterion of differences in operational marketing, it might be argued that there is as much or more difference between the small engineering firm – competing on service by adapting its offerings to individual customer specifications – and the national producer of packaged consumer goods, as between that last firm and the retailer marketing its packaged goods to the end user.

In fact, the major thrust of this paper is to suggest that such debates are largely superseded by other concerns. The concern of the literature has been with the tardiness of the service sector in adopting marketing departmentation and the outward signs of formalised marketing: 'It is ironic that service businesses, which are necessarily in the most direct contact with consumers, seek to be the last kind of firm to adopt a consumer marketing oriented marketing concern' [Bessom, 1973]. Others have emphasised the need to develop a new theory of services marketing [Rothwell, 1974; Grönroos, 1982], though largely in line with the traditional model provided for marketing products.

The interest here is in an issue of rather deeper significance: the impact of new information processing technology on marketing and, in particular, its impact on marketing at the level of retailing goods and services to consumers or other users. The point is that new technology undermines so much of the received model of corporate marketing systems – in organisation, information, distribution and communications – that new, different marketing structures and concepts are emerging in product marketing [Piercy, forthcoming], thus arguably invalidating much of the prescriptive marketing approach to the services sector. This last point emerges again at the end of the paper. The illustrations used here apply to the retailing of goods through stores to consumers, but the conclusions reached may easily be adapted to the context of many of the other industries served by *The Service Industries Journal* – particularly, for example, hotels and catering, tourism, business and financial services and the leisure industry.

Given this initial definition of context, it is also perhaps necessary to clarify the view being taken here of 'marketing'. As before, this is no proper setting for a debate about formal definition which has been attempted by others [e.g. Crosier, 1975]. The view taken here – however arbitrary it may be considered – is that marketing may be taken to include activities of three kinds: (a) *marketing strategy* – the formulation of product–market direction and competitive stance; (b) *marketing programmes* – the planning and implementation of policies at the customer interface in 'product' policy, pricing, communications and services; and (c) *marketing information* – the processing of data on markets, marketing effectiveness, and the environment.

While this paradigm may seem idiosyncratic, it has some foundation in businessmen's perceptions of marketing [e.g. Hague, 1971], and has the advantage of allowing for most views on and definitions of marketing.

In particular, this framework clears the way for the central argument to be developed here: that the impact of new technology on marketing is being, and will increasingly be, felt through its effect on marketing information, which feeds back to both marketing programme management, marketing strategy formulation and, hence, to organisational and corporate marketing issues.

With the underlying assumptions about the nature of services marketing declared, the structure of the article is built around this last contention. First, we examine the nature of new information technology (NIT) and the scope of its impact at operational and strategic levels. Second, we examine the specific implications of NIT for marketing information systems. Third, taking the retailing of consumer goods as context, it is possible to illustrate the strategic and political nature of the

NIT and marketing information interaction. This leads finally to the identification of a need for an explicit marketing/information technology strategy in retailing firms, and by implication others in the service sector.

NEW INFORMATION TECHNOLOGY

The case for adopting a proactive managerial or strategic – rather than technical or operational – stance towards new technology has recently been formulated by one writer in the following terms: (a) NIT is a high expenditure activity and continues to grow; (b) information processing is increasingly the means of 'delivering the services' which are central to many business operations; (c) NIT is offering new business and management opportunities of a strategic nature; (d) NIT is affecting all functions and levels of management; (e) NIT is obviously central to developing and upgrading management information systems; (f) as well as management, other stakeholders – unions, consumers, suppliers, and governments – are concerned with, and seeking to influence, the use of NIT; and (g) lack of management involvement has been associated with information processing failures [Earl, 1984].

To this list must be added concern for the increased potential for social control – in terms of measuring employee performance, restricting the way people do their work, collating information about employees, and affecting career development [Land, 1984] – and for changing, particularly centralising, management and organisational control systems [Mansfield, 1984].

Clearly interest here lies primarily in the impact of NIT on 'delivering services' and strategic issues in the marketing area, but the point should first be underlined that the nature of the changes created – or, at least, initiated – by NIT, are more fundamental than simply improving the speed and efficiency of operations.

The Nature of NIT-induced Change

That NIT induces change cannot be denied, but what should be emphasised is the progression or trend of that change, and its degree, with what this implies for business and marketing strategy.

In considering the way in which organisations use computing generally, Hedberg [1980] suggested three phases of change: a first phase where designers of information systems attempt to increase the efficiency of data processing tasks; a second phase, where systems are designed to avoid organisational change; and a third phase, in which systems designers attempt to use the technology to shape the structure and tasks of the organisation itself. Land [1984] suggests that most UK computer users are still in the first and second phases of the Hedberg model, implying that what is currently faced is the somewhat more fundamental disruption in organisations involved by a third phase change.

Long [1984] illustrates the progression of change in the case of a firm where field sales personnel have frequently to telephone a sales office to

THE IMPACT OF NEW TECHNOLOGY 67

obtain information for customers and to input orders. First phase auto-mation involves adopting microcomputers for the telephone clerks to store information for retrieval and to input orders. The second phase involves providing the sales force with portable terminals to access a central data base, thus eliminating the clerks and some salesmen. The third phase would involve direct electronic communication between the customer and the centralised data base, developing 'telemarketing', and removing the need for much of the sales force.

Partly as a result of such a progression, it is argued that NIT-induced change is deep-seated rather than peripheral, and of strategic rather than operational impact.

One may point to the diverse impacts of NIT on such issues as: the degree and type of control exercised by management in organisations – and hence, through management style the organisational climate; the structure of organisations – since structure may be conceived as a frame-work of information flows – and thus on the roles and relationships within that structure; the pattern of jobs – and thereby at the individual level on motivation, satisfaction and performance, and at the macro-level on employment and educational requirements; and thus on the entire nature of the organisation. Most particularly, the concept of organisational boundaries is weakened in the sense that electronic communications and information processing heighten the already existing trend towards 'quasi-integration' [Blois, 1977] between apparently independent organisations – the key interaction here is that between the environ-mental dependency of an organisation and the effect of electronic net-working, and this lies at the heart of the analysis pursued below.

Indeed, the central point is that in marketing as in other areas of business, many of our traditional, underlying assumptions about business and organisations are thrown into disarray [Handy, 1980].

Views about the direction of change faced vary from the pessimistic view of all-powerful multinational corporations and a 'technological elite' dominating business [Doll, 1981], to a scenario of 'democratic free enter-prise' and the growth of 'organic networks and multi-dimensional matrices combining rigorous accountability with autonomous operations' [Halal, 1982]. This said, it is also notable that some see the consequences of NIT as unavoidable, while others take a more deterministic view of managerial choices:

> The research shows that popular predictions about the radical and automatic advantages of new technologies are exaggerated ... management has a choice of means and ends in the use of new technology; these choices can and should be identified and evaluated in advance of change [Buchanan, 1982].

Indeed, it is the existence of such choice which underpins this present view of NIT-induced change in services marketing.

In addition, considering the general nature of NIT, Earl [1984] makes the point that new information technologies are: (a) *multiple* – since there are now many generic and specific information–communication technologies, each likely to stimulate its own portfolio of applications and management problems; (b) *dispersing* – for instance, into distributed, local, end-user and personal information processing; (c) *dynamic* – in that the rate of change continues to accelerate, bringing the risk of 'management and organisational dyspepsia'; and (d) *pervasive* – in the organisations, functions, and people affected and involved.

Taking the progressive and pervasive nature of NIT-induced change in business, its fundamental nature, and the significance of managerial choices, as given, the immediate strategic importance to the service sector has been illustrated by Earl [1984] in the following examples: (a) American Airlines placed terminals with travel agents for seat reservation enquiries which would display data on any subscribing airline but were programmed to show American Airlines first; (b) Commercial Union used a similar method to break into the American insurance broking business and – through the necessary work on developing special hardware and software – are now in the 'computing business' as well; (c) Merrill Lynch used NIT to enter and develop a market segment left by other financial institutions through the Cash Management Account; (d) Reuters invested in communications technology to develop a specialised, global information service for the financial sector – developing a new product-market and increasing profitability – at a time of poor performance by traditional news agencies. The implication of such cases is that NIT is both a competitive weapon and a key to increased productivity, but also a means of delivering new services and entering new businesses.

With these points relating to services marketing and NIT established, attention now turns to their interaction in one particular area of the services sector – the channel of distribution for consumer products – to demonstrate certain of the strategic implications for managers and researchers.

MARKETING INFORMATION SYSTEMS

It was noted that one element of marketing has concentrated on marketing information, perhaps typified by the prescriptive comment that 'good information is a facilitator of successful marketing action and indeed, seen in this light marketing management becomes first and foremost an information processing activity' [Christopher, 1980]. Indeed, this concept of marketing has been developed in a more analytical vein by others to evaluate the organisation of marketing:

> The organisation of a firm is designed for the purpose of processing environmental information . . . . Accordingly, we propose to look at the environment as a generator of information and at the marketing department as a processor of environmental information [Nonaka and Nicosia, 1979].

The implications of an information processing model of marketing have led to an information–structure–power model of the marketing organisation [Piercy, forthcoming], one element of which is pursued below.

The focus here is on information and environmental dependency. The central propositions are outlined below, and the practical implications are evaluated in the next section of the article.

First, an organisation 'knows' its competitor and market environments through the information system it operates – however formal or informal that system may be. Intervening variables include the process of 'enactment' in the sense that 'the human *creates* the environment to which the system then adapts. The human does not *react* to an environment, he enacts it' [Weick, 1969]. In addition to the technical inefficiencies of marketing information systems in scanning to provide 'valid' information (Aguilar, 1967; Piercy and Evans, 1983], more fundamentally the information system represents a structure imposed by an organisation on its environment:

> Theoretically information systems are designed and created to provide the information the decision maker requires, but that is an impossible task because the decision maker does not know what he needs, only what is available. The available information provides clues to what is considered organizationally important, and provides the information which will tend to be used by decision makers [Pfeffer and Salancik, 1978].

Thus, regardless of the technology, the information system involves construction or structuring of the environment.

Second, by implication the control of that process of structuring and construction is a source of power. At one level information is a source of power simply because it is a resource upon which others rely for their own activities, but the phenomenon is more pervasive still. If one accepts the notion that in organisational terms information is a source of: unity or common ground among decision makers; collective memory and cohesiveness among individuals; stability in decisions; re-assurance; delaying decisions; or ritual and conciliation [Piercy and Evans, 1983], then information may be seen also as a more covert source of influence on organisational functioning. Indeed, information has been increasingly recognised as a political weapon, used in the pursuit of goals through organisationally non-sanctioned behaviour through such activities as: the use of secrecy [Pfeffer, 1977]; the control of decision premises, alternatives, and information about alternatives [Pfeffer, 1981]; and the shaping of the 'agenda' for decision making [Bachrach and Baratz, 1962].

Third, and again by implication, control of information is central to obtaining formal power and less formally sanctioned political strength in an organisation. In the sense and to the extent that information is: a construction of the perceived environment; a source of uncertainty coping in relation to contingencies which are – or are perceived as – critical to organisational performance; and a source of control over the environment, and that decision making is surrounded by contingencies of uncertainty and conflict, then the party controlling information is in a powerful position to determine the agenda for decision making, to bargain with others and hence, to influence significant outcomes. This argument applies both intra-organisationally to determining the power and politics of the marketing department and other sub-units within a firm [Piercy, forthcoming], but also to inter-organisational relationships.

This brings us to a focus on the relationship between manufacturers and the wholesalers and retailers of their products, in terms of NIT-induced change in the location of information processing capacity and control.

MACRO-MARKETING INFORMATION SYSTEMS IN DISTRIBUTION CHANNELS

If the channel of distribution is seen as a service-filled space existing between manufacturers and consumers, then the contention may be advanced:

> If space in the channel is conceived not simply in geographical or physical terms, but also in terms of psychological and sociological distance – including such aspects as familiarity, trust, images, frequency of interaction and face-to-face communication – then it can be suggested that retailers enjoy a considerable advantage over suppliers. In particular, they enjoy a considerable *informational* advantage. [Piercy, 1983].

Firstly, that advantage relates simply to *access* to market and competitive data in terms of closeness to the market-place, but also in the availability of facilities and resources for market and product testing, advertising effectiveness evaluation, and the like.

However, the practical value of that access is far greater with the application of NIT. At present the parallel trends of adoption of electronic point-of-sale equipment – in particular scanning facilities – and the bar coding of manufacturer products suggest the development of an extremely powerful marketing information resource.

At the time of writing, the diffusion of these technological innovations appears to be accelerating. For instance, in the grocery market, by 1983, 80 per cent of packaged goods were source-coded, and the number of scanning stores had reached 75 (more than twice the number in 1981) [POS News, 1984].

To these specific innovations – adopted primarily for their impact on in-store operational efficiency – must be added the *networking* effect associated with NIT. This term is taken, for present purposes, to mean the electronic communication links between individuals and organisations, manifested in 'electronic mail', interactive television sets in the consumer's home, cable television, and so on. The ability to communicate electronically to numerous remote locations – virtually instantaneously – provides the catalyst which may lead in the very near future to the operationalisation of a major potential – the distributed or macro-marketing information system.

While the marketing information system (MkIS) has normally been seen as a corporate function, as noted above, the concept of organisational boundaries is becoming increasingly less relevant, and we may see the emergence of the type of distributed information system illustrated in Figure 1.

FIGURE 1

A MACRO-MARKETING INFORMATION SYSTEM

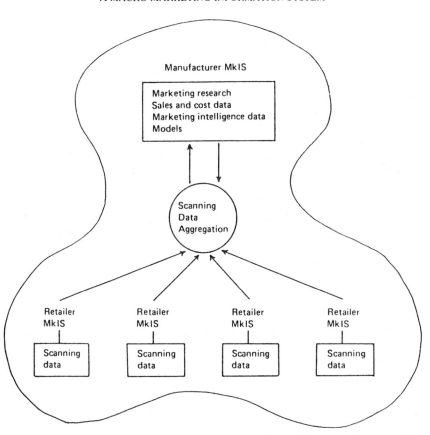

Source: Piercy and Evans [1983]

Conceptually, the channel may be seen as a network of information based on electronic links between manufacturers, distributors and consumers. However, as well as data access and networking, the retailer also enjoys the key advantage of information *control*. Bearing in mind the earlier commentary on the power and politics of information, one may identify retailer marketing information strategies of the type listed in Table 1.

TABLE 1
RETAILER MARKETING INFORMATION STRATEGIES

Strategies	Advantages to the Retailer
Conflict	Power in managing conflict for self-interest
Competition	Leverage in negotiation and bargaining
Commercial	Income from sales of marketing information
Co-operation	Reduction of total channel of distribution costs through integration and information sharing

Control by retailers of marketing information – or variations in the degree and type of information sharing – may be manifested in *conflict*: through building data monopolies, the retailer's informational advantages may be used simply as a competitive weapon in dealing with manufacturers – or less extremely in *competitive* behaviour, as part of the bargaining process. On the other hand, *commercial* information strategies are open – where information is sold to manufacturers – taking the service organisation into a new area of business as a marketing information processor and as a seller. Finally, the distributed information system may provide the basis for joint decision-making and *co-operative* marketing in the channel of distribution, with information-sharing in both directions and participation by manufacturers and retailers in participative strategic decisions. While empirical data remain limited, the American experience would seem to suggest the existence of all these strategies [Piercy, 1982].

Whichever situation prevails – and we return shortly to the importance of making an explicit choice of strategy – the underlying implication is that the NIT/marketing information interaction provides a further source of erosion of the position of the manufacturer and a corresponding elevation in that of the retailer. This has implications for the location of decision-making in the channel and for the organisational structures adopted for marketing.

First, informational advantages may be manifested in retailer marketing initiatives in product policy, pricing and communications typifying the channel of distribution for packaged goods. The well-known case of Marks and Spencer dominating R & D, product policy and pricing for goods, may well prove to be prototypical.

Second, this growing change in the locus of marketing decision-making power is likely to be manifested in organisational change – and indeed there are signs that the 'traditional' manufacturer marketing department is disintegrating: (a) some manufacturers are abandoning product and brand management – at one time the classic route to 'marketing orientation'; (b) marketing department responsibilities are being reduced – partly as a result of concentrated power in retailing – as the financial and strategic significance of decisions in such areas as advertising and promotion increases through greater top management intervention, cross-functional committees, and formal corporate planning; (c) in some areas the business sector or programme manager now comes between the chief executive and the marketing department, reducing the latter's role in strategy formulation and integration; (d) Trade Marketing departments are growing – separate from marketing – out of key account selling to deal directly with major retailer customers; (e) NIT is reducing the size of the marketing department and its co-ordinative and informational roles, and thus its power in the organisation, particularly in the key area of managing external interfaces and dependencies [Piercy, forthcoming].

The corollary is that the powerful, integrated marketing department may emerge in the channel of distribution – providing the source of formal management and control of product development – and branding, pricing, marketing communications and marketing information systems. The signs already evident are of increased unified departmentation of marketing, the greater use of product and brand management, more formally organised marketing research, and the appointment or designation of more chief marketing executives in retailing firms. The suggestion is therefore that the transfer of marketing power to the retailing firm is being accompanied by the relocation of the formal marketing organisation.

Finally, let us consider the implications of this type of change: first, for the retailer/manufacturer relationship, and second, more broadly for others in the service sector.

INFORMATION STRATEGY

If one accepts the premise that NIT-induced change affects: information systems, the structure of inter-organisational relationships, and intra-organisational structures, in the way argued above, then one is led to the conclusion that the change – in the phases now faced – is of a fundamental, strategic nature, rather than being peripheral or operational.

The implication in the retailer/manufacturer setting discussed above is that strategic choices are faced by management relating to: the conflictual or co-operative stance to be taken, the allocation of marketing decision-making initiative and power, and the reorganisation of marketing to reflect the new realities.

The suggestion here is that a proactive management approach to this area of change is likely to be more satisfactory than a reactive or passive attitude towards NIT. For this reason it is proposed that the issues above provide a management agenda, drawing on an analysis of the emerging NIT scenario and corporate needs and business opportunities, to make choices for the future [Piercy, 1984].

Secondly, and more broadly, a similar proposition may be advanced for other service organisations. The 'electronic market-place' suggests that the integration of marketing functions, the control of marketing decisions, and the formal organisation of marketing is emerging rapidly as a key strategic issue for the service organisation in many sectors. If this case is granted, then, as for retailers, the need is for a development of explicit strategies for marketing information and marketing organisation – the structure of which is detailed elsewhere [Piercy and Evans, 1983; Piercy, forthcoming].

Broadly, such a process involves a strategic analysis of (a) the technological scenario – the applications of NIT to operations and management in the long-term future [Benjamin, 1982]; (b) organisational impacts – in structural and management terms; (c) market impacts – on both customers and suppliers; (d) company needs and resources [Piercy, 1984]. While such a prescription is generally valid in all organisations, for the reasons noted above, it would be both particularly apt and urgent in the services sector marketing area.

REFERENCES

Aguilar, F.J., 1967, *Scanning the Business Environment*, New York: Macmillan.
Bachrach, P. and M.S. Baratz, 1962, 'Two Faces of Power', *American Political Science Review*, Vol.56.
Benjamin, R., 1982, 'Information Technology in the 1990s: A Long-Range Planning Scenario', *Management Information Systems Quarterly*, June.
Bessom, R.M., 1973, 'Unique Aspects of Marketing Services', *Arizona Business Bulletin*, November.
Blois, K.J., 1977, 'Problems in Applying Organizational Theory to Industrial Marketing', *Industrial Marketing Management*, Vol.6.
Buchanan, D.A., 1982, 'Using the New Technology: Management Objectives and Organizational Choices', *European Journal of Management*, Vol.1, No.2.
Christopher, M., Kennedy, S.H., McDonald M., and G. Wills, 1980, *Effective Marketing Management*, Farnborough: Gower.
Christopher, M., MacDonald, M., and G. Wills, 1980, *Introducing Marketing*, London: Pan.
Crosier, K., 1975, 'What Exactly Is Marketing?', *Quarterly Review of Marketing*, Vol.1, No.2.
Doll, R., 1981, 'Information Technology and its Socioeconomic and Academic Impact', *Online Review*, Vol.5, No.1.
Earl, M., 1984, 'Emerging Trends in Managing New Information Technologies', in Piercy, N. (ed.), *The Management Implications of New Information Technology*, Beckenham: Croom Helm.
Grönroos, C., 1982, 'An Applied Service Marketing Theory', *European Journal of Marketing*, Vol.16, No.7.
Hague, D.C., 1971, *Pricing in Business*, London: Allen & Unwin.
Halal, W.K., 1982, 'Information Technology and the Flowering of Enterprise', *European Journal of Management*, Vol.1, No.2.
Handy, C., 1980, 'Through the Organizational Looking Glass', *Harvard Business Review*, January/February.
Hedberg, B., 1980, 'The Design and Impact of Real-Time Computer Systems', in Bjorn-Anderson, N., Hedberg, B., Mercer, D., Mumford, E., and A. Sole, (eds.), *The Impact of Systems Change in Organizations*, Alphen: Sijtoff and Noordhoff.
Land, F., 1984, 'The Impact of Information Technology on the Work Place', in N. Piercy (ed.), *The Management Implications of New Information Technology*, Beckenham: Croom Helm.

Long, R., 1984, 'The Application of Microelectronics to the Office: Organisational and Human Implications', in N. Piercy (ed.), *The Management Implications of New Information Technology*, Beckenham: Croom Helm.

Mansfield, R., 1984, 'Changes in Information Technology, Organisational Design and Managerial Control', in N. Piercy (ed.), *The Management Implications of New Information Technology*, Beckenham: Croom Helm.

Middleton, V.T.C., 1983, 'Product Marketing – Goods and Services Compared', *Quarterly Review of Marketing*, Vol.8, No.4.

Nonaka, I., and F.M. Nicosia, 1979, 'Marketing Management, Its Environment and Information Processing: A Problem of Organizational Design', *Journal of Business Research*, Vol.7, No.4.

Pfeffer, J., 1977, 'Power and Resource Allocation in Organizations', in Staw, B.M., and G.R. Salancik (eds.), *New Directions in Organizational Behavior*, Chicago: St Clair.

Pfeffer, J., 1981, *Power in Organizations*, Marshfield, MA: Pitman.

Pfeffer, J., and G.R. Salancik, 1978, *The External Control of Organizations: A Resource Dependence Perspective*, New York: Harper & Row.

Piercy, N., 1982, 'How Retailers Use Marketing Information in the USA', *Retail and Distribution Management*, Vol.10, No.5.

Piercy, N., 1984, 'Retailer Marketing – Informational Strategies', *European Journal of Marketing*, Vol.17, No.6.

Piercy, N., forthcoming, *Marketing Organisation: An Analysis of Information Processing, Power and Politics*, London: Allen & Unwin.

Piercy, N., and M. Evans, 1983, *Managing Marketing Information*, Beckenham: Croom Helm.

POS News, 1984, 'The Progress in Bar-Coding and Scanning During 1983', *POS News*, No.1.

Rothwell, J.M., 1974, *Marketing in the Service Sector*, Cambridge, MA: Winthrop.

Weick, K.R., 1969, *The Social Psychology of Organizing*, Reading, MA: Addison-Wesley.

This chapter first appeared in *The Service Industries Journal*, Vol.4, No.3 (1984).

6
Customer Service in Retailing – the Next Leap Forward?

LEIGH SPARKS

Customer care is one of the phrases that appears to be sweeping British retailing For customers, however, this can often seem a bad joke. This paper presents a review of aspects of customer service in retailing, developing from the literature and research work in the United States to suggest how changed service orientations could improve customer relations. Examples of service are provided from the United States to illustrate the concepts.

INTRODUCTION

'You can't do that!' she barked, 'Customers cannot see anybody in Customer Service.'

(H H Kitasei 1985, reprinted in Mason, Mayer and Ezell, 1988, p. 529).

The American example quoted above is the kind of 'horror' story about customer service that almost everybody can embellish or 'cap' with their own version. Whether it is rude, gossiping shop assistants beloved of media caricaturists (Sharon and Tracey) or simply inefficiency in operation, there is widespread belief that service in British retailing is poor. And yet, retailers will quote for you the old adages of the 'customer is king' or the 'customer is always right'. Retailers are generally convinced that customer service is the coming management programme that will bring success in the 1990s. Gone are most 'ferocious' price-cutting programmes and price competition of the 1970s and in their place are the new, sparkling 'customer care', 'customer first' or 'customer service' programmes. In looking at the realities of British retailing, however, customers might be forgiven for believing that retailers understand only lip service rather than customer service. Figure 1 makes the point in an anecdotal fashion. The story is a personal experience with a Scottish retailer that advertises itself on the basis of its speed of response and service. The story illustrates how poor customer service is in that company and gives the customer a clear message about their status or place in the relationship with the retailer. In the early 1980s, concerns about service were being voiced in the United

FIGURE 1

SERVICE WITH A SMILE?

Our piece of furniture would be available for collection about six weeks after placing the order and paying. The shop would ring us when it was available.

Ten weeks later a post-card informed us we could collect from the shop. It was a few miles drive to the store. Their customer car park was locked. Admission was by asking in the store for the manager to open the barrier – which he promptly locked behind you. It took three minutes in the shop, we manhandled the piece to the car, and then we had to go back into the shop to get the manager to unlock the car park to get us out.

Upon opening the package at home, it was clear the piece was damaged. Furthermore, it was clear that it had been damaged in the factory and then wrapped up and sent out. We went straight back to the store. The same palaver with the car park took place. We received many apologies all round, along the lines of 'we cannot explain how it slipped through etc.' They promised to send it back and get a replacement within the week. They would ring me at work to tell me when I could collect it.

One week, two weeks, but still no phone call. Another personal appearance.at the store. 'Sorry sir, but it hasn't been collected by head office yet, but it will be this week, and we will ring you.'

One week, two weeks, but still no phone call. Another personal appearance. Another pantomime took place, but our furniture had not yet left the store.

Two months passed and finally something snapped. In words of few syllables I wrote to the managing director and copied in the store manager. I explained my problem; my four-month-plus wait; my views on customer service; my opinion of them holding my money and gaining interest; and threatened them with star-billing in my forthcoming article on customer service!

A second-class letter arrived from a very nice computer in the customer service department. They couldn't understand it; I was justified in my annoyance; the manager would be reprimanded; and my furniture would be available in my local branch for collection next Saturday.

We went to the store on Saturday, but the furniture wasn't there. We were promised it would be by mid-afternoon and we could collect it. We tried, but they had lost the key to the car park. By parking illegally I finally had my furniture in reasonable condition.

This is a true story from a Scottish company that advertises its rapid delivery and service. We have never set foot in the store again and have told as many people as we can about their service with a smile.

States. Retailers, amongst others, had allowed the situation where customer service desks were off limits to customers, for just one example! Through the decade, however, it has come to be recognised that in fact some American companies, including some retailers, are customer focused and driven and are applying customer care and service policies throughout their organisations. In this respect it can be suggested that *some* American retailers have lessons for British retailers about service, in the same way as there have been clear 'borrowings' in design, presentation and products.

It is important to state immediately however that there are difficulties in simply seeing 'good' things in America and importing them to Britain. Retailing in North America operates under very different conditions to Britain, with different costs and operating structures, as well as different employment situations. Customer flow patterns are very different and the amount and nature of competition varies considerably. It has also to be recognised that for some retailers their market positioning obviates a high degree of service, and indeed service is consciously excluded or diminished in their retail offering. Despite these caveats, however, it is useful and potentially instructive to consider the position in the United States.

This paper focuses on the positive and good aspects of customer service. That is not to say that bad service is unknown in America. It is not, and there are equally bad attempts at service in the United States as there are in the United Kingdom. The belief, however, is that British retail companies can learn from good service provision wherever it is found.

There are also social and cultural differences between the countries. All visitors to the United States are assailed by sayings or greetings as part of any exchange process. 'Have a nice day' or 'Enjoy!' are but examples of the genre. The important point is that such sayings are generally expected. A culturally specific aspect of customer service in this way is probably not meaningfully transferable. In Britain, however, beyond discussion of the weather, such rote greetings are now limited and reduce the comparative level of customer–staff interaction.

The structure of the paper is designed to focus attention on the positive aspects of customer service in America and to provoke thoughts about how retail management can apply and maintain customer service in the United Kingdom when appropriate. The aim is to provide examples to encourage thought about current offerings and possibly to lead on to changes in the future. The paper is structured into three sections. The first is a general review of the literature on customer service to ascertain the broad frameworks for understanding service. Second, examples from field work in the United States in the summer of 1989 are presented to suggest possibilities. Finally, broad lessons for British retailing are drawn. Throughout, the approach is one of using examples and illustrations to support themes rather than an exhaustive study of either the literature or retail companies in America.

WHAT IS CUSTOMER SERVICE?

Definitions of customer service abound and can be complicated. In the end, however, customer service is all about attracting, retaining and enhancing customer relationships. There are in turn a number of ways of considering this.

The attraction to customers could be in the price offer of the store or in the services that are provided, such as rest-rooms or gift wrapping. It is relatively easy to generate a list of such services that companies may (should?) provide. It can be argued that to attract certain customers to a store such services have to be provided as a 'qualifying' service package to enter the customer's consciousness or 'choice set' [Arnold, Capella and Smith 1983, Walters 1989]. This qualifying service will vary by customer segment and be dependent on the target market of the retailer.

It is important to accept, however, that merely providing services such as gift-wrapping or credit card acceptance is not enough. Customer service from a customer point-of-view is much more. Every time a customer comes into contact with a store, retail staff or merchandise, that customer is experiencing service and has certain expectations. Every time they deal with a store, its (your) staff or merchandise, they experience a 'moment of truth' [Carlzon, 1987]. Every moment of truth is an opportunity to attract, retain or enhance the relationship with the customer. Equally, every moment of truth is a potential disaster from a retailer's point-of-view and one that could put off a customer for life.

This is well-demonstrated by the illustration reported in Figure 1. The company, through its store staff, manager and ultimately computer, had a large number of 'moments of truth' in which to impress or satisfy the customer (me!). In almost every case they failed to satisfy the customer, keep to promises or even to remedy the situation. The continued inability to see the problem from the customer's viewpoint meant that they failed every moment of truth with the ultimate penalty of losing the business of the customer in the future. One dissatisfied customer tells many other potential and actual customers, thereby compounding the failure.

When a customer enters a store, they have expectations about what they will find and experience there. These expectations are based on received information and/or past experiences. If the expectations are not matched then the customer *may* take his/her custom elsewhere. Continued dissatisfaction will generally lead to loss of trade if there are competing opportunities. Retailers aim to meet these expectations and to keep their customers by binding them into a long-term relationship. To do this the company's offer must be positioned to meet the expectations of the target customer group and the in-store and out-of-store activities must match the expectations.

It is always possible for expectations of consumers to be depressed across an entire market. A good example of this is the contrast between grocery shopping at supermarkets and superstores in the United Kingdom and the United States of America. In the United Kingdom customers are expected to bag the groceries themselves and carry the goods to the car, possibly in the trolley. Their expectations of service are low. The last impression of the store the customer gets is often a long queue at the checkout, having to work themselves to pack their own purchases and then a trek to find the car and the resting place for the trolley. They may also have had to pay a returnable hire charge for the use of the trolley. In the United States, by contrast, many stores offer bagging and carry the products to the car or have a drive-up collection point. The last impression of the store is of a 'bag-boy' placing their groceries in their car, thanking them for shopping at the store and wishing them a good day. The contrast is extreme, but the expectations are extreme as well. This is why in the United States retailers are at pains to dispel any 'I'm *only* a bag-boy' statements from such staff, trying instead to impress on such employees that their final contact with the customer can be the crucial contact in meeting the expectations of the customer as it is the last thing they experience, and remember.

What should be evident from the foregoing is that emphasis needs to be placed in two main areas. First, it is crucial that the retailer knows and understands the customer. Many retailers claim to do this and to know what customers believe, but in fact it is debatable whether many retailers are truly pro-active when it comes to customer changes, research and requirements. How many retailers, for example, have a 'vice-president of listening and responding' as Burger King claim (*Guardian*, 31 March 1990)? Secondly, there has to be dedication to customer service, which in turn means a concentration on the service provided by sales employees to customers. The sales employee-customer relationship is crucial to the success of customer service policies as this is the area with major potential for problems. An element of this is the emphasis to be placed on seeing the service a company provides in the customer's terms – and not just on special occasions, but every occasion. How often do the managers of a retail company shop in their own stores, unannounced, unnoticed and as an 'ordinary' customer? How often do they try to return a product or ring up the customer service desk? What service levels are offered to the ordinary customers rather than seen on the flying (previously announced) visit of the company chief?

A customer service focus on customer-employee relationships, however, does not mean that the systems and procedures of customer service can be forgotten. The systems are drawn upon heavily by both staff and customers. But what is emphasised is the staff side of the provision of customer service – the people orientation. This can be seen in Figure 2 which is an attempt to model customer care [Thomas, 1987].

What the model illustrates is that there are a number of instances where customer service is provided or supported. The four main components identified are the customers, staff, management and systems. The interface between any of these has to be successful for proper customer service to be provided. The strength of this model is that it focuses attention not only on the systems (the physical service provision in most cases) but also on the people involved.

It also emphasises that the systems and the staff have to have shared direction or else they are pulling in opposite directions.

THE MANAGEMENT OF CUSTOMER SERVICE

The literature from the United States has seen a developing concern with the issues of customer service and particularly over how to provide good quality customer service. In many cases this initiative stems from the tub-thumping of people like Phil Crosby [e.g. Crosby, 1979] and particularly Tom Peters. Tom Peters' work on business excellence as a whole has been influential in causing managers and researchers to focus on the customer and service quality. His work [Peters and Waterman, 1982; Peters and Austin, 1985; Peters, 1988] contains elements on the management of service quality, but it is probably better to consider the specialist texts on the subject.

The recent book by Zeithaml et al.[1990] is a good example and the same authors have also pioneered the use of SERVQUAL [Parasuraman et al., 1988]. One of these authors has also produced some brief notes on delivering service in retailing [Berry, 1988]. In addition, there are a host of more populist books on the topic of customer service (e.g. Albrecht and Zemke 1985, Albrecht 1987, Hanan and Karp 1989, Lash 1989, Zemke and Schaaf 1989). There are also journal articles on the application of programmes to selected companies [e.g. Prouty, Roth and Nelson 1988, Burns 1989, Smith 1989].

Zeithaml et al. [1990] have concentrated on demonstrating the way in which customers' expectations are often not met by companies in terms of service and how companies can begin to remedy this. Their analysis is focused on the 'Gaps' model as illustrated in Figure 3. The model concentrates management effort on their identified gaps in service quality. What is apparent from the figure is that these gaps can develop from the mismatching of customers, management, staff and systems and that good service providers have closed these gaps. The similarity between the basic structure of Figures 2 and 3 should also be apparent.

The aim now is to show how some aspects of customer service in retailing are put into practice in the United States. Three retailers are illustrated below to demonstrate the overall orientation. These companies are: Harris-Teeter Supermarkets, Nordstrom and Palais Royal. It is not for one moment being suggested that these are the best service retailers in the United States, but rather that they illustrate well the aspects of the argument being developed here. The field work and interviews on which these brief profiles and the illustrations are based were carried out in the summer of 1989. The purpose of these brief profiles is to provide illustrations of the orientation of the three companies by singling out different aspects of their service provision. Each company does more on customer service than is illustrated here, but the aspect identified is an

FIGURE 2
A CUSTOMER CARE MODEL

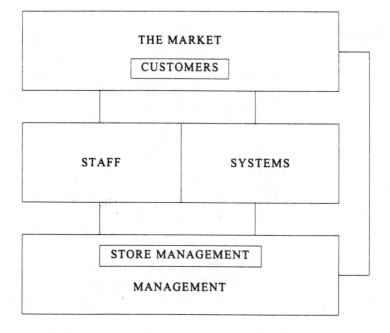

THE MARKET

CUSTOMERS

STAFF   SYSTEMS

STORE MANAGEMENT

MANAGEMENT

Source: after Thomas [1987], p. 290.

important element of the overall approach. The next section develops from these illustrations to examine the ways in which, and provide a framework to understand how, elements of customer service are applied in the United States. The aspects developed here are: customer contact and feedback in Harris-Teeter; customer service orientation in Nordstrom; and employee development in Palais Royal.

Harris-Teeter Supermarkets Inc.

Charlotte-based Harris-Teeter operate approximately 120 supermarkets in the Carolinas, Virginia and Tennessee. Originally founded in 1936, Harris-Teeter are now part of the Ruddick Corporation and are the second largest food chain in the Carolinas. The company is not one of the major food retailers in the United States but represents the leading regional-based style of operation. Its statement, prominently displayed in all company locations and activities, 'the only low-priced supermarket that refuses to act like one', is a fair reflection of the concern for customers that is felt throughout the company.

The company operates a small customer services department. The first goal

FIGURE 3
THE 'GAPS' MODEL

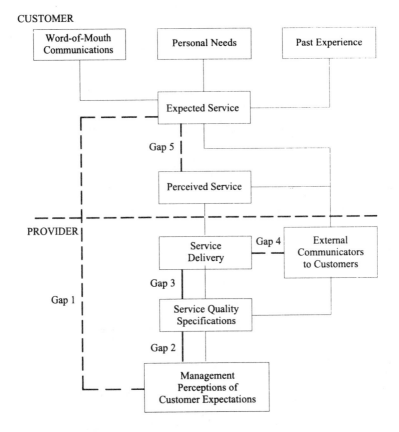

Source: Zeithaml *et al.*[1990], p. 46.

for the department is:

> to link management directly to the customers so they can know quickly what customers likes and dislikes are, as well as their requests. We will continue to actively seek input from our customers through:
> – comment cards made available in every store
> – toll-free numbers publicised on cash register receipts, all customer assistance literature and private label product labels.

This commitment to obtaining customer input is reflected in the way in which the customer service department has the ability to ring up anyone in the organisation to try to sort out problems. Customers can complain or simply

FIGURE 4
CUSTOMER COMMENT CARD – HARRIS-TEETER

Store No. ___288___
Eastland Mall Shopping Center,
Charlotte, NC 28205

Dear Customer,

You are number **ONE** at Harris Teeter. We want to make our store the **Very Best** it can be... for you!

HOW ARE WE DOING? Let us know. Your comments will encourage us to do a better job.

If our personnel have served you well, let us know so we can recognize a job well done.

Where you think we can improve, tell us. We guarantee that your opinions will receive careful consideration.

We at Harris Teeter are happy and proud to have you as our customer.

Sincerely,

Robert S. Goodale
President

Sincerely,

H. S. Dunn, Jr.
Executive Vice President

Dear Harris Teeter,   Date:

_____
_____
_____
_____
_____
_____
_____
_____
_____
_____

Name   **Phone**
Address

Drop in Suggestion Box Located On The Information Center Or Mail Postage Free

The Only
Low-Priced
Supermarket
That Refuses
To Act Like One!

BUSINESS REPLY CARD
FIRST CLASS PERMIT NO. 4871 CHARLOTTE, N.C. 28233

Postage Will Be Paid By—

HARRIS TEETER, INC
ATTENTION: PRESIDENT'S OFFICE
P.O. BOX 33129
CHARLOTTE, NORTH CAROLINA 28233

NO POSTAGE
NECESSARY
IF MAILED
IN THE
UNITED STATES

**Dear Customer,
We want to hear
from you!**

**Your Opinion
Counts!**

Harris Teeter

**Please fill out and
drop in our
Suggestion Box.**

comment in a number of ways. All these contacts have to be responded to and it is the responsibility of the customer service department to contact the customer within set time limits to attempt to remedy any problems and encourage the customer to return to the store/company. The belief is that a 'recovered' customer tends to be loyal – provided that repeat breakdowns are not made. Should there be a repeat, then the store manager can expect problems from both the customer service department and the 'higher' echelons of company management.

The company provides customer contact cards in every store through its customer information centre, which is a self-contained unit, generally on the inside front wall of the store. This centre, as well as containing comment cards, also contains product information, a newsletter, recipes, coupons and pens to complete the comment card. An example of the comment card is given in Figure 4.

On the staffing side, employees are trained in correct procedures for dealing with customers but are also told some things about customers:

- They are the most important people in our business.
- They are not an interruption in our daily work, but they are the reason for our work.
- When they bring us their wants and needs, it is our privilege to serve them.
- It is an honor for us to be able to serve them. They choose our store maybe it's because of the good service you gave them.
- They deserve and should receive our prompt, friendly attention.
- Our profits and job security depend on their business and loyalty.
- Whatever type of service they require, they tell their friends and neighbours – whether it is good or bad.
- Most importantly, they pay our wages! Without them, there would not be a need for us.

This message is constantly reinforced throughout training and in subsequent meetings and information briefings and so on. The message is simple: 'the customer is crucial to your pay packet. If the company and the staff don't deliver what the customer requires then the future is going to be bleak'.

Nordstrom Inc.

Nordstrom are a Seattle-based chain of department stores that have terrified their competitors by the service levels offered and customer loyalty engendered. They have also begun in the 1980s to move away from their north-west base and to open stores along the west coast and recently on the east coast. Nordstrom are a particular favourite of Tom Peters and are also profiled in the

Zemke and Schaaf (1989) list of best customer service companies. Whilst many of the stories about the company are undoubtedly apocryphal, there can be no doubting its success with its customers and its attraction for certain types of sales people. The company's draw is such that it can pick and choose its sales associates from a select pool of quality applicants.

This success has been attributed to many things, but it would seem that the real basis for Nordstrom is the overwhelming focus on the customer and the willingness to back and reward staff who put themselves out for their customers. Customer 'heroics' are welcomed, valued and celebrated as the pinnacle of salesmanship. The staff in Nordstrom tend to be very sharp, quick and responsive to customer needs. They are rewarded in commission and other terms for their success in selling. The message from Nordstrom is one of total commitment to the customer, focused through the sales staff.

Nordstrom claim that they do nothing very special in customer service terms, but simply put into practice what they have been doing since the company was founded. Being originally a shoe business, they argue that this gives them an attitude towards customers and inventory that is different to other retailers. Whether the attitude could now be grafted on to an existing retailer is doubtful. Their customer service approach can be defined in vague terms as a 'culture, background, chemistry, philosophy' or in simple terms as a 'wild dedication to taking care of the customers'. This dedication is generated by a complex reward and commission basis that treats every element of the company as responsible to its customers and rewards them on results. These rewards may be trophies, flowers, money, shares or enhanced discount, but they are cherished by employees. Such is the culture that even the accountants have customer service targets to achieve! This is reinforced by a management structure of decentralisation and a policy to restrict management hiring to within the business. The pressures are considerable, as is the responsibility, but equally the rewards and flexibility are considerable.

Palais Royal

Palais Royal are a long way from Nordstrom, both in geographical (Houston-based) and retail terms. They are a retailer of clothes at the lower and moderate end of the market and they focus on lower and moderate income people. The belief of the company, however, is that there is no reason why good customer service cannot be given to this target market as any other and that such service can be used to generate considerable customer loyalty and profitability. The service standards that are used by Palais Royal are all monitored and checked on a regular basis and staff are rewarded and promoted on the basis of their performance against agreed standards for the store and for the merchandise group which they sell. At the same time, the sales associates are constantly reminded about the importance of customers as people and not just as sales targets.

Palais Royal focus their efforts on customer service and taking care of the customer. The ways in which this is done is through the combination of 'training with follow-up and recognition for the people who achieve the standards'. At the same time, they try to listen to customers and make improvements at their behest, more hooks in the changing rooms, for example. The focus, however, is using the sales associates to deliver customer service by being sales professionals. To this end the systems in the company monitor staff performance in a number of elements of their job – both quantitative and qualitative – and reward staff for exceeding targets and standards. Such elements include not only sales volume per hour but items such as business card delivery, development of clientele books and sending of thank-you cards. In this way the system supports and monitors the staff whilst encouraging the sales associates to develop personal relationships with the clientele.

A good illustration of the importance the company places on the staff–customer relationship is given in Figure 5. The 'take note' document emphasises the way employees should treat customers and try to build a relationship with them over a long period. This is extended by the use of stickers and reminders on company literature, in staff rooms and throughout the store. These carry slogans such as:

- someplace special … because we care!
- never say no! if you can't say yes, call management
- we care
- customers are really everything (care)

The message is one of continuously reminding staff about the atmosphere, presentation and approach to the customers.

Figure 6 presents the customer service performance standards that are set for sales associates. Many of these can only be checked by store management watching the sales floor or by 'mystery' shoppers being employed to receive service as a customer and report on individual employees. Palais Royal in fact uses an extensive programme of such shoppers and rewards staff on performance on these. All staff know that the store is shopped on a regular basis. What Figure 6 also shows is the way in which service is used to extend the sale and to build the relationship. Sales associates are also monitored on items such as sales per hour, thank-you cards written, multiple item sales etc. The performance on these criteria against agreed standards affects the level of pay and staff entry or position on reward programmes.

One such programme is the STAR programme outlined in Figure 7. This shows both the standards to be achieved and the rewards to be gained by being a 'STAR'. Some of the standards are calculable on the basis of till data whilst others depend on agreement or assessment by managers and/or mystery shop-

FIGURE 5
TAKE NOTE – PALAIS ROYAL

TAKE NOTE

'THE SECRET IS ATMOSPHERE'

A pleasant shopping experience depends on the atmosphere we create. In a Palais Royal store the feeling is, 'I feel welcome here'. – 'I feel comfortable'. The store's layout, merchandise, and the way it is displayed, make important contributions. But first and foremost is the way customers are treated by the store's associates.
You are the all-important contact:

    – Your friendliness, a welcome smile, showing personal interest by using a customer's name, gives your customer a feeling of importance.
    – Your sincerity is evident in your efforts to find out a customer's needs, and once known, in quickly carrying out your customer's wishes.
    – Your honesty builds trust. Customers deserve the truth about merchandise ... about fit, fabric, and 'look'

These, and courtesy, create a pleasant shopping atmosphere that encourages our customers to come back again. That's the secret.

pers. In all cases the sales associate is interviewed about performance and appeals can take place. Sales associates themselves have records on their own performance agreed with management on a regular basis and available at all times. There are other programmes and awards that build on the STAR programme and develop other aspects of the employees performance.

CUSTOMER SERVICE DELIVERY

The illustrations of specific aspects of customer service in Harris-Teeter, Nordstrom and Palais Royal are important as they focus on three different aspects of the management and delivery of customer service. What they illustrate are the attention to detail and corporate culture that are needed to provide quality service. Physical items of this service provision can be copied or borrowed, but culture and attitudes are less transferable or require much more attention to develop. The argument is not that UK retailers should follow these illustrations slavishly but rather that they should begin to think about their customer service strategy.

Disaggregating customer service aspects for illustration as above can be somewhat misleading. This is because the approach in good service companies is not an aspect or a focus on one item but an overall orientation or strategy towards customers and customer satisfaction. All aspects of the company are tuned towards the customer and focus on satisfying customer needs. There is no management programme that can be used to bring customer service success.

FIGURE 6
CUSTOMER SERVICE PERFORMANCE STANDARDS
FOR SALES ASSOCIATES

1. Every customer is greeted or acknowledged within thirty seconds of entering the department.
2. Accompanies the customer to the fitting room.
3. Returns to the fitting room within five minutes to check with the customer while in the fitting room.
4. A minimum of two garments are presented to the customer while in the fitting room.
5. One additional item is suggested to the customer.
6. At the close of the sale, the customer is thanked by name, if available.
7. Presents a business card to all customers (except for regular/clientele customer).
8. Suggests a new account to every customer that does not have an account.
9. Two 'thank you' cards are written each day an associate is at work.
10. A minimum of one new clientele customer is added each week.

Rather, the service programme is one that involves all staff of the company and rewards on the basis of performance not just the managers but those that deliver the highest standards of service.

Whilst the argument that customer service is indivisible in any good service company is a powerful one, there seems little doubt that some core characteristics have to be achieved consistently. It is proposed here to discuss and illustrate these under five headings (which are presented in no ranked order). It is re-emphasised that these headings,whilst treated discretely here, are part of an integral service provision.

Attitudes

There are a number of different aspects to attitude that are demonstrated by the better service companies. One is a belief that the 'management' of a store and a company should have front-line experience of serving customers. This might be for only a few weeks a year or as a regular part of their job, but the important point is that they experience serving customers first hand. Wal-Mart insist that corporate staff spend a set time each year in their stores serving customers. Regional management at The Limited are required to sell in stores as part of their jobs. Attitudes such as these demonstrate a commitment to customer service and focus on the customer, not the corporate end of the business.

Equally, however, the attitude of sales staff in store is crucial towards the delivery of customer service. Disinterested sales staff speak volumes about the status of customers. On the contrary, however, sales staff who are motivated and have an customer attitude that focuses on providing service are vital in providing the correct atmosphere. One aspect of this attitude is in the way staff

FIGURE 7
STAR PROGRAMME

A: How to Reach the STARS

Standard	Senior Sales Associate	Sales Consultant	Senior Sales Consultant
	*In trailing 6 months	*In trailing 6 months	*In trailing 6 months
VPH	*Equals Dept's VPH	Is 10% above dept's VPH	Is 20% above dept's VPH
Multiple Sales %	*Equals dept's multiple %	Dept's multiple sales % + 1%	Dept's multiple sales % + 2%
New Accounts	*1 approved a month in 4 out of last 6 months.	2 approved a month in 3 out of last 6 months.	3 approved a month in 3 of last 6 months.
'Thank You' Cards	Average of 2 sent for 7 hours worked.	Average of 2 sent for 7 hours worked.	Average of 2 sent for 7 hours worked.
Loss Prevention Evaluation	'Satisfactory' rating	'Good' rating	'Outstanding' rating
Clientele Book Evaluation	'Excellent' rating	'Excellent' rating	'Excellent' rating
Overall Performance Evaluation	'Satisfactory' rating	'Good' rating	'Outstanding' rating
Shoppings (if none, 'no effect')	In trailing 4 months total score 75% or more.	In trailing 4 months total score 80% or more.	In trailing 4 months total score 85% or more.

B: STAR Benefits

Sales Associate	Senior Sales Associate	Sales Consultant	Senior Sales Consultant
			One additional paid floating holiday for each 6 months.
		Annual recognition breakfast with/top corporate executives.	Receives plaque at annual recognition breakfast with top corporate executives.
		Special Honor Roll Listing	Special Honor Roll Listing
		Once for each 6 months, Spring & Fall, can purchase PR merchandise at 50% of original price	One for each 6 months, Spring & Fall, can purchase PR merchandise at 50% off original price.
	Title engraved on name badge and on business card.	6-month bonus of 0.25% of trailing 6-month net sales	6-month bonus of 0.25% of trailing 6 months net sales.
	Special Honor Roll listing	Gold name badge title engraved on name badge and on business card.	Gold name badge with title and name engraved on it and on business card.
			0.25% monthly top of draw bonus on net sales.
Regular Palais Royal benefits and commissions.	Regular Palais Royal benefits and commissions.	Regular Palais Royal benefits and commissions.	Regular Palais Royal benefits and commissions.

speak to customers. In many stores staff are told to say certain phrases and to deal with customers in a set way. This is believed to be providing service. In fact, better service is provided by companies who tell staff 'this is what you must not say' and let them find their own phrases. This avoids the monotonous, repetitive, robotic form of 'service' that is currently prevalent in much retailing in the United Kingdom.

Sales Staff

Customer service is delivered mainly by the sales staff of a company. It is clear, therefore, that much effort has to be expended on recruiting and holding quality staff. In some instances this might be through the staff having the right 'attitude' or through a large degree of testing. Either way, it is a type of person that is being sought.

Engendering the motivation and attitude at the sales staff level is often seen as being a question of rewarding staff for good performance. Appraisal and reward systems such as those illustrated above are common in many American retailers, although their extent varies. Equally common is the payment of staff through commission systems. Staff are paid a basic salary and then are 'rewarded' by commission on the way in which they reach targets. Commission sales can be simply a percentage of volume, or can be rather more complex calculations that involve meeting targets on a variety of bases. Such targets could include multiple sales, thank-you cards and so on as well as simply volume. This is because volume-based measures alone can tend to lead to over-competitive staff chasing customers. It is also essential that there is no cap on the reward system. If staff sell enough product to make a very high wage then this should be encouraged and allowed. Sales staff earning large wages on the back of high levels of selling should lead to better performance for the company.

Such reward or commission systems should not be targeted solely at the sales floor staff. Store management, regional management and staff at corporate levels can also be made to be more dependent on performance, both personally and for the company as a whole. By so doing, all employees feel they have a stake in the simplest activity performed in the company.

Visibility

Customer service appears to have a much higher profile in the United States than it currently has in the United Kingdom. This is certainly the case inside retail outlets, where reference has already been made to customer information centres, the provision of toll-free numbers, store leaflets and notice boards, customer contact cards and so on. Visibility in this sense can be applied both to the physical visibility of service desks etc,and also to a less tangible visibility that comes from customer service attitudes. Whilst the physical visibility is important, it has to be combined with the correct attitude for customer service visibility. There is, for example, nothing quite so crass as a customer service desk that is closed or a customer contact card display that never has any cards. However, such things can be ameliorated by staff who are helpful and concerned about the customer. When there are physical and attitudinal attributes to visibility working together, then the message is one of service, care and concern.

Customer Contact

The examples given above have identified many ways in which retailers contact the customer. Most good service retailers are using a combination of these. In addition, however, there is also the use of staff to provide extra customer contact. The most obvious example of this is the way in which customers are greeted as they enter the store or certainly within their first few seconds in the store. This greeting acts both to acknowledge the presence of the customer and to begin the dialogue with the customer. It is not suggested here that such activity is applicable in all British retailers. It is instead the thinking behind customer contact activities that is crucial. In many British companies customer contact is the last thing on sales staff and management minds. This has obvious long-term implications.

Champions

The final component to be identified is that of champions for customer service. In one sense this has already been done by considering the staff and attitudes throughout the company. In another sense, though, this championing role is much more than this. It revolves, for example, around the significance given by the company to the customer service department. If the company truly believes that the customer is always right, then the status of the customer service division will be high and the authority they can wield will be considerable. In such companies the customer service division has the ability to impose solutions on the line management if the service has been less than perfect. In other companies it means an automatic referal upwards every day if complaints are not solved. The message is one that the company cares about its customers and will put things right and ensure that they don't go wrong again. Whilst getting it wrong first time should be avoided, repeating the mistake should be unnacceptable. Championing is about believing in customer heroics and encouraging all forms of excellent service.

CONCLUSIONS

This article has considered aspects of the customer service found in American retailing. The fundamental belief identified is that it is essential to build a long-term relationship with customers and that customer service is one way of doing this. The service illustrations used here are to an extent extreme in that they are interesting examples of service provision in North America. It does have to be remembered that not all American retailers practise good quality customer service and that 'gaps' can be identified quite readily (see Figure 3). It is a legitimate question to ask whether the better elements of service and the orientation could be introduced in the United Kingdom.

In some instances it is not difficult to imagine the problems that might ensue given the different trading environments of the United Kingdom and the United States. For example, the greeting of customers by staff members soon after they enter the store is probably only possible in the United States because of lower store volumes. It may not be practical in a real sense in the United Kingdom because customer volumes are much higher and no relationship between staff and customer is therefore commenced. This is not to say, however, that staff recognition of customers is not an achievable goal. Staff should be encouraged and rewarded to generate such an attitude.

On the other hand, however, it is undoubtedly true that many of the activities presented here should be basic to any retail company in the United Kingdom (and elsewhere). Some would claim to be 'doing customer service' already. Obtaining customer views, having high service visibility, rewarding staff for good service and ensuring good service attitudes throughout the company should be common place. Whilst many retailers may feel they are doing this, the reality from the customer's point of view is very different. Figure 1 reported a story that is not untypical of British retailing. Other examples could be used. Nowhere is it really possible to point to a multiple retailer which is totally service-oriented (although it does have to be recognised that some steps are being made). In one sense this does not really matter. It is seemingly part of the British psyche to enjoy poor service as it gives (us) something to complain about, but in the longer term it is probable that service levels and attitudes will have to rise as new companies exploit the British market and British consumers experience wider examples of good service. If this does happen then these companies that have already begun to digest the lessons of quality service retailing and are focusing on their customers will be those that will prosper. To do this retailers need to prepare a full customer service strategy and act all the time accordingly. This is easy to write, but is less easy to do, partly because it must affect everyone in a company to work properly. Tinkering through piecemeal quality programmes is not the way.

British retailing is characterised by low pay, poor levels of staff remuneration, sometimes inadequate working conditions and minimal staff levels, motivation and concern. This caricature is supported by high profit levels of many companies, even in difficult times, and relatively high margins. Management salaries and rewards are considerable. It is possible to suggest that the 'gap' is bridged by customer (dis)service and that it is customers who, by accepting inadequate standards, are helping to sustain inequities and suffering themselves in the process. What is likely to occur in the coming decade is that some retailers will begin to apply customer service as a strategic tool and profit accordingly and that customer segments will increasingly reject inadequate service provision. The winners in this process will see increased market share and profitability through satisfying customer requirements. The journey is not an easy one for companies to make and service provision and attitudes have a long way to go. It is hoped that this article will help in beginning to expand the consideration of service.

British retailing is poised to take a leap forward in customer service terms. This is not an easy step to take or journey to make, but it may be crucial in building successful retailing in the 1990s and beyond. There is no one answer and each company needs to work through its own customer service strategy and policies.

ACKNOWLEDGEMENTS

The author gratefully acknowledges the funding of the Winston Churchill Memorial Trust, which made possible this study. The assistance provided by many retailers, academics and consumers in North America is also acknowledged with thanks. The Carnegie Trust for Scottish Universities provided financial assistance for follow-up research, which is also gratefully acknowledged.

REFERENCES

Albrecht, K. and R. Zemke, 1985, *Service America!* Dow Jones-Irwin: Homewood, Illinois.
Albrecht, K. 1988, *At America's Service*. Dow Jones-Irwin: Homewood, Illinois.
Arnold, D. R., I. M. Capella and G. D. Smith, 1983 *Strategic Retail Management*. Addison-Wesley: Reading, Massachusetts.
Berry, L. L., 1988, 'Delivering Excellent Service in Retailing'. *Arthur Anderson and Co. Retail Issues Letter*, I(4), pp. 1–3.
Burns, R., 1989, 'Customer Service vs Customer Focused'. *Retail Control*, March, pp. 25–35.
Carlzon, J., 1987, *Moments of Truth*, Harper and Row: New York.
Crosby, P., 1979, *Quality is Free*. New American Library: New York.
Hanon, M., and P. Karp, 1989 *Customer Satisfaction*. Amacom: New York.
Lash, L., 1989, *The Complete Guide to Customer Service*, Wiley: New York.
Mason, J. B., M. L. Mayer and M. E. Ezell, 1988, *Retailing* (3rd edn.) Business Publications Inc: Plano, Texas.
Parasuraman, A., V. A. Zeithaml and L. L. Berry 1988, 'SERVQUAL: a multiple-item scale for measuring consumer perceptions of service quality. *Journal of Retailing*, vol. 64, No. 1, pp. 12–40.
Peters, T., 1988, *Thriving on Chaos*, Macmillan: London.
Peters, T. and N. Austin 1985, *A Passion for Excellence*, Random House: New York.
Peters, T. and R. Waterman, 1982, *In Search of Excellence*, Harper and Row: London.
Prouty, J., G. Roth and C. Nelson, 1988, 'An Evolving Obsession with Customer Service'. *Retail Control*, September, pp. 2–12.
Smith T. J., 1989, 'Nurturing a Customer Service Culture'. *Retail Control*, October, pp. 15–18.
Thomas, M., 1987, 'Customer Care: the ultimate marketing tool in Wensley, R. (ed.), *Reviewing Effective Research and Good Practice in Marketing Proceedings*, MEG, Warwick.
Walters, D. W. 1989, 'Customer Service as a Component of Retailing Strategy', pp. 209–26 of ESOMAR – *Adding Value to Retailing Offerings*, Esomar.

Zeithaml, V. A., A. Parasuraman and L. L. Berry, 1990, *Delivering Quality Service*. Free Press: New York.

Zemke R., and D. Schaaf, 1989, *The Service Edge*. New American Library: New York.Market Failure and Bank Regulation

This chapter first appeared in *The Service Industries Journal*, Vol.12, No.2 (1992).

7
Retail Location at the Micro-Scale: Inventory and Prospect

STEPHEN BROWN

Although the issue of retail location has attracted a great deal of academic attention, the bulk of this literature pertains to the national, regional and urban scales of analysis. An equally important, but comparatively neglected, consideration is micro-scale retail location; that is, location within planned shopping centres and unplanned shopping districts. This article reviews the literature on retail location at the micro-scale, summarises the current state of knowledge and sets out a future research agenda.

INTRODUCTION

It has often – perhaps too often – been said that the three secrets of success in retailing are location, location and location [Ghosh, 1990; Davies and Harris, 1990; Pearson, 1991]. Important though the other elements of the retail marketing mix undoubtedly are, the most sophisticated store designs, meticulous merchandise planning procedures, imaginative advertising campaigns, astute pricing policies and competent sales personnel all come to naught if a retailer's locational strategy is flawed. What is more, whereas errors in pricing, promotions, merchandise planning and so on can be comparatively easily adjusted, mistaken locational decisions are not readily rectified – indeed for some they can prove fatal – and only then at considerable expense, disruption and damage to a retailer's carefully nurtured reputation [Ghosh and McLafferty, 1987].

In keeping with its standing as a key component in the retailing mix, the locational issue is subject to intensive investigation and continual improvement [e.g. Ghosh and Ingene, 1991]. Although intuitive approaches to locational decision taking are still surprisingly prevalent [Simpkin, Doyle and Saunders, 1985; Anderson, Parker and Stanley, 1990], recent years have seen several sophisticated additions to the locational analyst's toolkit. Thanks to the virtual ubiquity of powerful, low cost computing facilities, a wide range of spatial databases and analytical techniques are now available [Beaumont, 1988; Goodchild, 1991; Curry, 1993]. Whether developed in-house or purchased from specialist providers like CACI and Pinpoint, these databases typically comprise a geographically organised (geocoded) amalgam of information from the population census statistics, postcodes file and surveys of shopper behaviour and buying power. They thus provide rapid, low cost means of assessing, profiling and comparing market opportunities, screening potential sites and defining catchment areas. This information, furthermore, is compatible with the new generation of store location models, such as SLAM, ILACS or FRANSYS, which facilitate the evaluation of multi-outlet networks operated by a single retail chain [Simpkin, 1989; Goodchild, 1984; Ghosh and Craig, 1991].

Despite the latter-day advances in location modelling and geographical information systems, the outcome of locational decisions ultimately rests on *micro-scale* considerations; that is, the appropriateness or otherwise of the precise location *within* the chosen city centre, regional shopping centre, inner city arterial, secondary shopping district, retail warehouse park or whatever. Indeed, it has often been said – though perhaps not often enough – that a few yards can make all the difference between success and failure in retailing [Parkes, 1987; Dewar and Watson, 1990]. The issue of micro-scale location, however, remains comparatively neglected by retailing researchers. True, the need for detailed study of retail location at the micro-scale has often been stressed [Shepherd and Thomas, 1980; Dawson, 1980; Potter, 1982; Breheny, 1988] and ample empirical evidence attests to its importance [Hansen and Weinberg, 1979; Hise *et al.*, 1983; Anderson, 1985]. Yet, compared to the extraordinarily voluminous literature on retail location at the national, regional and urban scales of analysis, the micro-scale placement of retail outlets within planned shopping centres and unplanned shopping districts has attracted relatively little academic discussion.

In an attempt to draw attention to this important, if somewhat neglected, research issue, this study will endeavour to bring together the extant literature on micro-scale retail location. It does so by, firstly, identifying and evaluating the available theoretical frameworks and associated empirical studies of shop patterns; secondly, exploring demand side analyses of within-centre shopper movement and behaviour; thirdly, highlighting the often imperceptible influence of supply side factors like town planning policies and the shopping centre development industry; and, fourthly, attempting to summarise the current state of knowledge on micro-scale retail location and set out a future research agenda. Before commencing the review proper, however, it is important to note that, despite its reputation as a 'cinderella' subject, the micro-scale literature is far from negligible. Its 'important but over-looked' status is entirely *relative* to the academic attention lavished on retail location at the meso- and macro-scales. As shall become apparent, a surprising amount of published material actually exists, though it tends to be scattered among a wide variety of academic specialisms – economics, geography, marketing, psychology, town planning and traffic engineering, to name but the most prominent.

THEORETICAL CONTEXT

If the literature on micro-scale retail location had to be summarised in a single word, that word would probably be agglomeration. Above all else, the spatial arrangement of retail outlets *within* shopping districts exhibits a tendency for similar 'types' of establishment – those selling similar categories of merchandise or orientated toward a similar target market – to cluster together into distinctive sub-areas. The department stores of Boulevard Haussmann, the outfitters of Oxford Street and the theatres and cinemas of Broadway are some of the best known examples of this phenomenon, but the agglomeration of analogous trade types is one of the most ubiquitous features of the commercial environment and a truly universal trait. It has been observed in suburban shopping centres [Jones, 1969; Maitland, 1985], traditional African markets [Miracle, 1962; Ukuw, 1969], Third World cities [Sendut, 1965; Beaujeu-Garnier and Delobez, 1979] and also times past. Nystrom [1930], for instance, noted 'natural groupings' of similar retail businesses in the centres of nineteenth-century American cities; Hassan [1972] has described the spatial proximity of retailers of books, incense, textiles and utensils in the Islamic cities of the late Middle Ages; and Davis [1966, p.108] cites an account of seventeenth-century Cheapside when it 'was beautiful to behold the glorious appearance of goldsmiths' shops . . . which in a continuous course reached from the Old Change to Buck-lesbury, exclusive of four shops only of other trades in all that space'.

Not unnaturally, the agglomerative tendencies of similar retail outlets and the intra-centre spatial arrangement of these clusters of activity have attracted a considerable amount of theoretical discussion and associated empirical analysis. The conceptual touchstones are two long-established and much-debated models, *the principle of minimum differentiation* and *bid rent theory*. Although different in many respects, both concepts are predicated on positivist, neoclassical premises, which presuppose, essentially, that there is an identifiable order in the material world, that people are rational, utility maximising decision-makers and that economic activity takes place in a freely competitive manner. The theories, what is more, are deductively derived and normative in ethos. In other words, they are based on stated, often highly simplified assumptions, not empirical observation, and as a result describe patterns of retail activity that ought to occur, given the underlying assumptions, not ones that necessarily do. That said, the models are by no means totally divorced from reality. On the contrary, they have given rise to numerous empirical investigations (the results of which are somewhat mixed but broadly supportive of the hypothesised patterns of retail activity) and several inductively derived attempts to combine and integrate the concepts into a more general *combination theory*.

The Principle of Minimum Differentiation

Although it is perhaps less well known than macro-scale locational concepts like central place theory and spatial interaction theory, Harold Hotelling's [1929] principle of minimum differentiation provides the conceptual foundations for the study of micro-scale retail location. Dealing initially with two profit maximising firms, selling identical products (with zero production costs) at f.o.b. prices from fixed locations in a bounded linear market where transport costs are constant, demand is completely inelastic and identical, utility maximising consumers are evenly distributed, bear the costs of distribution and patronise outlets solely on the basis of delivery prices, Hotelling demonstrated that an equilibrium existed where neither outlet could increase profits by altering its prices. He argued, moreover, that if one seller is free to relocate, it would maximise its hinterland (and hence its profit) by setting up shop adjacent to the other on the 'long' side of the market. If, as Chamberlin [1933] subsequently noted, both sellers are footloose, a process of mutual leapfrogging to the longer side of the market ensues, the upshot of which is a distinctive clustered arrangement in the centre of the market.

Since Hotelling's pioneering contribution, the principle of minimum differentiation has been applied to all manner of marketing phenomena, ranging from television programming and pricing conjectures to new product development [Brown, 1989; Ingene and Ghosh, 1991]. However, possibly as a result of its traditional textbook portrayal as the 'problem' of ice cream vendors on a beach, the concept is often taken to pertain to retail location at the micro-scale. In this respect, indeed, the associated empirical record lends considerable weight to Hotelling's agglomerative hypothesis. Shop pattern studies undertaken in a number of different countries, using a variety of statistical techniques and referring to a comprehensive cross-section of retail trade types, agree that sellers of the same category of merchandise (food, clothing, motor car dealers and so on) tend to cluster tightly together [Rogers, 1969; Lee, 1974; Okabe, Asami and Miki, 1985]. A number of empirical analyses also attest to the fact that compatible but contrasting store types (restaurants and cinemas, grocers and florists etc.) exhibit marked intra-centre agglomerative tendencies [Ratcliff, 1939; Parker, 1962; Brady, 1977].

Although Hotelling's clustering hypothesis appears to enjoy a high degree of empirical support, the agglomerated outcome of his model is a consequence of its initial assumptions concerning market conditions and competitor behaviour. Such conditions are rarely encountered in the real world, though the development of the western Canadian fur trade provides a fascinating exception to the rule [Freeman and Dungey, 1981], and, inevitably, this has prompted many attempts to relax the model's highly restrictive assumptions [e.g. Lerner and Singer, 1937; Devletoglou, 1965; Eaton and Lipsey, 1975]. Almost without exception, however, these adjustments give rise, not to the anticipated agglomerated pattern, but to *dispersed* spatial arrangements of competing firms. Apart from some evidence of pairing when large numbers of outlets are involved [Okabe and Susuki, 1987], the bulk of studies support Eaton and Lipsey's [1979, p.422] conclusion that, 'the Hotelling model is not able to explain the local clustering of firms . . . Indeed, once the assumptions are relaxed very slightly in the direction of realism, Hotelling's model predicts that no two firms should be clustered together'.

In recent years, however, the Hotelling model has been rehabilitated somewhat. This has been achieved through, firstly, the incorporation of agglomeration economies, positive externalities or cost reducing benefits that flow from spatial propinquity [Thill and Thomas, 1987; Fujita and Smith, 1990]; secondly, relaxing the traditional assumption that retailers and consumers are perfectly informed, and thus certain about the outcomes of their actions [Pascal and McCall, 1980; de Palma, Ginsburgh and Thisse, 1987]; and, thirdly, permitting these uncertain consumers to gather information and minimise costs by indulging in multi-purpose, multi-stop and comparison shopping behaviours [Fujita, Ogawa and Thisse, 1988; Ingene and Ghosh, 1990]. The upshot of these modifications is that the principle of minimum differentiation is once again capable of describing the much observed and statistically proven clustering of competitive and compatible retail outlets within unplanned shopping districts and planned shopping centres, though the conditions under which agglomeration occurs is somewhat at odds with Hotelling's original conception.

Bid Rent Theory

Although the principle of minimum differentiation has traditionally been associated with micro-scale retail location, the same cannot be said for bid rent theory, or at least not with the same conviction. It was originally developed at the macro-scale (regional/urban), and with respect to all manner of land use categories (residential, industrial, commercial, etc.), though it has since been applied with some success to retail land uses in general and micro-scale settings in particular. Dating from the celebrated agricultural model of von Thünen [1826], bid rent theory emphasises the paramount importance of accessibility to the patterning of urban land uses [see Jones, 1991; Thrall, 1991]. As the city centre is the focal point of transportation networks, it is the most accessible location in an urban area and consequently offers maximum market potential and optimum access to sources of labour and customers. Competition takes place for this, the most desirable of locations, and land goes to the highest bidders, those that can derive the greatest utility from the most central locations. Rents, therefore, are highest in the very centre of the city centre and decline with distance from the core area [Balchin, Kieve and Bull, 1988].

The need for a central location, however, varies between different categories of retail outlet and this affects the level of rents they are willing to bid for sites increasingly eccentric to the core. Assuming, as before, the existence of uniformly priced travel which is equally easy in all directions, a free market in property, perfectly informed, profit maximising buyers and sellers etc., bid rent curves can be constructed for each retailing function, their angle reflecting the sensitivity of that activity to changes in accessibility. Desiring to attract custom from the entire urban area and, as a result, requiring the most central sites of all, high order retailing functions such as department and speciality stores are prepared to bid the highest rentals, though the amount they are willing to pay falls off rapidly with distance. Low order retail functions, on the other hand, are more willing to trade off the accessibility of the primary shopping streets for the lower rentals available in secondary or peripheral shopping thoroughfares, and their bid rent curves are correspondingly shallower. Bid rent theory, in other words, postulates a concentric arrangement of intra-centre land uses with department stores and speciality retailers in the centre of the city centre and grocery stores and convenience goods retailers on the outer fringe [Scott, 1970]. A broadly similar model of the internal structure of suburban shopping districts has also been posited [Garner, 1966; Chudzynska, 1981].

Given its implausible assumptions of, amongst others, a monocentric city, accessibility that is maximised in the city centre and declines equally in all directions, a free market in property and the presence of a multiplicity of independent, rational, fully informed, utility maximising buyers and sellers, it is hardly surprising that the bid rent model has been subject to severe academic criticism [Harvey, 1974; Ball, 1979, 1985]. The empirical record, however, lends considerable support to the concentric zonation prediction, though the patterns are less clear cut in practice than they are in theory. Whether based upon land value or land use data, or utilising qualitative or quantitative analytical procedures, shop pattern studies undertaken in the centres of several American [Rannells, 1956; Weaver 1969], European [Davies, 1972a; Friedrichs and Goodman, 1987], African [Davies, 1965; Beavon, 1970], Asian [Khan and Uddin, 1967; Bellett, 1969] and Antipodean [Scott, 1959; Alexander, 1974] cities, concur that the retailing component of the city centre comprises a centrally located core devoted to high order functions and a peripheral fringe occupied by low order outlets and space extensive retailing establishments [Davies, 1976].

This intra-centre zonation, it must be emphasised, is not confined to western city centres, nor is it an artifact of the recent past. It has been reported in the market places and shopping parades of the developing world [Beaujeu-Garnier and Delobez, 1979], within the retailing assemblages at the exits of US interstate highways [Norris, 1987], in the centres of nineteenth-century European cities [Shaw, 1988] and the market towns of medieval England [Carter, 1983]. Indeed, its prevalence is nowhere better illustrated than in the recent emergence of 'suburban downtowns' in major US metropolitan areas, where, despite the ostensibly planned environment, competitive bidding for the most accessible micro-scale locations has become increasingly apparent [Buckwalter, 1989; Hartshorn and Muller, 1989]. When all is said and done, even the sternest critics of bid rent theory recognise that the pattern of retail land use it predicts provides a reasonably accurate reflection of reality [Harvey, 1973; Johnston, 1977; Whitehand, 1987].

Combination Theories

The concentric pattern of retail land use described by bid rent theory and the agglomerative proclivities enshrined in the principle of minimum differentiation do not, of course, operate in isolation. In fact, many empirical studies of micro-scale retail location, ranging from western city centres to traditional Moroccan souks, have noted that a combination of specialised clusters of activity and broad zonation from core to periphery tends to obtain in practice [Fogg, 1932; Scott, 1959; de Blij, 1962]. A number of attempts, therefore, have been made to develop significant combination theories of this state of affairs, though in sharp contrast to the deductively derived, neoclassical premises of both bid rent theory and the principle of minimum differentiation, these frameworks are almost without exception the outcome of inductive reasoning.

An early and much cited example of such theorising is the 'core-frame' model of Horwood and Boyce [1959]. Derived from a detailed literature review and land use surveys of the centres of eleven US cities, this model maintained that central areas comprised: firstly, an inner 'core' dominated by vertical development, pedestrian movement, internal linkages and an extreme concentration of shops, offices and other intensive land uses; and, secondly, an outer 'frame' which tended to be horizontally developed, motor vehicle orientated, externally linked and characterised by semi-intensive clusters of specialist land uses like wholesaling, light industry, transportation termini and automobile sales. Subsequent analyses in the United States [Horwood and McNair, 1961], Canada [Campbell, 1970], Germany [Hartenstein and Staack, 1967], Australia [Alexander, 1974] and the United Kingdom [Davies, 1976] have lent empirical weight to the concept and concluded that it has considerable descriptive and, indeed, prescriptive value [Davies, 1984].

Influential as it proved to be, the core-frame model – and its analogues [e.g. Davies, 1965; Herbert and Thomas, 1982] – was formulated with respect to a wide range of land use categories and thus tended to discuss retailing in crude aggregate terms. Another equally important but retail specific combination theory is Davies' [1972b] 'complex' model of city centre retailing. This not only incorporates the concentric zonation and specialist clusters of bid rent theory and the principle of minimum differentiation respectively, but also adds an arterial or linear component, which represents, in effect, a spatial manifestation of the countervailing forces of agglomeration and dispersion. Ostensibly an intra-centre adaptation of Berry's [1963] seminal typology of urban retail structure – though its roots are actually much older – empirical tests of Davies 'complex' model have proved remarkably successful. It was first employed to describe the central shopping district of Coventry [Davies, 1972a] and has since been successfully applied, albeit with a number of minor methodological and taxonomic adjustments, to the central areas of Newcastle-upon-Tyne [White, 1975], Stockport [Potter, 1982], Belfast [Brown, 1987a] and the west end of London [Davies, 1976].

DEMAND SIDE ANALYSES

Close though the correspondence appears to be between the normative predictions of the above theories and the associated empirical evidence

culled from studies of intra-centre shop patterns, it is incorrect to infer
that the latter, in some way, 'proves' the former – quite the reverse. Extant spatial patterns of retail activity may result from any number of
processes (inertia, cultural factors etc.) other than the behaviours of the
utility maximising decision takers and so on of the bid rent and PMD
models. While the commonplace clustering of (say) booksellers within
the central area of many European cities may well reflect consumers'
desire to reduce uncertainty through shopping around, this behavioural
process cannot be deduced from the study of spatial patterns alone. As
Scott [1970] rightly points out, 'the immediate juxtaposition of . . . shops
is not necessarily more indicative of the economies to be derived from
agglomeration than the juxtaposition of residents is indicative of neigh-
bourliness'.

   In these circumstances, it is not surprising that attempts have been
made to address the demand side of the locational equation; in other
words, to examine empirically and model the micro-scale movements of
consumers within planned and unplanned shopping centres. Broadly
speaking, these studies can be subdivided into three major categories:
empirical-behavioural, *cognitive-behavioural* and *conceptual*. The first
focuses entirely upon overt, acted-out consumer behaviour, the second
concentrates upon consumers' (covert) mental processes and appraisals
of retailing milieux whereas the third endeavours to derive meaningful
behavioural generalisations by drawing upon both overt and, to a lesser
extent, covert investigations.

Empirical-behavioural

Although micro-scale retail location is reputed to be a comparatively
underdeveloped field of study, the empirical-behavioural literature is far
from negligible. Dating from the early years of the present century,
when pedestrian counts for store location purposes first commenced
[Hurd, 1903; Brisco, 1927], this consists largely of analyses of shopper
behaviour within a variety of retailing environments, ranging from
regional shopping centres to neighbourhood parades, in contrasting
countries and employing all manner of research techniques [e.g. Bennison and Davies, 1977; Boal and Johnson, 1968; Churchman and Tzamir,
1981; Parker and McLaughlin, 1988]. Yet despite these major differences
in milieux and methodology, the principal findings of such studies are
remarkably consistent.

   The first of these is the influence of magnet or attractor stores.
Although the nature of the magnet many vary from environment to environment – department stores dominate in traditional town and city
centres, supermarkets hold sway in neighbourhood shopping complexes

and restaurants do likewise in festival malls etc. – the studies of micro-spatial shopper behaviour are as one in the key, customer-generating function of the magnet stores and the all-important influence they exert on shopper circulation patterns. To cite but two examples, a questionnaire survey of 1470 shoppers in central Newcastle-upon-Tyne, concluded that consumer movements were largely determined by the locations of the 13 major department and variety stores and Granger Market, which together accounted for 80 per cent of all 3193 reported purchases [Davies and Bennison, 1978]. In Canada, meanwhile, a study of shopper behaviour in the Whyte Center, an unplanned commercial agglomeration in inner city Edmonton, found that the bulk of consumers patronised either the Safeway supermarket or an Army and Navy department store – and many visited both [Johnson, 1978].

The second fundamental finding concerns the customer interchange that tends to occur between shops of a similar or compatible trade type. This tendency is amply illustrated by Toyne's [1971] detailed year-round examination of shopper behaviour in central Exeter, which revealed that the vast majority of inter-outlet linkages comprised movements from one outfitter, shoe shop, furniture retailer, cafe or whatever to another outfitter, shoe shop, furniture retailer and so on. Equally prominent were inter-type linkages between complementary retail establishments like supermarkets and greengrocers, greengrocers and bakers and shoe shops and outfitters. By far the best known study of shopper interchange, however, was that undertaken over 30 years ago by Nelson [1958]. After examining the shop-to-shop movements of around 100,000 customers in a host of planned and unplanned shopping centres in the US, he assembled his celebrated 'compatibility' tables in which retail business types were deemed to be highly compatible if between 10 and 20 per cent of the customers of both establishments were interchanged, moderately compatible if between 5 and 10 per cent interacted, slightly compatible if between 1 and 5 per cent of shoppers were shared and incompatible if very little customer interchange occurred. Another deleterious category was also devised, though no details on its calculation were supplied.

The third principal finding of the empirical-behavioural perspective pertains to the effects of entry and exit points on consumers' subsequent circulation patterns. As most intra-centre shopping trips commence and conclude at a car park, bus stop, railway terminus or, in certain cities, underground station, the precise location of these facilities has a major influence on the nuances of micro-spatial shopper movement, as indeed do alterations in the provision of transportation termini [Morris and Zisman, 1962]. This point is exemplified by the above mentioned longitudinal studies of shopper movement in central Newcastle-upon-Tyne [Bennison and Davies, 1980; Howard and Davies, 1986]. In the mid-1970s, the nature and geographical extent of consumers' within centre circulation behaviour was very closely related to the spatial arrangement of the three main bus stations. These activity patterns, however, were transformed by the opening of the Metro light rail system in 1982. The construction of the centrally located Monument station in particular ensured that shopper movements became increasingly confined to the core shopping area of Northumberland Street and Eldon Square. Although retailers in the primary shopping thoroughfares undoubtedly benefited from this change, the shopping streets on the peripheries of the city centre suffered severe downturns in trade as a consequence.

The final key finding of the studies of micro-scale consumer behaviour is the frictional effect of distance. Despite the fact that the distances involved are often comparatively short, shoppers appear determined, in line with Zipf's [1949] famous principle, to minimise the expenditure of effort [Johnston, 1973]. In the United States, for instance, the complaint is increasingly being heard that the new generation of mega-scale shopping developments – West Edmonton Mall, Mall of the Americas etc. – is proving just too large for comfort with shoppers being forced to walk what are deemed to be 'excessive' distances [Rogers, 1987; Turchiano, 1990]. Similar charges have recently been laid at the (widely separated) doors of European megacentres [Howard and Reynolds, 1991; McGoldrick and Thompson, 1992], though a friction of distance effect is apparent within even the smallest shopping milieux [Johnston and Kissling, 1971]. Indeed, numerous commentators have concluded that a maximum inter-outlet walking distance exists, with 200 metres being perhaps the most frequently cited spatial limit [Nelson, 1958; Gruen 1973; McKeever and Griffin, 1977].

Cognitive-behavioural

The wellspring of the cognitive-behavioural school of thought is unquestionably Kevin Lynch's [1960] seminal study of city centre images in the United States. By means of interviews, conducted tours and, most significantly for the body of research that was to follow, requiring respondents to draw freehand sketch maps of the locality in question, he managed to elicit the mental constructs of the downtown area held by citizens of Boston, Los Angeles and Jersey City. Although the details of the Lynchian 'mental mapping' methodology have been subject to considerable subsequent criticism [Pocock and Hudson, 1978], his investigations stimulated a spate of similar sketch map studies and the mental maps of many city centres have since been investigated. These include Washington DC [Zawawi, 1970], Chicago [Saarinen, 1977], Toronto [Jones and Simmons, 1987], Berlin [Sieverts, 1967], Amsterdam, Rotterdam and the Hague [de Jonge, 1962], Bristol [Smith, Shaw and Huckle, 1979] and, once again, Newcastle-upon-Tyne [Davies and Bennison, 1978]. Despite the inevitable variations from study to study, most analyses agree that retailing facilities figure prominently in mental representations of the city centre. Shop elements featured strongly in Lynch's [1960] pioneering investigation and over 90 per cent of the respondents to de Jonge's [1962] study of central Rotterdam mentioned the Lijnbann, the major shopping street. Similarly, Sieverts [1967] was able to distinguish between primary and secondary cognitive shopping streets in Berlin, whereas the undergraduate interviewees in Newcastle described some streets in terms of the particular retailing specialisms found therein, as did students in Toronto [Davies and Bennison, 1978; Jones and Simmons, 1987]. Most significantly perhaps, large stores and transportation termini have consistently emerged as important cognitive features in individual images of the city centre [Goodey, 1973; Matthews, 1980; Jansen, 1989].

Consumers' mental representations of retailing at the micro-scale thus appear to lend weight to the principal empirical-behavioural revelations, though the images themselves are far from Elucidean. As a rule, Lynchian style sketches tend towards normalisation, in that complex shapes are rearranged into patterns of straight lines and right angles, and simplification, through the omission of many minor details. The extent of normalisation and simplification, however, depends upon the 'legibility' of the locality; in other words, the simplicity/complexity of the city's spatial configuration and thus the degree to which it can be readily organised into a coherent cognitive pattern [see Marchand, 1974].

Important though mental mapping and similar exercises, such as 'cognitive distance', have proved [see Golledge and Timmermans, 1990], consumer cognitions are not confined to inventories of imperfect information about the micro-scale spatial arrangement of retailing facilities. They also comprise evaluations of, attitudes towards and emotional involvements with the shops and shopping centres that make up their retailing schemata. Indeed, as patronage decisions are determined, at least in part, by consumers' likes, dislikes, attitudes and so on, it is not surprising that such appraisive issues have been studied at length. The bulk of these analyses, however, refer to shopping centres as a whole or individual retail outlets (cf. the vast store image literature), though there are a limited number of micro-scale exceptions to the rule.

These include studies of consumer attitudes towards contrasting shopping streets and shopping centres within the same city centre [Allpass and Agergaard, 1979; Smith and Dolman, 1981], attitudes towards the same street before and after pedestrianisation and refurbishment programmes [Roberts, 1989], and attitudes towards different sub-areas *within* the same shopping street [Moles, 1979].

Just as contrasts in *consumers'* attitudes are apparent, so too *retailers* differ in their intra-centre assessments. An attitude survey of 1000 plus retail organisations in the centre of Belfast, for example, revealed that the micro-spatial cognitions of store managers were dominated; firstly, by the customer attracting ability of nearby magnet stores; secondly, the compatibility or incompatibility of adjacent shop types (outlets belonging to the same retail trade were especially favoured); thirdly, the importance of proximate transportation facilities (car parks, bus stops) and potential sources of custom (office blocks, schools); and, fourthly, by a cognitive distance decay effect, wherein 200 metres was the maximum perceived distance over which one retail outlet could generate spin-off trade for another [Brown, 1987b]. Broadly similar findings have been reported in surveys of retailer attitudes in Holland [Timmermans, 1986], Germany [Heinritz and Sittenauer, 1991] and Singapore [Wing and Lee, 1980].

Behavioural Generalisations

Despite the many and varied research procedures employed and retailing environments examined by students of micro-scale consumer behaviour and cognition, the above analyses nonetheless concur on the importance of magnet stores, the friction of distance effect, the positioning of points of ingress and egress and the customer interchange that occurs between complementary outlets. This has prompted several attempts to formulate meaningful models of micro-scale consumer behaviour. Perhaps the best known and certainly the most widely cited of these behavioural generalisations are the various locational 'rules' that R.L. Nelson [1958] derived from his extensive surveys of consumer shop-to-shop movement.

In an attempt to encapsulate the substantial volumes of shopper interchange between retail establishments selling related categories of merchandise (theatres and restaurants, outfitters and jewellers etc.), Nelson [1958, p.66] posited his 'rule of retail compatibility', which states that,

> two compatible businesses in close proximity will show an increase
> in business volume directly proportionate to the incidence of
> customer interchange between them, inversely proportional to the

ratio of business volume of the larger store to that of the smaller store and directly proportionate to the sum of the ratios of purposeful purchasing to total purchasing in each of the two stores.

Similarly, consumers' apparent desire to compare the offerings of several stores before purchase, especially for items where price, pattern, quality and fashion are important considerations, prompted the proposal of the 'theory of cumulative attraction'. This contends that, 'a given number of stores dealing in the same merchandise will do more business if they are located adjacent, or in proximity to each other than if they are widely scattered' [Nelson, 1958, p.58].

Although Nelson's generalisations have been subject to severe criticism [Applebaum and Kaylin, 1974; Okabe and Miki, 1984], the empirical record lends substantial weight to their veracity. As noted earlier, several studies have highlighted the extensive customer interchange that occurs between compatible and competitive retail outlets, and shown, moreover, that the volume of interchange is strongly influenced by the distance between the establishments concerned [Hawes and Lewison, 1984; Bromley and Thomas, 1989; McNeal and Madden, 1987].

These countervailing forces of compatibility (or attraction) and distance are encapsulated in a familiar and much-used macro-scale behavioural generalisation, the gravity model or spatial interaction theory [Haynes and Fotheringham, 1984; Fotheringham and O'Kelly, 1989]. One of the earliest micro-scale adaptations of the gravity model was Morris and Zisman's [1962] study of pedestrian movement in Washington DC. They argued that the volume of customers city centre retail establishments attracted from adjoining office blocks and other places of employment was directly proportional to the size of the retail outlets (and the office blocks) and inversely proportional to the square of the distances between them. A similar model, which also took the locations of transportation termini into account was employed by Ness, Morall and Hutchinson [1969] to estimate journey to work and lunchtime pedestrian movements in downtown Toronto. Other applications include the entropy maximising procedure advanced by Scott [1974], Butler's [1978] less than totally successful attempt to adapt this framework to the movement of shoppers in central Liverpool and Rutherford's [1979] comprehensive analysis of the spatial behaviour of 11,632 individuals in downtown Chicago, which produced a 'reasonable replication of observed trip patterns' (p.57). More recently, Hagishima, Mitsuyoshi and Kurose [1987] have used spatial interaction theory successfully to simulate the micro-scale movements of shoppers in Fukouka City, Japan, though they found that the model, as Rutherford discovered in Chicago, underestimated pedestrian flows in several main streets due to the large traffic volumes generated by transport termini therein.

Apart from spatial interaction theory, other attempts have been made to develop models of micro-scale consumer movement [see May, Turvey and Hopkinson, 1985]. These include the O-D (origin-destination) procedures beloved by traffic planners [Barrett, 1972; Thornton, McCullagh and Bradshaw, 1992], analyses of the relationship between land uses and pedestrian flows [Behnam and Patel, 1977; Sandrock, 1988] and, most notably, the trip chaining models of Borgers and Timmermans [1986a,b]. The last of these comprised a Monte Carlo simulation of the destination choice, route choice and stopping behaviour of 345 shoppers in the centre of Maastricht, Holland. Although the model provided a 'satisfactory' correspondence between predicted and observed pedestrian movement, more recent research suggests that the decision heuristics employed by shoppers are strongly influenced by the complexity of the extant retailing environment and the idiosyncrasies of the individual location [van der Hagen, Borgers and Timmermans, 1991].

SUPPLY SIDE STUDIES

While it is true, as Craig, Ghosh and McLafferty [1984:12] point out, that 'the aggregate choices of consumers shape the overall pattern of retail activity', it is equally undeniable that the patronage decisions of consumers are themselves shaped by the locational choices of retail organisations and analogous supply side decision takers. Thus the distinctive agglomerations of (say) cattle dealers within the marketplaces of the developing world or estate agents and building societies in British city centres may well be a manifestation of consumers' desire to compare the offerings of several competing establishments before purchase. In reality, however, the placement of the stallholders or purveyors of property services is often an outcome of the locational policies adopted by the marketplace administrators and local town planners respectively. These retail establishments, in other words, are not free to choose their locations but are allocated sites according to the preferred spatial arrangement of the appropriate legislative authority. True, the legislators may have devised their optimal layout on the basis of theoretical principles or in an attempt to simplify the consumer's task. Nevertheless, the fact remains that the spatial pattern of cattle dealers or property service outlets is primarily a manifestation of the supply side of the locational equation.

Of all the manifold supply side influences upon retail location perhaps the most important, and certainly the most thoroughly investigated, are; firstly, the policies of shopping centre developers; secondly, the spatial strategies of multiple retail organisations; and, thirdly, the controls of central and local government and equivalent administrators. Although a substantive literature exists in each of these areas, detailed micro-scale considerations remain, as ever, *comparatively* few in number.

Shopping Centre Development

From a micro-scale standpoint, perhaps the most important aspect of the planned shopping centre is the fact that – as the 'planned' epithet implies – it is a totally controlled environment in which everything is pre-ordained by the developer and designer, and manipulated to maximise customer expenditure and ultimately the returns of the owners and investors. Contrary to the assumptions of land value theory and so on, a free market in property does not obtain. The 'highest and best use' of any given location within a centre is determined by some combination of developer, property consultant and letting agent, *not* by the workings of the bid rent mechanism. Similarly, the intra-centre circulation of shoppers is an effect not a cause of the micro-spatial placement of the centre's occupants. In fact, it has often been asserted that the shopping centre ideal is a controlled flow of pedestrians past as many of the outlets as possible [Martin, 1982; Northen, 1984; Abratt, Fourie and Pitt, 1985].

In the quest for the shopping centre grail of controlled pedestrian flow, a host of 'principles' of tenant placement have been posited. These comprise such well-known rules of thumb as: place the magnet stores at opposite ends of the mall and line the intervening space with smaller outlets; ensure that the main entrances and anchor stores are sufficiently far apart to pull shoppers past the unit shops; avoid culs de sac if at all possible, as they inhibit the free flow of shoppers; place service outlets on the side malls close to the entrances and exits; keep pet shops and dry cleaners away from food shops, and food shops separate from outfitters; and, achieve an even distribution of shoppers in multi-level centres through the judicious arrangement of escalators and eating facilities and by manipulating the tier at which consumers enter the complex [Dawson, 1983; Casazza and Spink, 1985; Maitland, 1990].

Useful though these rules of tenant placement have proved, they are the outcome of a long and expensive trial and error process [Beddington, 1982]. As such, they are subject to fashion effects and have given rise to sterile and specious debate. A consensus, for example, has long been lacking over the efficacy of placing similar types of outlet, such as fashion or food retailers, or stores of comparable quality levels, in close spatial proximity within the centre. Shopping centre developers in the United States have been variously advised to separate similar shop types in order to maximise consumer movement within the centre, thereby increasing their exposure to its attractions [Rouse Company, 1969; Stambaugh, 1978; McKeever and Griffin, 1977], and to cluster compatible shop types in order to ease the shopper's task and to enable certain areas of the centre to become magnets in their own right [Smith, 1956; Berman, 1970; Gruen, 1973]. A zonal compromise between the two extremes has also been suggested and this appears to be the preferred approach at present, at least in the larger regional, super-regional and mega-regional schemes [Jackson and Johnson, 1991].

Although it is easy to condemn the shopping centre industry for its continuing reliance upon the received wisdom of tenant placement, it must be appreciated that the placement process, constrained as it is by the financial plan and overall design, is a highly complex undertaking [Gosling and Maitland, 1976]. Equally importantly perhaps, the comparatively few published studies that there are lend weight to the saws of tenant placement [see Anderson, 1985; Sim and Way, 1989; Brown, 1992]. Guthrie [1980a,b], for example, conducted a multiple regression analysis of the sales figures of 848 stores in ten US regional centres and concluded that certain locations within the malls performed substantially better than others. Central courtyards and corner sites proved to be the best overall locations in the selected shopping complexes, though mid-mall and ground floor situations also produced above average sales performances. Somewhat surprisingly, locations adjacent to anchor stores tended to underperform, as, rather less surprisingly, did sites in the side malls. Of all the micro-scale options, however, culs de sac were by far the worst performers. Stores in these dead ends averaged as little as 53 per cent of the sales figures of equivalent establishments in superior spatial settings. Besides his analysis of broad sub-areas within regional shopping centres, Guthrie explored the extent to which similar types of retail store benefited from geographical juxtaposition. He found: firstly, that clusters of ladieswear outlets have substantial synergistic effects: secondly, that menswear outlets gain considerably from close geographical proximity; and, thirdly, that retailers of menswear and ladieswear mix well. Agglomeration, in short, pays dividends.

Retailers' Spatial Strategies

Just as the planned shopping centre has attracted considerable academic attention, so too an extensive empirical literature exists on the spatial strategies of individual retail firms and the diffusion of innovative retailing institutions [Allaway, Mason and Black, 1991]. These include analyses of regional and off-price shopping centres in the USA [Cohen, 1972; Lord, 1985], hypermarkets in Europe [Dawson, 1984] and retail organisations as diverse as McDonalds [Aspbury, 1984], Macys [Laulajainen, 1987], Marshall Field [Laulajainen, 1990] and Marks and Spencer [Bird and Witherwick, 1986].

Useful though such studies have proved, however, they have tended to overlook the competitive aspect of retailers' spatial strategies. With the possible exceptions of market leaders, such as Toys R Us or IKEA, and the unreal multiple retailers of most neoclassical models [Teitz, 1968; Ghosh and Buchanan, 1988], very few organisations can afford to ignore their competitors when taking locational decisions. Indeed, several competitor orientated spatial strategies can be identified, most notably 'avoidance', 'matching' and 'predation'. The avoidance approach, which, as the name implies, simply involves keeping away from the competition, is exemplified by the growth of variety stores in the central belt of Sweden [Laulajainen and Gadde, 1986], branch banks in Charlotte, North Carolina [Lord and Wright, 1981] and the development of the Kwik Save discount grocery chain in Great Britain [Sparks, 1990]. A matching or competitor-seeking stance, by contrast, has been pursued by co-operative retailing organisations in Finland [Laulajainen, 1981], fast food restaurants in Atlanta [Pillsbury, 1987] and Filene's speciality department store chain in Boston [Cohen and Lewis, 1967]. Safeway, meanwhile, was once renowned for its predation approach which comprised buying up all the available sites in a market, thereby pre-empting its competitors, or by locating in very close proximity to established supermarkets and precipitating a price war, thus driving out the rival [West and von Hohenbalken, 1984]. A similar strategy of 'keeping out the competition' has been deduced from longitudinal studies of the spatial patterns of convenience stores and petrol stations in Denver and Hong Kong [Lee and Koutsopoulos, 1976; Lee and Schmidt, 1980].

As with so much of the locational literature, most of the above investigations of retailers' spatial strategies have been conducted at the meso- and macro-scales of analysis. Yet micro-scale considerations are vitally important and are clearly taken into account by retail organisations. It is not unusual, after all, to find several branches of the same chain or conglomerate retailing organisation in the same shopping district or centre. There are two branches of Marks and Spencer, six branches of Benetton, three branches of Burger King and eighteen outlets belonging to the Burton Group alone in Oxford Street, London, for example, and the West Edmonton Mall is similarly endowed [Johnson, 1991]. Micro-scale locational decisions, moreover, are often taken with regard to competitive or complementary establishments. In Britain, 'as close as possible to Marks and Spencer' remains a widely espoused spatial strategy [Peters, 1990] and a 'parasitic' approach, where firms locate themselves in very close proximity to outlets in entirely different sectors of the retail industry (supermarkets adjacent to drug stores, for instance), has been reported on numerous occasions [Cohen and Lewis, 1967; Berman and Evans, 1991]. For example, the chairman of T & S Stores, a chain of some 600 discount convenience stores, has recently stated that he prefers to site his outlets 'next to shops which have a high customer flow such as bakers or greengrocers, rather than banks or building societies' [Thornhill, 1992, p.14]. Beavon [1970], Brown [1987b] and Brous [1981] have also described how the micro-locational decisions of retail organisations in South Africa, Great Britain and the United States respectively are made with reference to propinquitous outlets, especially major magnet stores. Yet anecdotal evidence aside this issue has been all but neglected by students of spatial strategy hitherto and must be considered a major priority for future research.

Government and Administrative Influences

Important though the foregoing supply side factors have proved, the location of retailing activities is not simply a reflection of the tenant placement policies of shopping centre developers, nor an artefact of the spatial machinations of multiple retailers intent on optimising branch networks whilst confounding their competitors. It is also attributable to the locational policies or the locational outcomes of the policies of central and local governments and other legislative authorities, such as the administrators of marketplaces in the developed, developing and indeed ancient worlds.

As discussed in detail by several commentators [Boddewyn and Hollander, 1972; Dholakia and Dholakia, 1978], the retail industry is subject to a plethora of direct and indirect policy controls, some of which have micro-scale locational implications. In the United Kingdom, for instance, these include the Betting, Gaming and Lotteries Act of 1963 and the Town and Country Planning Use Classes Orders of 1972 and 1988. The former controls the number, appearance and location of betting shops, which are prohibited in close proximity to churches, schools or premises patronised by persons of 'known bad character'. The latter serve to permit or prohibit proposed changes of land use, such as from 'shop' to 'office' or, more specifically, from certain types of retail outlet to others (e.g. bookseller to bank, or grocer to hot food facility). The upshot of these micro-scale interventions, according to Davies and Bennison [1978], is that the internal spatial organisation of British shopping districts is more a manifestation of retail planning policies than the market forces the plans were designed to accommodate.

In the United States, furthermore, the territorial exclusivity clauses of franchise agreements are subject to state and federal law [Stern and El-Ansary, 1988], zoning ordinances are ubiquitous, albeit circumventable [Kane and Belkin, 1981] and, to cite arguably the best known example, the tenant mix planning procedures of shopping centre developers have attracted detailed government scrutiny. In the early years of the shopping centre industry the emerging concept of a controlled tenant mix was accompanied by the addition of a variety of 'restrictions and exclusives' clauses to centre leases. Introduced at the insistence of the all-powerful anchor stores, these 'inducement' clauses allowed the magnets effectively to determine the merchandise range, pricing policy, space allocation and precise location within the complex of the centre's other occupants [ICSC, 1974; Cutler and Reilly, 1976]. Equally commonplace were covenants concerning store opening hours, permitted advertising and promotional activities, membership of the merchant's association and the prohibition of other branches of the same organisation within a specified radius of the centre [see Cooper, 1975; Mason, 1975; Mallen and Savitt, 1979]. Such restraints of trade attracted the attention of the FTC which issued, after a landmark investigation of leasing practices at Tyson's Corner regional shopping centre, a series of consent decrees relating to proscribed activities [Savitt, 1985].

Although the spatial organisation of British shopping districts and American shopping centres cannot be understood without an appreciation of the regulatory context, the degree of administrative control in the western world pales by comparison with that exercised in the fixed and periodic markets of the developing and ancient worlds. Whether it be the *souks* of Kuwait City [Al-Otaibi, 1990], the *tamus* of Sabah [Burrough, 1978], the *tianguis* of Mexico City [Pyle, 1978], the *raun* of New Guinea [Ward *et al.*, 1978], the *zoma* of Madagasgar [Donque, 1966] or the *nien-shih* of T'ang dynasty China [Braudel, 1982], the internal spatial organisation of these urban, rural, formal and informal marketplaces leaves very little to chance and is often minutely controlled [Moore, 1985]. Once again, however, the predominant micro-scale organising principle is the clustering of sellers of similar wares and the separation of purveyors of incompatible merchandise. It has been observed in the markets of Manila [McIntyre, 1955], Madras [Lessinger, 1985], Mali [Harts-Broekhuis and Verkoren, 1987] and pre-conquest Mexico [Berdan, 1985], the medinas of Morocco, Algeria and Tunisia [Troin, 1990; Thompson, 1982; Miossec, 1990], the forums of ancient Rome [Allix, 1922], the fairs and marketplaces of medieval Europe [Alexander, 1970; Moore, 1985] and many more besides.

CURRENT STATUS AND FUTURE PROSPECTS

This article has endeavoured to demonstrate that, although minute by meso- and macro-scale standards, the literature on micro-scale retail location is far from negligible. It is, admittedly, scattered throughout a diverse mix of academic specialisms such as marketing, geography, economics, psychology, operations research, urban planning, architecture, estate management and regional science. The material, moreover, is characterised by definitional and methodological disputation, whether it be the most appropriate procedures for delimiting shopping districts, the comparative advantages of nearest neighbour analysis or quadrat analysis in the statistical assessment of shop patterns, the existence or otherwise of mental maps, the bogus calibration and spatial non-stationarity problems of the gravity model, or, simply, disentangling the relationship between the spatial patterns of retail activity and the processes of supply and demand which appear to give rise to them.

TABLE 1
RETAIL LOCATION AT THE MICRO-SCALE: APPROACHES AND INSIGHTS

	Centripetal	Centrifugal	Combination
Theory	principle of minimum differentiation	bid rent theory	complex model
Pattern	cluster	dispersed	linear
Demand	comparison	multi-purpose	convenience
Supply	match	mix	intercept

Yet despite the above methodological differences and marked variations in approach – be it theoretical and associated shop pattern analysis, demand side led or supply side orientated – the micro-scale literature exhibits a surprisingly high degree of commonality. Summarised in Table 1, retail location at the micro-scale is characterised by centripetal and centrifugal tendencies, and the interaction or combination of these two opposing forces. Centripetal tendencies are inherent in the theoretical underpinnings provided by the principle of minimum differentiation, the empirically observable and all but universal clusters of specialised retail activities (bookshops, electrical goods suppliers, kola nut dealers etc.), consumers' demonstrable desire to compare the wares of several competing outlets before purchase and the policy of 'matching', clustering or locating adjacent to outlets of a similar trade type/quality level widely espoused by shopping centre developers, town planners and retail organisations respectively. Centrifugal tendencies, on the other hand, are implicit in bid rent theory (in

that competition for the prime central locations pushes lower order retailing functions progressively to the peripheries of unplanned shopping
districts), the mixed pattern of shop types that characterises most non-
specialist shopping districts and centres, consumers' everpresent preference for variety, a choice of *different* shop types within easy reach,
and, not least, the belief long held by many retailers, developers and
planners that direct competition is best avoided or kept at arms' length
and that a balanced and carefully managed 'mix' of compatible shop
types is always preferable to the uncertain (and invariably agglomerated) outcome of the free play of market forces.

Centripetal and centrifugal forces, of course, do not act in isolation
and, as exemplified by Davies' 'complex' model of city centre retailing,
attempts have been made to strike a meaningful balance between the
two. Thus the linear component of the complex model can be viewed as
the spatial manifestation of the countervailing tendencies towards
agglomeration and dispersal, insofar as it combines the clustering of retail outlets on an edge-of-town-centre arterial and their spatial extension
alongside it. Similarly, shoppers' overarching desire for convenience
and effort minimisation underpins *both* their comparison shopping activities (e.g. several shoe shops in close spatial proximity) and their
multi-purpose trips for different items (indeed, the wide range but
limited assortment offered by hypermarkets and department stores
represents the same principle under a single roof). Likewise, it is arguable that the supply side equivalent of this phenomenon is the parasitic or
interceptor location, where a retail outlet is interposed (as a consequence of the organisation's spatial strategy or the activities of a
surrogate supply side decision taker) between the consumers' point of
entry into the shopping environment and their primary or ultimate destination, usually the magnet store.

Given the high degree of commonality in the literature, irrespective
of the diverse approaches adopted by individual researchers, it is tempt-
ing to conclude that micro-scale retail location is characterised, above
all, by the agglomeration of similar shop types and the dispersal of these
clusters throughout the said shopping district. Indeed, as a basic organising principle, this appears to have much to commend it. The reality of
micro-scale retail location, however, is rather less straightforward, in
that – theoretical assumptions notwithstanding – all retailing outlets are
not created equal. Even though they may belong to the same trade
'type', retail establishments differ enormously in terms of size, reputation, range of goods, pricing policy, service quality, promotional
activity, customer pulling power and so on. In fact, much of the attraction of a specialist retailing cluster derives from these non-locational

differences between the various neighbouring outlets. After all, if every establishment offered precisely the same goods, at exactly the same prices and so on, there would be nothing to choose between them and no reason to compare their wares. Indeed, shop pattern studies have shown that when outlets of the same type are comparatively undifferentiated – e.g. CTNs – there is a tendency towards spatial dispersal.

In other words, the legitimacy of the entire body of micro-scale locational literature rests ultimately on the veracity of 'trade type' taxonomies. Although long established and still in widespread use, such classifications invariably fail to withstand close scrutiny. Apart from the advent of 'scrambled merchandising', which has prompted many commentators to question the continuing relevance of trade type distinctions *per se* [Dawson, 1982; Dawson and Sparks, 1986; O' Brien and Harris, 1991], the number of categories in the classification and the subtlety, or otherwise, of their gradation can prove equally problematical. The frequently noted clustering of 'food' outlets, for example, disguises the fact that individual butchers or greengrocers tend to avoid locations adjacent to direct competitors, but are often situated in close proximity to compatible 'food' purveyors like bakeries, grocers and so on. The characteristics of the classification, in short, influence the outcome of the empirical analysis, whether it be the study of shop patterns, consumers' store-to-store movements or the placement policies of town planners and shopping centre developers.

Thus, although Table 1 represents an attempt to transcend trade type considerations by summarising the theoretical (and associated pattern analysis), demand side and supply side approaches, it must also be appreciated that the realities of micro-scale location are by no means as clearly delineated as the table suggests. Centrifugal and centripetal tendencies not only overlap, as noted above, but the relationship between the various components is multifaceted and reflexive. It is, for example, an oversimplification to assume that the spatial pattern of retailing is an *outcome* of the forces of demand and supply. The reality, of course, is that the patronisation and locational decisions of consumers and retailers (or their supply side surrogates such as urban planners, shopping centre developers and marketplace administrators) are influenced if not determined by extant patterns of retail activity. Likewise, land use planners and so on plan on the basis of existing conceptualisations such as the core-frame model or, at a different scale, central place theory, and which determine in turn the spatial patterns of retailing activity. In other words, the processes of supply and demand, the geography of retailing and theoretical insights are intimately intertwined. The study of micro-scale retail location is thus entangled in what Giddens [1990] terms the 'double hermeneutic', where the very existence of a concept (or classification) influences and alters the phenomena to which it pertains.

Just as the relationships between demand, supply and the spatial arrangement of retail outlets are not definitive, neither is our understanding of retail location at the micro-scale. Despite the enormous literature that already exists on the subject of retail location generally and, to a much lesser extent, the specifics of the micro-scale, there remains ample scope for additional research activity within each of the theoretical (and associated pattern analysis), demand side and supply side traditions. With regard to the first of these, recent years have witnessed enormous strides in the study of bid rent theory and the principle of minimum differentiation. Multi-stop and multi-purpose shopping behaviours, dynamic dimensions, uncertainty reduction and a host of other more realistic assumptions have been successfully incorporated within the models. Set against these normative insights, however, latter-day shop pattern analyses have been less than impressive. The bulk of the empirical 'tests' of the bid rent, PMD and 'complex' models are 20 to 30 years old (e.g. Berry's [1963] classic Chicago study and Davies' [1972a] landmark analysis of Coventry). Given the enormous changes in the spatial structure of retailing since then, it may be worthwhile attempting to address, once again, the most basic of questions: is the bid rent model still applicable to the spatial organisation of urban retailing and the micro-geography shopping districts? Do stores of the same retail trade and of similar quality levels still cluster together within planned and unplanned shopping centres? Is the complex model still applicable to the internal spatial organisation of central shopping districts or have latter-day planning interventions rendered it all but redundant?

In a similar vein, the empirical, cognitive and conceptual variants of the demand side perspective have much to offer today's micro-scale research workers. The empirical-behavioural approach, for instance, remains beset by a basic methodological problem concerning the lack of correspondence between consumers' observed and reported behaviour [Shepherd and Thomas, 1980]. Researchers have traditionally utilised the latter technique, which is substantially cheaper if less reliable than the former, though asking retail managers to provide insights into micro-scale shopper movement may provide a cost-effective alternative [Heinritz and Sittenauer, 1991]. On the cognitive side, moreover, mental mapping exercises relevant to retailing have hitherto been confined to central business districts or, on occasion, the internal layout of individual retail outlets [Sommer and Aitkens, 1982]. Consumers' cognitions of planned suburban shopping environments have yet to be fully explored, as indeed have retailers' [though see Foxall and Hackett,

1992]. Likewise, despite widespread agreement on the principal characteristics of micro-scale shopper behaviour, attempts to model the
movements of shoppers within centres remain few and far between.
There are, admittedly, a number of important exceptions to this over-
sight, but as Baron [1991, p.3] has recently and tantalisingly pointed out
'if you can find a workable model of pedestrian flows in shopping
centres, you can make a fortune'.

   Last but not least, the supply side of the intra-centre locational equation is in particular need of further investigation. As discussed above,
micro-scale factors manifestly impinge upon the spatial strategies of retail organisations, yet this issue has hardly featured in the locational
literature. The rules of thumb employed in the internal spatial organisation of planned shopping centres are also comparatively
under-researched, as are the specific micro-scale effects of legislative
change. A final component of the locational canon that has been sorely
neglected by retailing researchers is the unique character of the micro-
site (i.e. the individual site as opposed to the location's situation relative
to the whole shopping centre or district). The significance of site specific
factors like street layout, alignment, aspect, slope, pavement width,
prevailing wind, foot frontage, visibility, proximity to car parking, pedestrian crossings, street corners and so on were recognised and discussed
at length over 60 years ago [Pyle, 1926; Parkins, 1930]. Yet the bulk of
the subsequent micro-scale literature has overlooked these essentially
idiographic elements in the search for meaningful generalisations.
Generalisations, moreover, that in many cases comprise uncritical adaptations of concepts developed at the macro- and meso-locational scales
(bid rent theory, spatial interaction theory etc.). It is arguable, therefore, that until such times as students of micro-scale location come up
with meaningful concepts of their own, the subject will continue to lan-
guish as an 'interesting but ignored' component of the retailing mix.

CONCLUSION

It has often been said that a few yards can make all the difference between success and failure in retailing. This article has reviewed the
literature on retail location at the micro-scale, arguing that theoretical,
demand side and supply side approaches can be discerned. The theoretical approach comprises two long-established, normative conceptualisations, bid rent theory and the principle of minimum
differentiation, various inductively derived attempts to integrate the two
into a plausible combination theory and a body of associated empirical
research which is broadly supportive of the hypothesised spatial patterns

of retail activity. Demand side studies range from the analysis of consumer movements within planned and unplanned shopping centres and mental mapping exercises, to micro-scale adaptations of the gravity model and analyses of the much-lauded locational dicta of R.L. Nelson. Supply side perspectives include the tenant placement policies practised by owners and developers of planned shopping centres, the micro-scale locational strategies of conglomerate retailing organisations and, not least, the (often imperceptible) influence of government legislation and analogous administrators.

Albeit small in meso- or macro-scale terms, the subject of micro-scale location has generated a surprisingly sizeable literature, though it is scattered across a number of academic specialisms from economics to architecture. There is, none the less, ample scope for additional research activity within each of the theoretical, demand side and supply side schools of thought. If, however, the study of micro-scale location is to develop beyond its current status of 'interesting but ignored', a meaningful reformulation of long-established but increasingly outmoded trade type taxonomies is urgently required, as are attempts to develop models and theories that are micro-scale specific rather than straightforward applications of macro-scale concepts. Further research, as they say, is clearly necessary.

REFERENCES

Abratt, R., J. L. C. Fourie and L. F. Pitt, 1985, 'Tenant Mix: The Key to a Successful Shopping Centre', *Quarterly Review of Marketing*, Vol.10, No.3.

Alexander, D., 1970, *Retailing in England During the Industrial Revolution*, London: Athlone Press.

Alexander, I. C., 1974, *The City Centre: Patterns and Problems*, Nedlands: University of Western Australia Press.

Allaway, A. W., J. B. Mason and W. C. Black, 1991, 'The Dynamics of Spatial and Temporal Diffusion in a Retail Setting', in A. Ghosh and C. A. Ingene (eds.), *Spatial Analysis in Marketing: Theory, Methods and Applications*, Greenwich: JAI Press.

Allix, A., 1922, 'The Geography of Fairs: Illustrated by Old-World Examples', *Geographical Review*, Vol.12.

Allpass, J., and E. Agergaard, 1979, 'The City Centre – For Whom?', in I. Hammarstrom and T. Hall (eds.), *Growth and Transformation of the Modern City*, Stockholm: Swedish Council for Building Research.

Al-Otaibi, O., 1990, 'The Development of Planned Shopping Centres in Kuwait', in A. M. Findlay, R. Paddison and J. A. Dawson (eds.), *Retailing Environments in Developing Countries*, London: Routledge.

Anderson, C. H., T. H. Parker and S. R. Stanley, 1990, '1990 Site Selection Study: Summary of Results', paper presented at Applied Geography Conference, Charlotte, October.

Anderson, P. M., 1985, 'Association of Shopping Centre Anchors with Performance of a Non-anchor Speciality Chain's Stores', *Journal of Retailing*, Vol.61, No.2.

Applebaum, W., and S. O. Kaylin, 1974, *Case Studies in Shopping Centre Development and Operation*, New York: International Council of Shopping Centres.

Aspbury, G. F., 1984, 'The Geography of Franchise Expansion: An Illinois Example', *Bulletin of the Illinois Geographical Society*, Vol.26, No.2.

Balchin, P. N., J. L. Kieve and G. H. Bull, 1988, *Urban Land Economics and Public Policy*, Basingstoke: Macmillan.

Ball, M., 1979, 'A Critique of Urban Economics', *International Journal of Urban and Regional Research*, Vol.3, No.3.

Ball, M., 1985, 'The Urban Rent Question', *Environment and Planning A*, Vol.17, No.4.

Baron, S., 1991, 'No Accounting for Shoppers?', *O R Insight*, Vol.4, No.1.

Barrett, R., 1972, 'Moving Pedestrians in a Traffic-Free Environment', *Traffic Engineering and Control*, Vol.14.

Beaujeu-Garnier, J., and A. Delobez, 1979, *Geography of Marketing*, London: Longman, translated by S. H. Beaver.

Beaumont, J. R., 1988, 'Store Location Analysis: Problems and Progress', in N. Wrigley (ed.), *Store Choice, Store Location and Market Analysis*, London: Routledge.

Beavon, K. S. O., 1970, *Land Use Patterns in Port Elizabeth: A Geographical Analysis in the Environs of Main Street*, Cape Town: Balkema.

Beddington, N., 1982, *Design for Shopping Centres*, London: Butterworth Scientific.

Behnam, J. and B. G. Patel, 1977, 'A Method for Estimating Pedestrian Volume in a Central Business District', *Transportation Research Record*, Vol.629.

Bellett, J., 1969, 'Singapore's Central Area Retail Pattern in Transition', *Journal of Tropical Geography*, Vol.28, No.1.

Bennison, D. J. and R. L. Davies, 1977, *The Movement of Shoppers Within the Central Area of Newcastle-upon-Tyne*, Department of Geography, Seminar Papers No.34, Newcastle: University of Newcastle-upon-Tyne.

Bennison, D. J. and R. L. Davies, 1980, 'The Impact of Town Centre Shopping Schemes in Britain', *Progress in Planning*, Vol.14.

Berdan, F., 1985, 'Markets in the economy of Aztec Mexico', in S. Plattner (ed.), *Markets and Marketing*, New York: University Press of America.

Berman, B., 1970, 'Location Analysis within Regional Shopping Centres', in D. J. Rachman (ed.), *Retail Management Strategy: Selected Readings*, Englewood Cliffs: Prentice Hall.

Berman, B. and J. R. Evans, 1991, *Retail Management: A Strategic Approach*, New York: Macmillan, fifth edition.

Berry, B. J. L., 1963, *Commercial Structure and Commercial Blight: Retail Patterns and Processes in the City of Chicago*, Department of Geography, Research Paper No.85, Chicago: University of Chicago.

Bird, J. and M. E. Witherwick, 1986, 'Marks and Spencer: The Geography of an Image', *Geography*, Vol.71, No.4.

Boal, F. W. and D. B. Johnson, 1968, 'Nondescript Streets', *Traffic Quarterly*, Vol.22.

Boddewyn, J. J. and S. C. Hollander, 1972, *Public Policy Toward Retailing: An International Symposium*, Lexington: D. C. Heath.

Borgers, A. and H. J. P. Timmermans, 1986a, 'City Centre Entry Points, Store Location Patterns and Pedestrian Route Choice Behaviour: A Microlevel Simulation Model', *Socio Economic Planning Science*, Vol.20, No.1.

Borgers, A. and H. J. P. Timmermans, 1986b, 'A Model of Pedestrian Route Choice and Demand for Retail Facilities within Inner-city Shopping Areas', *Geographical Analysis*, Vol.18.

Brady, J. E. M., 1977, 'The Pattern of Retailing in Central Dublin', unpublished MA thesis, Dublin: University College Dublin.

Braudel, F., 1982, *The Wheels of Commerce*, London: Collins, trans. S. Reynolds.

Breheny, M. J., 1988, 'Practical Methods of Retail Location Analysis: A Review', in N. Wrigley (ed.), *Store Choice, Store Location and Market Analysis*, London: Routledge.

Brisco, N.A., 1927, *Principles of Retailing*, New York: Prentice-Hall.

Bromley, R. D. F. and C. J. Thomas, 1989, 'The Impact of Shop Type and Spatial Structure on Shopping Linkages in Retail Parks', *Town Planning Review*, Vol.60, No.1.

Brous, P., 1981, 'The Chain Store Looks at the Future', in G. Sternlieb and J. W. Hughes (eds.), *Shopping Centres USA*, Centre for Urban Policy Research, New Jersey: Rutgers.

Brown, S., 1987a, 'The Complex Model of City Centre Retailing: An Historical Interpretation', *Transactions, Institute of British Geographers*, Vol.12, No.1.

Brown, S., 1987b, 'Retailers and Micro-Retail Location: A Perceptual Perspective', *International Journal of Retailing*, Vol.2, No.3.

Brown, S., 1988, 'Information Seeking, External Search and "Shopping" Behaviour: Preliminary Evidence from a Planned Shopping Centre', *Journal of Marketing Management*, Vol.4, No.1.

Brown, S., 1989, 'Retail Location Theory: The Legacy of Harold Hotelling', *Journal of Retailing*, Vol.65, No.4.

Brown, S., 1992, 'Tenant Mix, Tenant Placement and Shopper Behaviour in a Planned Shopping Centre', *Service Industries Journal*, Vol.12, No.3.

Buckwalter, D. W., 1989, 'Effects of Competition on the Patterns of Retail Districts in the Chattanooga, Tennessee, Metropolitan Area', *Southeastern Geographer*, Vol.29, No.1.

Burrough, J. B., 1978, 'The Tamus of Sabah', in R. H. T. Smith (ed.), *Market Place Trade – Periodic Markets, Hawkers and Traders in Africa, Asia and Latin America*, Centre for Transportation Studies, Vancouver: University of British Columbia.

Butler, S., 1978, *Modelling Pedestrian Movements in Central Liverpool*, Working Paper 98, Institute for Transport Studies, Leeds: University of Leeds.

Campbell, N., 1970, 'An Application of the Core-Frame Concept to the CBD, London, Ontario, in Three Dimensions', *Ontario Geography*, Vol.5.

Carter, H., 1983, *An Introduction to Urban Historical Geography*, London: Edward Arnold.

Casazza, J. A. and F. H. Spink, 1985, *Shopping Centre Development Handbook*, Washington DC: Urban Land Institute, second edition.

Chamberlin, E. H., 1933, *The Theory of Monopolistic Competition: A Re-orientation of the Theory of Value*, Cambridge: Harvard University Press, eighth edition.

Chudzynska, I., 1981, 'Locational Specialisation of Retail Trade Functions in Warszawa', *Environment and Planning A*, Vol.13, No.8.

Churchman, A. and Tzamir, Y., 1981, 'Traffic Segregation and Pedestrian Behaviour in a Shopping Centre', *Man-Environment Systems*, Vol.11.

Cohen, S. B. and G. K. Lewis, 1967, 'Form and Function in the Geography of Retailing', *Economic Geography*, Vol.43, No.1.

Cohen, Y. S., 1972, *Diffusion of an Innovation in an Urban System: The Spread of Planned Regional Shopping Centres in the United States, 1949–1968*, Department of Geography, Research Paper 140, Chicago: University of Chicago.

Cooper, M. B., 1975, 'Shopping Centre Lease Agreements: Participants and Perceptions of Selected Operating Policies', in H. W. Nash and D. P. Rodin (eds.), *Proceedings: Southern Marketing Association 1975 Conference*, Mississippi: Mississippi State University.

Craig, C. S., A. Ghosh and S. McLafferty, 1984, 'Models of the Retail Location Process: A Review', *Journal of Retailing*, Vol.60, No.1.

Curry, D. J., 1993, *The New Marketing Research Systems*, New York: Wiley.

Cutler, E. R. and J. R. Reilly, 1976, *The Anti-trust Aspects of Restrictive Covenants in Shopping Centre Leases*, New York: International Council of Shopping Centres.

Davies, D. H., 1965, *Land Use in Central Cape Town: A Study in Urban Geography*, Cape Town: Longmans.

Davies, G. J. and K. Harris, 1990, *Small Business: The Independent Retailer*, Basingstoke: Macmillan.

Davies, R. L., 1972a, 'The Retail Pattern of the Central Area of Coventry', in *The Retail Structure of Cities*, Occasional Publication No.1, London: Institute of British Geographers.

Davies, R. L., 1972b, 'Structural Models of Retail Distribution: Analogies with Settlement and Land Use Theories', *Transactions, Institute of British Geographers*, Vol.57, No.1.

Davies, R. L., 1976, *Marketing Geography: With Special Reference to Retailing*, Corbridge: Retail and Planning Associates.

Davies, R. L., 1984, *Retail and Commercial Planning*, London: Croom Helm.

Davies, R. L., and D. J. Bennison, 1978, 'Retailing in the City Centre: The Characters of Shopping Streets', *Tijdschrift voor Economische en Sociale Geografie*, Vol.69, No.5.

Davis, D., 1966, *A History of Shopping*, London: Routledge and Kegan Paul.

Dawson, J. A., 1980, 'Introduction', in J. A. Dawson (ed.), *Retail Geography*, London: Croom Helm.

Dawson, J. A., 1982, *Commercial Distribution in Europe*, London: Croom Helm.

Dawson, J. A., 1983, *Shopping Centre Development*, London: Longman.

Dawson, J. A., 1984, 'Structural-Spatial Relationships in the Spread of Hypermarket Retailing', in E. Kaynak and R. Savitt (eds.), *Comparative Marketing Systems*, New York: Praeger.

Dawson, J. A. and L. Sparks, 1986, 'Issues for the Planning of Retailing in Scotland', *Scottish Planning Law and Practice*, Vol.18.

De Blij, H. J., 1962, 'The Functional Structure and Central Business Direct of Laurenço, Marques, Mocambique', *Economic Geography*, Vol.38, No.1.

De Jonge, D., 1962, 'Images of Urban Areas, their Structures and Psychological Foundations', *Journal of the American Institute of Planners*, Vol.28.

De Palma, A., V. Ginsburgh and J-F. Thisse, 1987, 'On the Existence of Location Equilibria in the 3-Firm Hotelling Problem', *Journal of Industrial Economics*, Vol.36, No.2.

Devletoglou, N. E., 1965, 'A Dissenting View of Duopoly and Spatial Competition', *Economica*, Vol.32, May.

Dewar, D. and V. Watson, 1990, *Urban Markets: Developing Informal Retailing*, London: Routledge.

Dholakia, N. and R. R. Dholakia, 1978, 'A Comparative View of Public Policy Toward Distribution', *European Journal of Marketing*, Vol.12, No.8.

Donque, G., 1966, 'Le zoma de Tananarive: étude géographique d'un marche urbain', *Madagascar Revue de Géographie*, Vol.8.

Eaton, B. C. and R. G. Lipsey, 1975, 'The Principle of Minimum Differentiation Revisited: Some New Developments in the Theory of Spatial Competition', *Review of Economic Studies*, Vol.42, No.1.

Eaton, B. C. and R. G. Lipsey, 1979, 'Comparison Shopping and the Clustering of Homogeneous Firms', *Journal of Regional Science*, Vol.19, No.4.

Fogg, W., 1932, 'The Suq: A Study in the Human Geography of Morocco', *Geography*, Vol.17, Nov.

Fotheringham, A. S. and M. E. O'Kelly, 1989, *Spatial Interaction Models: Formulations and Applications*, Dordrect: Kluwer.

Foxall, G. R. and P. Hackett, 1992, 'Consumer Perceptions of Micro-Retail Location: Way Finding and Cognitive Mapping in Planned and Organic Shopping Environments', *International Review of Retail, Distribution and Consumer Research*, Vol.2, No.3.

Freeman, D. B. and F. L. Dungey, 1981, 'A Spatial Duopoly: Competition in the Western Canadian Fur Trade, 1770–1835', *Journal of Historical Geography*, Vol.7, No.3.

Friedrichs, J. and A. C. Goodman, 1987, *The Changing Downtown: A Comparative Study of Baltimore and Hamburg*, Berlin: de Gruyter.

Fujita, M., H. Ogawa and J-F. Thisse, 1988, 'A Spatial Competition Approach to Central Place Theory: Some Basic Principles', *Journal of Regional Science*, Vol.28.

Fujita, M. and T. E. Smith, 1990, 'Additive-interaction Models of Spatial Agglomeration', *Journal of Regional Science*, Vol.30, No.1.

Garner, B. J., 1966, *The Internal Structure of Retail Nucleations*, Northwestern University Studies in Geography, No.12, Department of Geography, Evanston: Northwestern University.

Ghosh, A., 1990, *Retail Management*, Hinsdale: Dryden.

Ghosh, A. and B. Buchanan, 1988, 'Multiple Outlets in a Duopoly: A First Entry Paradox', *Geographical Analysis*, Vol.20, No.2.

Ghosh, A. and C. S. Craig, 1991, 'FRANSYS: A Franchise Distribution System Location Model', *Journal of Retailing*, Vol.67, No.4.

Ghosh, A. and C. A. Ingene, 1991, *Spatial Analysis in Marketing: Theory, Methods and Applications*, Greenwich: JAI Press.

Ghosh, A. and S. McLafferty, 1987, *Location Strategies for Retail and Service Firms*, Lexington: Lexington Books.

Giddens, A., 1990, *The Consequences of Modernity*, London: Polity Press.

Golledge, R. G. and H. Timmermans, 1990, 'Applications of Behavioural Research on Spatial Problems I: Cognition', *Progress in Human Geography*, Vol.14, No.1.

Goodchild, M. F., 1984, 'ILACS: A Location-Allocation Model for Retail Site Selection', *Journal of Retailing*, Vol.60, No.1.

Goodchild, M. F., 1991, 'Geographic Information Systems', *Journal of Retailing*, Vol.67, No.1.

Goodey, B., 1973, *Perception of the Environment*, Centre for Urban and Regional Studies, Occasional Paper 17, Birmingham: University of Birmingham.

Gosling, D. and B. Maitland, 1976, *Design and Planning of Retail Systems*, London: Architectural Press.

Gruen, V., 1973, *Centres for the Urban Environment: Survival of the Cities*, New York: Van Nostrand Reinhold.

Guthrie, P. R., 1980a, 'Statistical Survey Reveals Effect on Sales of Store Location Inside Mall', *Shopping Centre World*, Vol.9, May.

Guthrie, P. R., 1980b, '"Zone" Location in Mall May Affect Sales Performance', *Shopping Centre World*, Vol.9, June.

Hagishima, S., K. Mitsuyoshi and S. Kurose, 1987, 'Estimation of Pedestrian Shopping Trips in a Neighbourhood by Using a Spatial Interaction Model', *Environment and Planning A*, Vol.19, No.9.

Hansen, M. H. and C. B. Weinberg, 1979, 'Retail Market Share in a Competitive Market', *Journal of Retailing*, Vol.55, No.1.

Hartenstein, W. and G. Staack, 1967, 'Land Use in the Urban Core', in W. F. Heinemeijer, M. van Hulten and H. D. de Vries Reilingh (eds.), *Urban Core and Inner City*, Leiden: Brill.

Harts-Broekhuis, E. J. A. and O. Verkoren, 1987, 'Gender Differentiation among Market-traders in Central Mali', *Tijdschrift voor Economische en Sociale Geografie*, Vol.78, No.3.

Hartshorn, T. A. and P. O. Muller, 1989, 'Suburban Downtowns and the Transformation of Metropolitan Atlanta's Business Landscape', *Urban Geography*, Vol.10, No.4.

Harvey, D., 1973, *Social Justice and the City*, London: Edward Arnold.

Harvey, D., 1974, 'Class-monopoly Rent, Finance Capital and the Urban Resolution', *Regional Studies*, Vol.8.

Hassan, R., 1972, 'Islam and Urbanisation in the Medieval Middle East', *Ekistics*, Vol.33, Feb.

Hawes, J. M. and D. M. Lewison, 1984, 'Retail Site Evaluation: An Examination of the Principle of Accessibility', in R. W. Belk (ed.), *A.M.A. Educators' Proceedings*, Chicago: American Marketing Association.

Haynes, K. E. and A. S. Fotheringham, 1984, *Gravity and Spatial Interaction Models*, Beverly Hills: Sage.

Heinritz, G. and R. Sittenauer, 1991, 'Linkage Behaviour and Mix of Goods and Services in Shopping Centres: Observations in the PEP, Munich', paper presented at IGU Commission, *Geography of Commercial Activities Conference*, Munich, Aug.

Herbert, D. T. and C. J. Thomas, 1990, *Urban Geography: A First Approach*, London: Wiley.

Hise, R. T., J. P. Kelly, M. Gable and J. B. McDonald, 1983, 'Factors Affecting the Performance of Individual Chain Store Units: An Empirical Analysis', *Journal of Retailing*, Vol.59, No.2.

Horwood, E. M. and R. R. Boyce, 1959, *Studies of the Central Business District and Urban Freeway Development*, Seattle: University of Washington Press.

Horwood, E. M. and M. D. McNair, 1961, 'The Core of the City: Emerging Concepts', *Plan*, Vol.2, No.2.

Hotelling, H., 1929, 'Stability in Competition', *Economic Journal*, Vol.39, March.

Howard, E. B. and R. L. Davies, 1986, *Contemporary Change in Newcastle City Centre and the Impact of the Metro System*, CURDS, Discussion Paper No.77, Newcastle: University of Newcastle-upon-Tyne.

Howard, E. B. and J. Reynolds, 1991, 'Understanding the Challenge of the UK Regional Shopping Centre', in R. A. Thurik and H. J. Gianotten (eds.), *Proceedings of the Sixth World Conference on Research in the Distributive Trades*, The Hague: Institute for Small and Medium-Sized Business.

Hurd, R. M., 1903, *Principles of City Land Values*, New York: The Record and Guide, 1924 reprint.

ICSC, 1974, *Anti-trust Update: The Shopping Centre Industry and Anti-trust Laws*, New York: International Council of Shopping Centres.

Ingene, C. A. and A. Ghosh, 1990, 'Consumer and Producer Behaviour in a Multipurpose Shopping Environment', *Geographical Analysis*, Vol.22, No.1.

Ingene, C. A. and A. Ghosh, 1991, 'Conclusions', in A. Ghosh and C. A. Ingene (eds.), *Spatial Analysis in Marketing: Theory, Methods and Application*, Greenwich: JAI Press.

Jackson, E. L. and D. B. Johnson, 1991, 'The West Edmonton Mall and Mega-malls', *Canadian Geographer*, Vol.35, No.3.

Jansen, A. C. M., 1989, '"Funshopping" as a Geographical Notion, or: The Attractiveness of the Inner City of Amsterdam as a Shopping Area', *Tijdschrift voor Economische en Sociale Geografie*, Vol.80, No.3.

Johnson, D. B., 1978, 'The Unplanned Commercial Nucleation as a Regional Shopping Centre', in P. J. Smith (ed.), *Edmonton: The Emerging Metropolitan Pattern*, Western Geographical Series, Vol.15, Department of Geography, Victoria: University of Victoria.

Johnson, D. B., 1991, 'Structural Features of West Edmonton Mall', *Canadian Geographer*, Vol.35, No.3.

Johnston, R. J., 1973, *Spatial Structures*, London: Methuen.

Johnston, R. J., 1977, 'Conceiving the Geography of Land Values in Cities', *South African Geographer*, Vol.5, April.

Johnston, R. J. and C. C. Kissling, 1971, 'Establishment Use Patterns within Central Places', *Australian Geographical Studies*, Vol.9.

Jones, C. S., 1969, *Regional Shopping Centres: Their Location, Planning and Design*, London: Business Books.

Jones, D. W., 1991, 'An Introduction to the Thünen Location and Land Use Model', in A. Ghosh and C. A. Ingene (eds.), *Spatial Analysis in Marketing: Theory, Methods and Applications*, Greenwich: JAI Press.

Jones, K. G. and J. Simmons, 1987, *Location, Location, Location*, Toronto: Methuen.

Kane, H. E. and E. H. Belkin, 1981, 'Legal and Land Use Tissues: Suburb versus Central City', in G. Sternlieb and J. W. Hughes (eds.), *Shopping Centres USA*, Centre for Urban Policy Research, New Jersey: Rutgers.

Khan, F. K. and A. S. Uddin, 1967, 'The City Centre of Chittagong', *The Original Geographer*, Vol.11, No.1.

Laulajainen, R., 1981, 'Three Tests on Locational Matching', *Geografiska Annaler*, Vol.63B., No.1.

Laulajainen, R., 1987, *Spatial Strategies in Retailing*, Dordrecht: Reidel.

Laulajainen, R., 1990, 'Defense by Expansion: The Case of Marshall Field', *Professional Geographer*, Vol.42, No.3.

Laulajainen, R. and L-E. Gadde, 1986, 'Locational Avoidance: A Case Study of Three Swedish Retail Chains', *Regional Studies*, Vol.20, No.2.

Lee, Y., 1974, 'An Analysis of Spatial Mobility of Urban Activities in Downtown Denver', *Annals of Regional Science*, Vol.8, No.1.

Lee, Y. and K. Koutsopoulos, 1976, 'A Locational Analysis of Convenience Food Stores in Metropolitan Denver', *Annals of Regional Science*, Vol.10.

Lee, Y. and C. G. Schmidt, 1980, 'A Comparative Location Analysis of a Retail Activity: The Gasoline Service Station', *Annals of Regional Science*, Vol.14, No.2.

Lerner, A. P. and H. W. Singer, 1937, 'Some Notes on Duopoly and Spatial Competition', *Journal of Political Economy*, Vol.45, No.2.

Lessinger, J., 1985, '"Nobody here to yell at me"': Political Activism among Petty Retail Traders in an Indian City', in S. Plattner (ed.), *Markets and Marketing*, New York: University Press of America.

Lord, J. D., 1985, 'The Malling of the American Landscape', in J. A. Dawson and J. D. Lord (eds.), *Shopping Centre Development: Policies and Prospects*, London: Croom Helm.

Lord, J. D. and D. B. Wright, 1981, 'Competition and Location Strategy in Branch Banking: Spatial Advoidance or Clustering?', *Urban Geography*, Vol.2, No.3.

Lynch, K., 1960, *The Image of the City*, Cambridge: MIT Press.

Maitland, B., 1985, *Shopping Malls: Planning and Design*, London: Construction Press.

Maitland, B., 1990, *The New Architecture of the Retail Mall*, London: Architecture Design and Technology Press.

Mallen, B. and R. Savitt, 1979, *A Study of Leasing Practices and Retail Tenant Selection and Restriction in Shopping Centres in Canada*, Research Branch, Bureau of Competition Policy, Ottawa: Department of Consumer and Corporate Affairs.

Marchand, B., 1974, 'Pedestrian Traffic Planning and the Perception of the Urban Environment: A French Example', *Environment and Planning A*, Vol.6, No.5.

Martin, P. G., 1982, *Shopping Centre Management*, London: Spon.

Mason, J. B., 1975, 'Power and Channel Conflicts in Shopping Centre Development', *Journal of Marketing*, Vol.39, April.

Matthews, M. H., 1980, 'The Mental Maps of Children: Images of Coventry's City Centre', *Geography*, Vol.65.

May, A. D., I. G. Turvey and P. G. Hopkinson, 1985, *Studies of Pedestrian Amenity*, Institute for Transport Studies, Working Paper 204, Leeds: University of Leeds.

McGoldrick, P. J. and M. G. Thompson, 1992, *Regional Shopping Centres: In-town Versus Out-of-Town*, Aldershot: Avebury.

McIntyre, W. E., 1955, 'The Retail Pattern of Manila', *Geographical Review*, Vol.45, No.1.

McKeever, J. R. and N. M. Griffin, 1977, *The Community Builder's Handbook*, Washington DC: Urban Land Institute.

McNeal, J. U. and C. S. Madden, 1987, 'Retail Failure: A Site Selection Perspective', *Southwest Journal of Business and Economics*, Vol.4, No.3.

Miossec, J-M., 1990, 'From Suq to Supermarket in Tunis', in A. M. Findlay, R. Paddison, and J. A. Dawson (eds.), *Retailing Environments in Developing Countries*, London: Routledge.

Miracle, M. P., 1962, 'African Markets and Trade in the Copperbelt', in P. Bohannan and G. Dalton (eds.), *Markets in Africa*, Evanston: Northwestern University Press.

Moles, A. A., 1979, 'The Human Perception of Urban Streets', *Planification Habitat Information*, Vol.94, April.

Moore, E. W., 1985, *The Fairs of Medieval England: An Introductory Study*, Toronto: Pontifical Institute of Medieval Studies.

Morris, R. L. and S. B. Zisman, 1962, 'The Pedestrian Downtown, and the Planner', *Journal of the American Institute of Planners*, Vol.28, No.3.

Nelson, R. L., 1958, *The Selection of Retail Locations*, New York: Dodge.

Ness, M. P., J. F. Morrall and B. G. Hutchinson, 1969, 'An Analysis of Central Business District Pedestrian Circulation Patterns', *Highway Research Record*, Vol.283.

Norris, D. A., 1987, 'Interstate Highway Exit Morphology: Non-Metropolitan Exit Commerce on I-75', *Professional Geographer*, Vol.39, No.1.

Northen, R. I., 1984, *Shopping Centre Development*, London: Spon.

Nystrom, P., 1930, *The Economics of Retailing*, New York: The Roland Press.

O'Brien, L. and Harris, F., 1991, *Retailing: Shopping, Society, Space*, London: David Fulton.

Okabe, A., Y. Asami and F. Miki, 1985, 'Statistical Analysis of the Spatial Association of Convenience-Goods Stores by Use of a Random Clumping Model', *Journal of Regional Science*, Vol.25, No.1.

Okabe, A. and F. Miki, 1984, 'A Conditional Nearest-Neighbour Spatial-Association Measure for the Analysis of Conditional Locational Interdependence', *Environment and Planning A*, Vol.16, No.2.

Okabe, A. and A. Suzuki, 1987, 'Stability of Spatial Competition for a Large Number of Firms on a Bounded Two-Dimensional Space', *Environment and Planning A*, Vol.19, No.8.

Parker, A. J. and M. McLoughlin, 1988, *Shoppers in Dublin: Grafton Street*, Dublin: Research Report 88/3, Centre for Retail Studies, University College Dublin.

Parker, H. R., 1962, 'Suburban Shopping Facilities in Liverpool', *Town Planning Review*, Vol.33.

Parkes, C., 1987, 'Problems Facing Out-of-Town Shopping Developers', *Financial Times*, Thursday, 18 June.

Parkins, A. E., 1930, 'Profiles of the Retail Business Section of Nashville, Tenn., and their Interpretation', *Annals of the Association of American Geographers*, Vol.20.

Pascal, A. H. and J. J. McCall, 1980, 'Agglomeration Economies, Search Costs and Industrial Location', *Journal of Urban Economics*, Vol.8, No.3.

Pearson, T. D., 1991, 'Location! Location! Location! What is Location?', *The Appraisal Journal*, January.

Peters, J., 1990, 'Managing Shopping Centre Retailer Mix: Some Considerations for Retailers', *International Journal of Retail and Distribution Management*, Vol.18, No.1.

Pillsbury, R., 1987, 'From Hamburger Alley to Hedgerose Heights: Toward a Model of Restaurant Location Dynamics', *Professional Geographer*, Vol.39, No.3.

Pocock, D. C. D. and R. Hudson, 1978, *Images of the Urban Environment*, London: Macmillan.

Potter, R. B., 1982, *The Urban Retailing System: Location, Cognition and Behaviour*, Aldershot: Gower.

Pyle, J., 1926, 'The Determination of Location Standards for Retail Concerns', *Harvard Business Review*, Vol.4, April.

Pyle, J., 1978, 'Tianguis: Periodic Markets of Mexico City', in R. H. T. Smith (ed.) *Market Place Trade – Periodic Markets, Hawkers and Traders in Africa, Asia and Latin America*, Centre for Transportation Studies, Vancouver: University of British Columbia.

Rannells, J., 1956, *The Core of the City: A Pilot Study of Changing Land Uses in Central Business Districts*, New York: Columbia University.

Ratcliff, R. U., 1939, *The Problem of Retail Site Selection*, School of Business Administration, Ann Arbor: University of Michigan.

Roberts, J., 1989, *Talking About Walking*, London: TEST.

Rogers, A., 1969, 'Quadrat Analysis of Urban Dispersion: 2. Case Studies of Urban Retail Systems', *Environment and Planning*, Vol.1, No.2.

Rogers, D. S., 1987, 'America's Shopping Centres: A Mid-life Crisis?', *Retail and Distribution Management*, Vol.15, No.6.

Rouse Company, 1969, *Amalgam Mall: A Case Study in the Development of a Regional Shopping Centre*, New York: International Council of Shopping Centres.

Rutherford, G. S., 1979, 'Use of the Gravity Model for Pedestrian Travel Distribution', *Transportation Research Record*, Vol.728.

Saarinen, T. F., 1977, *Maps in Minds: Reflections on Cognitive Mapping*, New York: Harper and Row.

Sandrock, K., 1988, 'Heuristic Estimation of Pedestrian Traffic Volumes', *Transportation Research*, Vol.22A.

Savitt, R., 1985, 'Issues of Tenant Policy Control: The American Perspective', in J. A. Dawson and J. D. Lord (eds.), *Shopping Centre Development: Policies and Prospects*, London: Croom Helm.

Scott, A. J., 1974, 'A Theoretical Model of Pedestrian Flow', *Socio-Economic Planning Sciences*, Vol.8.

Scott, P., 1959, 'The Australian CBD', *Economic Geography*, Vol.35.

Scott, P., 1970, *Geography and Retailing*, London: Hutchinson.

Sendut, H., 1965, 'The Structure of Kuala Lumpur', *Town Planning Review*, Vol.36.

Shaw G., 1988, 'Recent Research on the Commercial Structure of Nineteenth-Century British Cities', in D. Denecke and G. Shaw (eds.), *Urban Historical Geography: Recent Progress in Britain and Germany*, Cambridge: Cambridge University Press.

Shepherd, I. D. H. and C. J. Thomas, 1980, 'Urban Consumer Behaviour', in J. A. Dawson (ed.), *Retail Geography*, London: Croom Helm.

Sieverts, T., 1967, 'Perceptual Images of the City of Berlin', in W. F. Heinemeijer, M. van Hulten, and H. D. de Vries Reilingh (eds.), *Urban Core and Inner City*, Leiden: E. J. Brill.

Sim, L. L. and C. R. Way, 1989, 'Tenant Placement in a Singapore Shopping Centre', *International Journal of Retailing*, Vol.4, No.1.

Simpkin, L. P., 1989, 'SLAM: Store Location Assessment Model: Theory and Practice', *Omega*, Vol.7, No.1.

Simpkin, L. P., P. Doyle and J. Saunders, 1985, 'UK Retail Store Location Assessment', *Journal of the Market Research Society*, Vol.27, No.2.

Smith, G. C. and N. K. Dolman, 1981, 'Consumer Responses to Alternative Retail Environments in Nottingham's Central Area', *East Midland Geographer*, Vol.7/8.

Smith, G. C., D. J. B. Shaw and P. R. Huckle, 1979, 'Children's Perception of a Downtown Shopping Centre', *Professional Geographer*, Vol.31, No.2.

Smith, P. E. 1956, *Shopping Centres: Planning and Management*, New York: National Dry Goods Association.

Sommer, R. and S. Aitkens, 1982, 'Mental Mapping of Two Supermarkets', *Journal of Consumer Research*, Vol.9, No.2.

Sparks, L., 1990, 'Spatial Structural Relationships in Retail Corporate Growth: A Case Study of Kwik Save Group PLC', *Service Industries Journal*, Vol.10, No.1.

Stambaugh, D., 1978, 'Proper Tenant Mix: How to Put It all Together', *Shopping Centre World*, Vol.7, No.4.

Stern, L. W. and A. I. El-Ansary, 1988, *Marketing Channels*, Englewood Cliffs, Prentice Hall.

Teitz, M. B., 1968, 'Locational Strategies for Competitive Systems', *Journal of Regional Science*, Vol.8, No.2.

Thill, J-C. and I. Thomas, 1987, 'Toward Conceptualising Trip Chaining Behaviour: A Review', *Geographical Analysis*, Vol.19, No.1.

Thompson, I. B., 1982, *The Commercial Centre of Oran*, Geography Department, Occasional Papers No.9, Glasgow, University of Glasgow.

Thornhill, J., 1992, 'Why Location Counts', *Financial Times*, Thursday 27 Feb.

Thornton, S. J., M. J. McCullagh and R. P. Bradshaw, 1992, 'Pedestrian Flows and Retail Turnover', *British Food Journal*, Vol.93, No.9.

Thrall, G. I., 1991, 'Production Theory of Land Rent', *Environment and Planning A*, Vol.23, No.8.

Timmermans, H., 1986, 'Locational Choice Behaviour of Entrepreneurs: An Experimental Analysis', *Urban Studies*, Vol.23, No.2.

Toyne, P., 1971, 'Customer Trips to Retail Business in Exeter', in K. J. Gregory and W. C. D. Ravenhill (eds.), *Exeter Essays in Geography*, Exeter: University of Exeter Press.

Troin, J-F., 1990, 'New Trends in Commercial Locations in Morocco', in A. M. Findlay, R. Paddison and J. A. Dawson (eds.), *Retailing Environments in Developing Countries*, London: Routledge.

Turchiano, F., 1990, 'Farewell Field of Dreams: "Build it and they will come" Era Ends for Shopping Centres', *Retailing Issues Letter*, Vol.2, No.9.

Ukuw, U.I., 1969, 'Markets in Iboland', in B. W. Hodder and U. I. Ukuw, *Markets in West Africa*, Ibadan University Press: Ibadan.

Van der Hagen, X., A. Borgers and H. Timmermans, 1991, 'Spatio-Temporal Sequencing Processes of Pedestrians in Urban Retail Environments', *Papers in Regional Science*, Vol.70.

Von Thünen, J. H., 1826, *Der Isolierte Staat in Beziehung auf Landwirtschaft und Nationalokonomie, 1. Teil*, Hamburg: Perthes.

Ward, R. G., D. Howlett, C. C. Kissling and H. C. Weinand, 1978, 'Maket Raun: The Introduction of Periodic Markets to Papua, New Guinea', in R. H. T. Smith (ed.), *Market Place Trade – Periodic Markets, Hawkers and Traders in Africa, Asia and Latin America*, Centre for Transportation Studies, Vancouver: University of British Columbia.

Weaver, D. C., 1969, 'Changes in the Morphology of Three American Central Business Districts 1952–1966', *Professional Geographer*, Vol.21, No.6.

West, D. S. and B. von Hohenbalken, 1984, 'Spatial Predation in a Canadian Retail Oligopoly', *Journal of Regional Science*, Vol.24, No.3.

White, P. G., 1975, *The Composite Structure of the Central Area*, Newcastle: University of Newcastle-upon-Tyne, Department of Geography, Seminar Papers No.30.

Whitehand, J. W. R., 1987, *The Changing Face of Cities: A Study of Development Cycles and Urban Form*, Oxford: Basil Blackwell.

Wing, H. C. and S. L. Lee, 1980, 'The Characteristics and Locational Patterns of Wholesale and Service Trades in the Central Area of Singapore', *Singapore Journal of Tropical Geography*, Vol.1, No.1.

Zawawi, M., 1970, 'Perception of Downtown: A Case Study of Washington DC.' unpublished MA thesis, Washington DC: George Washington University.

Zipf, G. K., 1949, *Human Behaviour and the Principle of Least Effort*, Cambridge: Harvard University Press.

This chapter first appeared in *The Service Industries Journal*, Vol.14, No.4 (1994).

8

The Retail Park: Customer Usage and Perceptions of a Retailing Innovation

by
Stephen Brown

Recently described as a 'peculiarly British innovation', retail parks are an increasingly important element of the UK's urban retail structure. Yet relatively little is known about customer usage and perceptions of this innovative retail form. A study of the Abbey Trading Centre, an unplanned retail park on the outskirts of Belfast, reveals that the complex is patronised by middle-class families of one-stop-shoppers. The perceived advantages and disadvantages of shopping in the retail park are also explored and it is argued that these may help explain the evolution of retailing innovations.

INTRODUCTION

One of the most contentious issues in UK retailing is shopping out-of-centre, or 'megacentre madness' as it is sometimes called [Johnston, 1987]. Since 1985 approximately 11.5 million sq. ft. of retailing floorspace has been constructed in suburban or out-of-town locations and a staggering 64 million is proposed [Hillier Parker, 1988a, 1988b]. Although much of this is speculative and unlikely to be built in practice, the very prospect is giving rise to widespread concern about the impact on existing High Streets and led to predictions of the 'hole in the doughnut' syndrome, wherein the town centre is destroyed by a ring of outlying shopping complexes [Cochrane, 1987; Schiller, 1987].

Much of the debate, and moreover academic research, on out-of-centre shopping development has centred upon mega-scale developments of 1 million sq. ft. plus [Davies and Howard, 1987; Shaw, 1987]. Yet, as Hillier Parker [1988a, 1988b] have demonstrated, the bulk of latter-day development comprises planned and unplanned retail parks, loose agglomerations of retail warehouses – and occasionally superstores – with shared car parking facilities. Indeed, they accounted for 50 per cent of the total out-of-town retailing floorspace in 1986, 77 per cent in 1987 and an estimated 79 per cent of the 7.4 million sq. ft. currently under construction. Examples include Cribbs Causeway in

FIGURE 1

	DISPERSED	COMPACT
UNPLANNED	CRIBBS CAUSEWAY (BRISTOL) SWANSEA ENTERPRISE ZONE	CHEETHAM HILL ROAD (MANCHESTER) NEWPORT ROAD (CARDIFF)
PLANNED	RETAIL WORLD (ROTHERHAM) MERRY HILL (DUDLEY)	PRIORY FIELDS (TAUNTON) JUNCTION 10 RETAIL CENTRE (WALSALL)

Bristol, Retail World in Rotherham, the Meteor Centre, Derby and the Aireside Centre, Leeds.

Despite their ubiquity, retail parks come in a wide variety of forms, ranging from the spatially compact and carefully planned to the spatially extensive and poorly co-ordinated (Figure 1). What is more, they contain an increasingly diverse mix of retailing outlets. What began with flat-pack furniture, DIY materials and gardening equipment has expanded into the retailing of toys, apparel, soft furnishings, electrical equipment, motor accessories and much more besides. Surprisingly, however, relatively little is known about customer usage and, perhaps more importantly, their perceptions of retail parks, though noteworthy exceptions are the studies of Bromley and Thomas [1987], Bernard Thorpe [1985] and Leicester City Council [1987] in Swansea, Leeds and Leicester respectively. These reveal that retail parks have a distinctive customer profile – car-borne, family groupings of the early middle-aged middle classes, who live within approximately five miles and patronise the facility on an irregular basis.

THE ABBEY TRADING CENTRE

Important as the foregoing exercises are, they make little attempt to explore customer perceptions of the advantages and disadvantages of shopping in retail parks. This neglect is somewhat unfortunate in that it may provide some insight into the evolution of innovative retailing forms (see below). In order to further this area of research, a study was undertaken in the Abbey Trading Centre, an unplanned, retail park in

FIGURE 2
THE ABBEY TRADING CENTRE

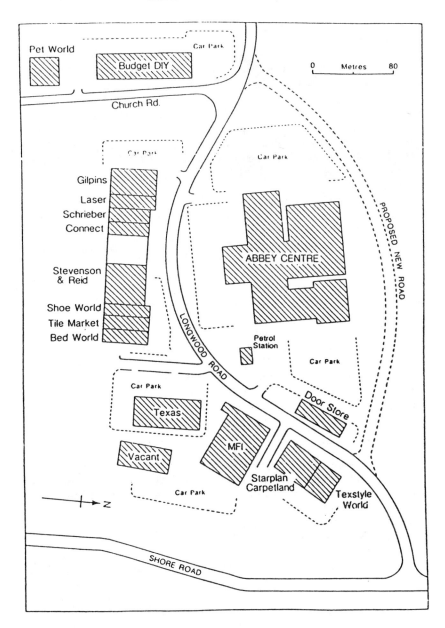

the northern suburbs of Belfast and one of the largest concentrations of retail floorspace in Northern Ireland. Employing almost 900 people, the Abbey Trading Centre comprises a 176,000 sq. ft. gross district centre – The Abbeycentre – and 16 retail warehouses totalling 246,800 sq. ft. gross (Figure 2).

Identified as a potential district centre site in the Belfast Urban Area Plan of the late 1960s (Building Design Partnership, 1969), the Abbeycentre opened in November 1978 and was extended to its present size two years later. The first retail warehouse, Texas Homecare, began trading in August 1980 and since then the retail warehouse element of the park has developed in an incremental fashion. It now comprises two DIY stores, two electrical retailers, six household goods specialists, three furniture stores, two other specialist outlets (pets and shoes) and one vacant unit,[1] though at least two additional warehouses are planned.

Little attempt has been made to integrate the Abbey Trading Centre, though a walkway was constructed from Gilpins to Bed World in order to improve pedestrian access. Nevertheless, the net effect of the piecemeal development is an unplanned agglomeration of stores with individual, and arguably inadequate, car parking facilities. Remarkably, the car parking ratio at the Abbey Trading Centre (3.9 spaces per 1,000 sq. ft. of gross floorspace) is lower than the centre of Belfast (5.0 spaces per 1,000 sq. ft), although it varies considerably from store to store. Indeed, the unplanned form of the park gives rise to peak-time traffic congestion (1,500 vehicles per hour) which the Department of the Environment has tried to alleviate through the installation of traffic lights and the construction of slip roads at the Shore Road and Church Road intersections. Plans for a relief road to the rear of the Abbeycentre and the introduction of a one-way traffic system are also well advanced (Figure 2).

SURVEY METHODOLOGY

In order to investigate customer usage and perceptions of the Abbey Trading Centre, a pilot survey, comprising 40 face-to-face interviews, was undertaken in February 1988. This was followed by the main survey exercise on a Saturday in early March. The interviewers were stationed at 13 survey points in the retail park – including all three entrances to the Abbeycentre – thereby ensuring that every store was incorporated into the study. A systematic sample of shoppers was interviewed at each outlet and, as a result, the number of interviews is approximately proportional to the volume of shoppers at that location. Thus almost 30 per cent of the 688 interviews took place in the Abbeycentre, a further 30 per cent were conducted at Texas, MFI and Budget DIY, and the remainder were spread among the smaller, more specialised outlets.

TABLE 1
FREQUENCY OF VISITS, DISTANCE TRAVELLED AND MEANS OF TRANSPORT

Frequency of Visits

	Total		Warehouses		Abbeycentre	
	N	%	N	%	N	%
More than 1 per week	118	18.0	61	13.2	57	29.4
1 per week	180	27.5	117	25.4	63	32.5
2-3 per month	99	15.1	77	16.7	22	11.3
1 per month	100	15.3	77	16.7	23	11.9
Less than 1 per month	158	24.1	129	28.0	29	14.9

Distance Travelled

	Total		Warehouses		Abbeycentre	
	N	%	N	%	N	%
Less than 1 mile	97	14.2	57	11.8	40	20.0
2-5 miles	287	41.9	201	41.4	86	43.0
6-10 miles	154	22.5	110	22.7	44	22.0
11-20 miles	102	14.9	81	16.7	21	10.5
20+ miles	45	6.6	36	7.4	9	4.5

Means of Transport

	Total		Warehouses		Abbeycentre	
	N	%	N	%	N	%
Private Car	630	91.6	453	92.8	177	88.5
Public transport	33	4.8	21	4.3	12	6.0
Walk	25	3.6	14	2.9	11	5.5

FINDINGS

Usage of Centre

The results of the questionnaire survey reveal that 43 per cent of respondents are regular users of the Abbeycentre, visiting the complex one or more times per week (Table 1). At the same time, a sizeable minority of shoppers (37 per cent) patronise the retail park on an irregular basis, once per month or less. As Bromley and Thomas [1987] discovered in Swansea, this duality in customer usage is indicative of a functional dichotomy between the superstore anchored district centre and the retail warehouses (chi square significant at .0001). The former is

TABLE 2
VISITS TO OTHER SHOPPING CENTRES

Intention to Visit

	Total		Warehouses		Abbeycentre	
	N	%	N	%	N	%
Visited/Intend to Visit Other Centres	140	20.4	108	22.2	32	16.0
One-stop shoppers	547	79.6	379	77.8	168	84.0

Most Frequently Visited Centres on Day of Interview

	N	%
Northcott	50	35.7
Belfast city centre	25	17.8
Park centre	15	10.7
Ards shopping centre	13	9.3
Connswater	8	5.7
Others	34	24.3

characterised by regular (weekly or more often) convenience-orientated shopping trips, whereas the durable goods retailers in the latter are frequented on a much less regular basis. Noteworthy exceptions, however, are Budget DIY and Pet World where over 50 per cent of respondents visit once per week or more. Budget, in effect, appears to be functioning as a convenience DIY retailer while the newly opened Pet World is experiencing a high level of repeat visits as a result, presumably, of its curiosity value.

The district centre–retail warehouse dichotomy is also evident when the trade area of the retail park is examined (chi square significant at .05). Sixty-three per cent of the Abbeycentre's customers reside within five miles of the complex and only 15 per cent travel more than ten miles. By contrast, almost one quarter of those interviewed at the retail warehouses reside more than ten miles distant and just over half live within a five mile radius (Table 1). Once again, Pet World and Budget DIY are the major exceptions with respectively, 77 per cent and 65 per cent of respondents travelling less than five miles. This emphasises the localised, convenience nature of Budget's clientele and, doubtless, the low level of awareness of Pet World (although open for business it had not been 'launched' at the time of the survey). At the opposite extreme, the Door Store, being highly specialised, attracts custom from an exceptionally wide catchment area. Approximately half its customers reside more than ten miles distant.

Given its car orientation, it is not surprising that the vast majority of respondents (91.6 per cent) travel to the Abbey Trading Centre by private car (Table 1). Another 3.6 per cent are walk-in customers and the remainder use public transport or the private hire taxi services that ply between the Abbeycentre and nearby housing estates. This is reflected in the slightly lower usage of private cars at the Abbeycentre (88.5 per cent) than the retail warehouses (92.8 per cent), though the difference is not statistically significant.

Despite the preponderance of highly mobile shoppers, the survey reveals relatively little evidence of multi-centre shopping expeditions (Table 2). As in Swansea, though in contrast to Leicester and Leeds, only around 20 per cent of respondents had visited or intended to visit another shopping district on the day of the interview. Although this pattern of behaviour is more evident among customers of the retail warehouses

TABLE 3

AGE AND SOCIO-ECONOMIC GROUP OF RESPONDENTS

Age

	Total		Warehouses		Abbeycentre		NI
	N	%	N	%	N	%	%
Less than 25	71	10.4	49	10.1	22	11.1	22
25 - 44	374	54.6	272	56.0	102	51.3	34
45 - 64	204	29.8	146	30.0	58	29.1	21
65+	36	5.2	19	3.9	17	8.5	23

Socio-Economic Group

	Total		Warehouses		Abbeycentre		NI
	N	%	N	%	N	%	%
AB	139	20.4	96	20.0	43	21.5)	
							) 35
C1	160	23.5	116	24.2	44	22.0)	
C2	196	28.8	139	29.0	57	28.5)	
							) 67
DE	185	27.2	129	26.9	56	28.0)	

TABLE 4

SHOPPER GROUP COMPOSITION

	Total		Warehouses		Abbeycentre	
	N	%	N	%	N	%
Adult male only	130	18.9	101	20.7	29	14.5
Adult female only	135	19.6	85	17.5	50	25.0
Adult male and children	22	3.2	15	3.1	7	3.5
Adult female and children	57	8.3	31	6.4	26	13.0
Adult male, adult female and children	101	14.7	75	15.4	26	13.0
Adult male and female	242 .	35.2	180	37.0	62	31.0

(22 per cent) than the district centre (16 per cent), the difference is not statistically significant. It appears, in other words, that the Abbey Trading Centre is providing a 'one-stop-shopping' experience, though it is interesting to note that, in contrast to Swansea, Leicester and Leeds the city centre is *not* the shopping area most frequently patronised by multi-centre shoppers. They tend rather to visit the nearest planned centre, the 100,000 sq. ft. Northcott Shopping Centre in Glengormley.

Customer Profile

In terms of customer profile, the bulk of shoppers at the Abbey Trading Centre fall into the 25–44 age category and the C1-C2 socio-economic groups. Thus, compared with the profile of the population as a whole, young adults and the very old are under-represented, as are the lowest socio-economic groups (Table 3). In this respect the Abbey Trading

TABLE 5

PERCEIVED ADVANTAGES AND DISADVANTAGES OF THE
ABBEY TRADING CENTRE

Advantages

	Total		Warehouses		Abbeycentre	
	N	%	N	%	N	%
Shops together	416	61.0	285	59.2	131	65.5
Choice	253	37.1	197	40.9	56	28.0
Convenient	180	26.4	108	22.4	72	36.0
Car Parking	105	15.4	77	16.0	28	14.0
Named Shops	29	4.2	21	4.4	8	4.0
Nothing	25	3.7	15	3.1	10	5.0
Late/Sunday opening	16	2.3	15	3.1	1	0.5
Other	58	8.5	37	7.7	21	10.5

Disadvantages

	Total		Warehouses		Abbeycentre	
	N	%	N	%	N	%
Nothing	235	34.9	164	34.6	71	35.7
Access Roads	173	25.7	141	29.7	32	16.1
Crowds	119	17.7	73	15.4	46	23.1
Car Parking	77	11.4	53	11.2	24	12.1
Lack of Shops	35	5.2	18	3.8	17	8.5
Lack of Cohesion	16	2.4	15	3.2	1	0.5
Lack of Pedestrian Crossings	8	1.2	7	1.5	1	0.5
Other	91	13.5	59	12.4	32	16.1

Centre is similar to most suburban shopping centres in the UK and, as noted earlier, the retail parks in Leicester, Leeds and Swansea.

Although there is no statistically significant difference between the overall age and socio-economic profile of the district centre and retail warehouses, an interesting contrast exists between the adjacent outlets Texstyle World and Starplan. The former has the most affluent customer profile in the entire retail park (54 per cent ABC1) whereas the latter is patronised by the least affluent shopper groups (31 per cent ABC1), thereby indicating that both are successfully appealing to their respective target markets. Texstyle World, what is more, has the highest proportion of female customers, though the Abbeycentre is not far behind. In fact, the district centre is something of a female preserve compared to the male orientated DIY and electrical goods warehouses (chi square significant at .01). However, the majority of shopper groups in the retail park are mixed, with the family groupings of males and females, and males, females and children being dominant at both the district centre and retail warehouses (Table 4).

Perceptions of Centre

In order to explore customer perceptions of the retail park, respondents were asked, in an umprompted, open-ended question format, to state the major advantages and disadvantages of shopping in the Abbey Trading Centre. As Table 5 demonstrates the overwhelming perceived advantage is the 'grouping together' or agglomeration of such a wide range of retail outlets, and, indeed, the closely related factor of 'wide choice' is the second most frequently cited advantage. The centre's convenient or handy location is also of some importance, albeit more for the Abbeycentre's essentially localised, convenience goods-orientated shoppers than the less regular and further-flung users of the non-food retail warehouses. Other important but less frequently mentioned advantages include: the presence of certain (named) shops; late night and Sunday trading; and the availability of car parking facilities. Interestingly, the last-named did not emerge as the major perceived advantage, in contrast to many other studies of out-of-town shopping complexes. However, this is possibly a reflection of the retail park's relative paucity of car parking spaces. The parking ratio at the Abbey Trading Centre is lower than most of the other large shopping complexes in Northern Ireland and, as outlined earlier, lower even than the centre of Belfast.

Turning to the disadvantages, approximately one third of the respondents reported no particular problems, though overcrowding in the Abbeycentre, a perceived lack of car parking spaces and the need for a wider range of shops figure prominently (Table 5). Nevertheless, the single most frequently stated disadvantage, especially for those interviewed at the retail warehouses, is the traffic congestion on the access roads. It would appear that despite the Department of the

Environment's attempts to improve traffic flow, it remains a major headache for drivers. Indeed when subsequently asked, 'have you ever found the roads around the Abbey Trading Centre congested, or not', no less than 87 per cent of car users claimed they had (Table 6). As one might expect, this belief is particularly strongly marked among those who live nearby and frequent the shopping complex most often (chi square significant at .001). Forty per cent of these respondents also report that the traffic congestion has caused them to alter their shopping behaviour, most notably changing the time of their visit, cutting short their shopping trip, visiting less often, altering their approach route, or, in 36 per cent of cases, going elsewhere (Table 6).

TABLE 6

PERCEIVED CONGESTION AMONG CAR USERS AND INFLUENCE ON BEHAVIOUR
(BASE 627)

	Total N	Total %	Warehouses N	Warehouses %	Abbeycentre N	Abbeycentre %
Roads congested	552	88.0	396	88.4	156	87.2
Roads not congested	75	12.0	52	11.6	23	12.8

Influence of Congestion on Shopping Behaviour (Base 217)

	N	%
Change time	79	36.4
Go elsewhere	78	35.9
Visit less often	45	20.7
Cut short visit	40	18.4
Change approach road	6	2.8
Other	4	1.8

DISCUSSION

The retail park, according to Schiller [1988: 184], is a peculiarly British innovation, a retailing enigma unknown in Europe, Africa or Australia. This may be so, but the retail park has evolved in time-honoured fashion. As Figure 3 illustrates, most retail innovations are initially characterised by the sale of a narrow range of cut-price wares which gradually expands to incorporate a more diverse mix of merchandise. A period of 'trading-up' then transpires and this eventually gives way to a narrower focus due to the emergence of a new breed of cut-price specialists [Brown, 1988]. These stages of development are very clearly demonstrated by the retail park, though the fourth and final phase is perhaps some way distant. What began with free-standing discount retail warehouses selling flat-pack furniture and DIY materials from low-rent, redundant premises such as warehouses and cinemas, has developed into the retailing of toys, apparel, textiles, sports equipment, optical goods, fast food, etc. etc. from landscaped, sophisticated and carefully integrated clusters of purpose-built structures [see Gibbs, 1985, 1987; Schiller, 1988].

FIGURE 3

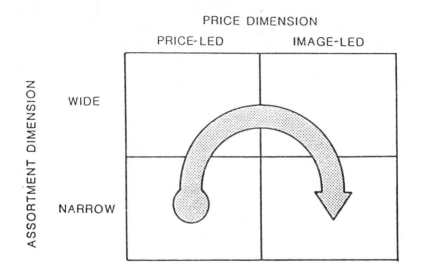

Although these evolutionary stages are reasonably well established in retailing theory, the reasons for this pattern of development have generated prolonged academic debate. Some consider it a result of managerial deterioration, others say it is a function of inter-institutional competition and yet others contend it is nothing less than a natural law [see Brown, 1987]. The evidence from the Abbey Trading Centre, which showed that the major perceived advantages and disadvantages were the wide choice and traffic congestion respectively, suggests that the evolution of the retail park has been driven, in the main, by retailers' response to consumer demand. Thus, the early free-standing facilities, though cheap, lacked the variety of merchandise provided by the agglomerated, second-phase parks such as Swansea Enterprise Zone or, indeed, the Abbey Trading Centre. However, these in turn are beset by problems associated with their unplanned, uncoordinated layout – notably traffic congestion, which has given rise to the latest generation of carefully integrated 'user-friendly' retail parks (e.g. West Thurrock,

Retail World). True, several other factors including the availability of low-cost land in suburban locations, the bulky nature of the goods sold in retail warehouses, and the changing attitudes of both town planning authorities and funding institutions, have contributed to the emergence of the retail park [Gibbs, 1987; Schiller, 1988], yet it is arguable that the *evolution* of this retailing innovation is, ultimately, driven by consumer demand.

CONCLUSION

The retail park is an increasingly important element of the British urban retailing system, more so, arguably, than the headline-grabbing mega-scale schemes of 1 million sq. ft. plus. Despite their ubiquity, relatively little is known about consumer perceptions and usage of this novel form of retailing. This article has examined the functioning of an unplanned retail park, the Abbey Trading Centre, on the outskirts of Belfast. A face-to-face survey of 688 shoppers revealed that, as in Swansea, Leeds and Leicester, the complex was patronised by middle-class family groups of (largely) one-stop shoppers. Furthermore, a functional dichotomy, in terms of frequency of visit, distance travelled and gender of respondent, was evident between the convenience-orientated district centre and the non-food retail warehouses. The perceived advantages and disadvantages of shopping in the retail park were also explored, and it appeared that the wide choice of retail outlets brought together in the unplanned retail park was offset by the attendant traffic congestion. It was argued that these factors help to explain, albeit tentatively, the evolution of innovative retailing forms.

NOTE

1. The vacant unit has since been occupied by General George (carpets).

REFERENCES

Bernard Thorpe and Partners, 1985, *Retail Warehouse Parks: An Approach to Planned Development*, London: Bernard Thorpe.

Bromley, R.D.F. and C.J. Thomas, 1987, *Retail Parks, Enterprise Zone Policy and Retail Planning: A Case Study of the Swansea Enterprise Zone Retail Park*, SEREN, University College of Swansea.

Brown, S., 1987, 'Institutional Change in Retailing: A Review and Synthesis', *European Journal of Marketing*, Vol. 21, No. 6.

Brown, S., 1988, 'Retailing Change: Cycles and Strategy', *Quarterly Review of Marketing*, Vol. 13, No. 3.

Building Design Partnership (1969), *Belfast Urban Area Plan*, Belfast: BDP.

Cochrane, W., 1986, 'Sour Taste at the Edge of the Doughnut', *Financial Times*, Saturday, 18 October, p.9.

Cochrane, W. and E. Howard, 1987, 'Retail Change on Tyneside and the Early Effects of the Metro Centre', in *Retail Planning and Development*, PTRC, P298, London.

Gibbs, A., 1985, 'Planners and Retail Innovation', *The Planner*, Vol. 71, No. 5.

Gibbs, A., 1987, Retail Warehouses: Development Pressure and the Planning Response', *Estates Gazette*, 284 (6358), pp. 588–9, 596.

Hillier Parker, 1988a, *British Shopping Developments, 1987 Supplement*, London: Hillier Parker, May and Rowden.

Hillier Parker, 1988b, *Shopping Schemes in the Pipeline, May 1988*, London: Hillier Parker, May and Rowden.

Johnston, B., 1987, 'Megacentre Madness', *Housing and Planning Review*, Vol. 42, No. 3.

Leicester City Council, 1988, 'Trading Patterns of Retail Warehouses in Leicester', Leicester: City Planning Department.

Schiller, R., 1987, 'Out-of-Town Exodus', in E. McFadyen (ed.), *The Changing Face of British Retailing*, London: Newman Books.

Schiller, R. 1988, 'Quality Going Out of Town', *Town and Country Planning*, Vol. 57, No. 6.

Shaw, G., 1987, 'Shopping Centre Developments in Small Town Environments', paper presented at UGSG Conference, May 1987.

This chapter first appeared in *The Service Industries Journal*, Vol.10, No.2 (1990).

9

Tenant Mix, Tenant Placement and Shopper Behaviour in a Planned Shopping Centre

STEPHEN BROWN

*The planned shopping centre is one of the most widely studied re-
tailing phenomena, yet comparatively little empirical research
has addressed the issue of tenant placement, the relative location
of retail outlets within centres. In an attempt to increase our
understanding of placement issues and the behaviour of shoppers
within centres, a week-long observation study of 250 shopping
groups was undertaken in a suburban district centre. Amongst
other things, this reveals that shopper circulation tends to be
limited to a small section of the mall. In addition, the key,
customer-attracting role of the magnet stores is highlighted, as
are the benefits to be gained from locating compatible outlets in
close spatial proximity. The implications of the findings for
tenant placement in general and the surveyed centre in particular
are discussed and the important social side of the shopping centre
'experience' is explored.*

Recently described as 'the secular cathedrals of the late twentieth
century, dedicated to the twin gods of commerce and profit' [Gardner
and Sheppard, 1989: 97], shopping centres rank among the most re-
vered, reviled and indeed researched retailing phenomena of our time.
An enormous number of words have been processed and paper con-
sumed by commentators on the development [Gayler, 1984; Morgan
and Walker, 1988], planning [Davies, 1984; Schiller, 1985], management
[Martin, 1982; McKenna, 1985], impact [Guy, 1987; Howard, 1989], evolution [Brown, 1989a; Rogers, 1990], aesthetics [Maitland, 1985; Scott,
1989] and almost every other feature of this particular retailing institution [for example, Dawson, 1983; Casazza and Spink, 1985].

Surprisingly, however, the issue of tenant mix – the combination of
retail establishments occupying space in the centre – has generated comparatively little published research. It has of course frequently been
asserted that the mix of tenants is the single most important determinant

of a shopping centre's success or failure [NEDO, 1971; Tindale, 1980; Beddington, 1982; Abratt *et al.*, 1985; Lewis, 1987]. What is more, the concept of a carefully controlled tenant mix can be dated back to the opening of the New Exchange in London in 1609 [Davis, 1966]. Yet it is arguable that almost four hundred years after the New Exchange, tenant mix remains not only one of the most important aspects of shopping centre development but also one of those about which least is known [Northern and Haskoll, 1977; Sim and Way, 1989].

TENANT MIX CONSIDERATIONS

According to Dawson [1983], tenant mix considerations revolve around two major questions: the number, nature and size of the outlets within the centre; and, the placement of these outlets relative to each other and the points of entry into the complex. Although both of these issues are crucial, the former has been simplified in recent years through the availability of sophisticated databases, such as those of Chas. Goad and the Data Consultancy. By quantifying the extent of retail under- and over-provision in a given catchment area, these facilitate the identification of an appropriate assemblage of tenants, be it for a festival mall, retail warehouse park or traditional town centre shopping complex. True, this 'optimum' mix is usually subject to substantial subsequent modification thanks to the intercession of the funding institutions, the demands of the magnet stores, the availability of tenants and the overall state of the property market [see Dawson, 1983; Lewis, 1987; Morgan and Walker, 1988]. Nevertheless, the formulation of an inventory of apposite tenants is a much less onerous and subjective task than previously.

Just as the difficult decisions concerning the number and nature of centre occupants have been expedited by the technological advances of recent years, so too our appreciation of the significance and subtleties of tenant placement has increased substantially. Despite the restrictions inherent in the provision of the Landlord and Tenant Act and the relative paucity of turnover rental arrangements, which facilitate tenant mix adjustments, the traditional 'come as you please' approach to the selection and placement of centre occupants has been largely superseded of late, though the current plight of the retail property market will undoubtedly test developers' determination to wait for the right tenants rather than resort to space-filling tactics [Morgan and Walker, 1988; Walsh, 1989; Goddard and Smith, 1990; Peters, 1990].

Although awareness of the importance and nuances of tenant placement has increased significantly, the science of space management is still very much in its infancy. Whereas issues like centre impact, design and, increasingly, tenant composition are conceptually, technologically and methodologically well established, the intra-centre location of outlets remains heavily reliant upon the 'received wisdom' of the shopping centre industry. This comprises such well-known rules of thumb as: place the magnet stores at opposite ends of the mall and line the intervening space with smaller outlets; ensure that the main entrances and anchor stores are sufficiently far apart to pull shoppers past the unit shops; avoid culs-de-sac if possible as they inhibit the free flow of customers; place service outlets on the side malls close to the entrances and exits; keep pet shops and dry cleaners away from food shops, and food shops separate from outfitters; and, achieve an even distribution of shoppers in multi-level centres through judicious placement of escalators and eating facilities and the manipulation of the floor at which shoppers enter the complex [Gruen, 1973; Beddington, 1982; Abratt et al., 1985; Lewis, 1987; Sim and Way, 1989].

Useful though the above dicta proved in the past, they are in danger of being elevated, on the basis of relatively little published research, into unbreakable shopping centre axioms. They are thus inimical to imaginative tenant placement, subject to fashion effects and, inevitably, give rise to sterile and specious debate. The provision and location of restaurants, for example, was once deemed relatively unimportant by British shopping centre developers [Capital and Counties, 1969; Greenbury, 1974]. Today, however, the first-floor food court is as much a shopping centre cliché as the atrium, the water feature and the glass-sided wall-climber lift.

Likewise, there has long been a debate over the efficacy of placing similar types of outlet, such as fashion or food retailers, in close spatial proximity within the centre. The influential Capital and Counties and NEDO reports of 1970 and 1971 respectively, recommended separating similar shop types in order to maximise shopper movement within, and exposure to the wares of, the centre. Jones [1970] and Darlow [1972], on the other hand, endorsed the clustering of compatible shop types in order to ease the shoppers' task and enable certain areas of the centre to become magnets in their own right. A zonal compromise between the two extremes has also been suggested [Orchard-Lislie, 1980] and this appears to be the preferred approach at present, at least in the larger schemes like Metrocentre, Meadowhall and Merry Hill. Without the reassurance of empirical research, however, the current fashion for themed areas may well go the way of the subterranean lighting, glycerine waterfalls and fibreglass sculptures of the Arndale centres of old.

RESEARCH ISSUES

One of the major reasons for the continuing reliance upon time-honoured 'principles' of tenant placement (besides, of course, the fact that much proprietary research remains unpublished), is the sheer difficulty of conducting empirical research in this area. Questionnaire surveys of shoppers, though easily mounted, are highly unreliable as the methodology is incapable of revealing the subtleties of the spatial pattern of shopper behaviour within the centre. This technique, furthermore, relies upon respondents' notoriously unreliable ability to recall their shopping experiences. A recent comparison of observed and reported consumer behaviour, for example, revealed that less than half the retail outlets entered in a shopping centre were subsequently recalled by the individuals concerned, even though the interview was conducted within minutes of the conclusion of the shopping episode [Brown, 1989b].

Research techniques that do not depend upon the frailties of human memory, most notably observation exercises, are an obvious alternative. But these in turn are fraught with difficulty. Pedestrian counts, though useful and widely employed to examine the pattern of shopper circulation and reveal the existence of 'dead spots' within the centre [for example, Sim and Way, 1989], suffer from the fact that they only record gross flows and not the behaviour of individual shoppers and shopping groups. Similarly, participant observation, whereby shoppers are accompanied by researchers and a concurrent 'protocol' of the behaviour constructed, is encumbered by respondents' inability to articulate fully their ongoing mental processes and, moreover, the behavioural distortions that inevitably ensue when a third party is present. It has long been recognised that the presence of an observer results in a modification of the behaviour of those under scrutiny [Webb et al., 1966; Alt, 1980; East, 1990].

Unobtrusive observation or 'tracking' studies, where the shopper is unaware of the observer, present yet another possibility though this approach is no less problematical than pedestrian counts and participant protocols. Whether based on human or mechanical (photographs, video, etc.) recording instruments, unobtrusive observation exercises tend to be time consuming, expensive to mount, difficult to analyse and, ultimately, only capable of revealing *what* people do, not their *reasons* for so doing. The ethics of observing an individual's behaviour, without their knowledge or prior consent, are also questionable [Finn, 1989], though it should be stressed that such studies are permissable under the code of practice of the Market Research Society. This states that un-

FIGURE 1
THE ABBEYCENTRE, USE OF FLOORSPACE

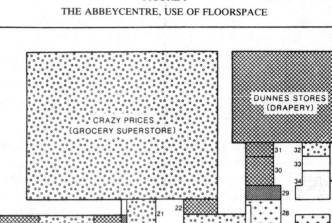
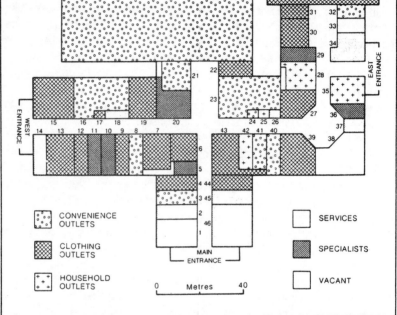

obtrusive observation is allowed provided the subjects are in an environment (a shop, airport or other public space, for instance) where they can reasonably expect to be observed [MRS, 1989].

Despite the difficult methodological issues and, moreover, moral dilemmas surrounding the use of the unobtrusive observation research technique, it provides the only *practical* method of assessing intra-centre shopper behaviour. As tenant placement is ultimately dependent upon shopper behaviour and shopper behaviour upon tenant placement, the necessity for observation exercises cannot be gainsaid. Indeed, several prominent commentators at a recent retailing conference (including Dennis Cassidy and Robb Hamson of Gillow and House of Fraser respectively) concluded that the biggest single weakness of shopping centre layout and design was the overall lack of thought given to the movement and behaviour of shoppers [McColl, 1989]. If the principles of intra-centre retail location are to be empirically established, therefore, observation surveys of shopper behaviour are vitally necessary.

RESEARCH DESIGN

In an attempt to increase our understanding of the nature of shopper behaviour within shopping centres and, hence, the implications for tenant placement principles, a week-long observation study was conducted in the Abbeycentre, a substantial district centre in the northern suburbs of Belfast. Opened in 1978, extended to its present size two years later and refurbished at a cost of £1 million in 1987, the Abbeycentre totals 180,000 sq. ft. of gross retail floorspace. This is occupied by two anchor stores, Crazy Prices (grocery) and Dunnes Stores (drapery), and 44 unit shops comprising 8 convenience outlets, 15 outfitters, 5 household goods retailers, 7 specialists and 9 service facilities including a bank, building society and two restaurants (Figure 1). A ring of retail warehouses, totalling 250,000 sq. ft. of gross retail floorspace, has developed in an incremental fashion on land adjacent to the centre, making it one of the largest concentrations of retailing facilities in Northern Ireland. Indeed, with its 1,000 car parking spaces, 312 metres of covered, air conditioned malls and three late night openings per week, the Abbeycentre has proved enormously successful, attracting approximately 80,000 shoppers per week and up to 110,000 at peak trading periods.

From the perspective of this article, however, perhaps the most interesting feature of the Abbeycentre is the spatial arrangement of its retailing occupants. Although the tenant mix typifies the traditional 'come as you please' approach to space management, albeit with the magnets spatially separated, several groupings of compatible retail outlets have evolved over the years. As Figure 1 illustrates, an agglomeration of ladies fashions and fashion related retailers is evident adjacent to the Dunnes Stores drapery magnet. Clusters of convenience outlets and male orientated establishments straddle the eastern and western malls respectively and a concentration of retail services surrounds the main entrance. However, as the bulk of the occupants have been located with little thought to the influence of propinquity, the Abbeycentre provides an opportunity to compare the 'cluster' and 'separate' (or, 'match' and 'mix') approaches to tenant placement.

The observation exercise was conducted in March 1988, prior to the onset of the Easter rush, by final year Business Studies students at the University of Ulster. A systematic sample of shoppers was un-

TABLE 1

GROUP COMPOSITION AND TIME EXPENDED

Group Composition	N	%	Time Expended
Adult male only	17	7.8	27.5 minutes
Adult female only	85	39.2	52.6 minutes
Adult male and children	2	0.9	27.0 minutes
Adult female and children	33	15.2	62.9 minutes
Adult male and female	60	27.6	51.1 minutes
Adult male, female and children	20	9.2	65.0 minutes
Total	217	100.0	52.7 minutes

obtrusively observed from their time of entry to their time of departure and the information recorded included time elapsed, shops entered, purchases made, window-shopping behaviour, non-shopping activities and the size and composition of the shopper group. Circulation patterns were also traced on a base map of the centre. A total of 250 shopper groups were observed over an entire trading week from Monday morning to Saturday evening, including three late nights. Strictly speaking, this number of shopping episodes represents a relatively small sample size (with a confidence limit of + 6.2 per cent at the 95 per cent level), but in terms of observation exercises, which necessitate substantial inputs of observer time for each behavioural record, 250 is considered an unusually large sample. Indeed, had the same amount of time been devoted to 'traditional' face-to-face interviewing, the sample size would have been in the order of 3,000 respondents.

RESULTS

Of the 250 shopper groups observed, 8 were not in the centre to shop (members of staff on breaks, sales reps, etc.) and a further 25 were either lost in the course of the exercise or their observation record was incomplete. These groups were excluded from the analysis and thus the results presented below refer to 217 shopping groups, comprising 436 people.

Group Size and Time Expended

The mean size of the observed shopper groups was 2.0 people, though it ranged from as many as six individuals to solitary shoppers. The composition of the groups was equally variable. Adult females formed the single largest category with 39.2 per cent of the total. Another 42.8 per cent of the groups comprised either adult males and females, or adult females and children. The remainder were made up of family groups of adult males, females and children, adult males only, or, on very rare occasions, adult males and children (Table 1).

Just as group composition exhibited considerable variation, so too did the amount of time expended in the centre. This ranged from as little as one minute to two and a half hours, with an average of 52.7 minutes. Indeed, a clear relationship between group size and composition and total time expended can also be discerned. Broadly speaking, the larger the group the longer the visit. Single person groups spent 38.3 minutes on average, two person groups averaged 55.0 minutes and groups comprising three or more persons spent 66.9 minutes on average in the centre. Likewise, the shopping expeditions of groups that contained children tended to be considerably longer than the norm (62.4 mins), whereas those with men were just the opposite (49.3 mins). In fact, the typical male only shopping trip took less than 30 minutes (Table 1).

As might be anticipated, the observation study revealed substantial variations in the amount of time spent in the individual retail outlets. The magnet stores, Crazy Prices and Dunnes, averaged 33.9 and 14.4 minutes respectively, while visits to the unit shops averaged 5.5 minutes. Differences, moreover, are discernible from trade to trade and outlet to outlet, though sample sizes are quite small in some cases of the latter. Not unexpectedly given the nature of their business, service outlets in general (14.5 mins) and restaurants in particular (19.4 mins) enjoyed especially lengthy customer stays. Convenience outlets, on the other hand, turned around the typical customer in a fraction over four minutes, as did the majority of comparison retailers – albeit for different reasons (see below).

However, perhaps the most interesting revelation of the observation exercise was the fact that in an average 50-minute shopping visit to the Abbeycentre, no less than 20 per cent of the total time was spent not in the shops but in the malls. Much of this time admittedly was devoted to the simple physical act of walking from one shop to another. Yet a surprising amount of non-ambulatory activity also took place. This ranged from indulging children's desire to ride the centre's selection of mechanised fauna to queuing for the autobank and, at peak times, the restaurants. But most prominent in this respect was window shopping. Almost 60 per cent of the groups indulged in some form of window shopping, though, as many retailers do not possess display windows, this behaviour tended to concentrate on certain outlets. Needless to say, Ratners the jeweller, Trueform shoes and Chinacraft (which had an attractive display of glass and crystal housewares) proved especially popular with the window shopping fraternity.

TABLE 2

TENANT MIX, SHOP TYPE AND PATRONISATION BEHAVIOUR

Unit Number[1]	Shop Name	Shop Type	ENTER %	ENTER Rank	BUY %	BUY Rank	Enter-Buy Ratio[2]
—	Crazy prices	Grocery	46.1	1	45.2	1	.98
—	Dunnes Stores	Drapery	41.5	2	22.1	3	.53
1	Northern	Bank	0.5	45	0.5	41	1.00
2	Peter Mark	Hairstylist	0.9	43	0.9	32	1.00
3	Countryscene	Fruitshop	18.4	7	16.6	5	.90
4	Roundabout	Ladieswear	12.9	13	2.3	21	.18
5	Uneeda	Records	3.7	36	1.4	27	.37
6	Chicago	Ladieswear	13.4	11	1.4	27	.10
7	Fosters	Menswear	4.1	33	1.4	27	.33
8	Winemark	Off-Licence	6.9	25	4.6	10	.67
9	Centre-man	Menswear	2.3	40	0.0	44	.00
10	Autospares	Car Accessories	5.1	31	2.3	21	.45
11	Body Shop	Cosmetics	8.3	22	6.0	14	.72
12	Sting	Meanswear	3.2	37	0.9	32	0.29
13	Saxone	Shoeshop	5.1	31	0.5	41	.09
14	Leeds	Building Society	1.4	42	1.4	27	1.00
15	Dorothy Perkins	Ladieswear	19.8	5	3.2	19	.16
16	Boots	Chemist	25.3	4	18.9	4	.75
17	Tie Rack	Menswear	3.2	37	1.4	27	.43
18	Motorway	Insurance	0.9	43	0.9	32	1.00
19	LQ Shop	Menswear	6.0	27	0.9	32	.15
20	Ratners	Jewellers	7.8	17	2.3	21	.29
21	Logans	Chemist	13.8	10	8.7	10	
22	Exhibit	Ladieswear	5.5	29	0.9	32	.17
23	NPO	Stationers	35.0	3	24.0	2	.68
24	Scoop	Confectioners	6.9	25	6.9	12	1.00
25	Dacora	Window Blinds	0.5	45	0.0	44	0.00
26	Mr Minit	Cobblers	4.1	33	4.1	16	1.00
27	Chelsea Girl	Ladieswear	12.0	15	2.3	21	.19
28	Harry Corry	Textiles	10.1	18	0.9	32	.09
29	Abbeytat	Cards/Gifts	17.5	8	9.7	9	.55
30	Square One	Ladieswear	15.2	9	0.9	32	.06
31	Miselle	Ladieswear	7.4	23	0.5	41	.06
32	Options	Chemist	10.1	18	10.1	8	1.00
33	Vacant	—	—	—	—	—	—
34	Bumpers	Restaurant	10.1	18	10.1	8	1.00
35	Chinacraft	Housewares	6.0	27	0.9	32	.15
36	Playtime	Toys	5.5	29	2.3	21	.42
37	Contact	Travel Agent	2.8	39	0.0	44	0.00
38	Vacant	—	—	—	—	—	—
39	Pricewise	Ladieswear	18.9	6	6.5	13	.34
40	O'Haras	Bakery	12.9	13	11.5	6	.89
41	Nicholl	Butchers	8.8	231	7.8	11	.89
42	Radio Rentals	T.V. Hire	1.8	41	0.9	32	.50
43	Trueform	Shoeshop	13.4	11	3.2	19	.24
44	Harry Corry	Drapery	11.5	17	2.3	21	.20
45	Cleanland	Dry Cleaner	4.1	33	4.1	16	1.00
46	Skandia	Restaurant	12.0	15	11.0	7	.92

Notes:
1. Refer to Figure 1.
2. Proportion of shop entrants who made purchases therein.

Socialisation proved to be another particularly common form of non-circulation behaviour. Approximately one quarter of the groups under observation stopped to socialise with other (non-group) shoppers at some stage during their visit. When this is added to the (unobserved) in-store socialisation and the numerous salutations and brief acknowledgements of acquaintances that also occurred during the visit, it provides overwhelming evidence of the important, if often overlooked, social and recreational side of consumer behaviour [see, for example, Bellenger and Korgoankar, 1980].

Judging from the observation exercise, the Abbeycentre clearly functions as a meeting place, an environment to see and be seen, and a locale for social interchange and the reinforcement of personal networks.

Shop Visits

As was the case with group size and time spent in the centre, the number of shops visited varied from group to group. It ranged from none to more than twenty, though the majority of visits comprised five shops or fewer. Not unexpectedly, a strong and statistically significant relationship between the number of shops entered and time expended is discernible. Visits to two shops or less took 26.5 minutes on average, whereas some 94.4 minutes was expended by visitors to ten or more stores.

When the pattern of shop visits is examined, the key role of the magnet stores and the 'secondary attractors' becomes apparent. Over 45 per cent of the shopping groups patronised the Crazy Prices superstore and 41.5 per cent Dunnes Stores. Moreover, more than a third of the subjects entered NPO, the newsagent-stationery, and Boots the Chemist attracted just over one quarter of those observed. The most infrequently visited outlets, on the other hand, were the service trades – banks, building society, insurance brokers, travel agent, hairdressers, etc. – none of which attracted more than 5 per cent of those under scrutiny (Table 2).

In addition to noting the outlets entered by the shopping groups, the observers were instructed to record the establishments in which purchases were made. Despite some understandable concerns over the possibility of drawing shoppers' attention to the survey exercise, the task proved remarkably straightforward. The shopping groups had no idea that they were under observation and the recording of in-store purchasing behaviour posed few methodological problems. The results reveal that purchases were made in 2.6 outlets on average, though, as Table 2 indicates, the rankings of individual retailers change considerably when purchasing – as opposed to visiting – behaviour becomes the focus of attention. Dunnes Stores and Dorothy Perkins, for example, slipped from second and fifth to third and seventh places in the rankings respectively. Pricewise (cut price clothing) fell from sixth to thirteenth, Trueform Shoes from eleventh to nineteenth and Harry Corry (household textiles) from eighteenth to thirty-second. NPO, by contrast, took over second place, Countryscene, the fruit and vegetable shop, rose from seventh to fifth, O'Hara's home bakery moved from thirteenth to sixth and Winemark, the off-licence, jumped ten places to fifteenth.

As a rule, the falls tended to be concentrated among retailers of comparison goods and rises among the convenience outlets. This corroborates the frequently drawn contrast between the shopping behaviours associated with these two categories of merchandise. Comparison goods shopping is relatively infrequent and necessitates extensive information gathering ('shopping around') before purchase, whereas convenience shopping is a regular act requiring relatively little forethought or information seeking. Indeed, this also helps explain the surprisingly short visits (referred to earlier) that appear to characterise comparison goods retailers. In the main, purchasers spend considerably longer in these types of outlet than information gatherers, though as the latter are much more numerous than the former, the average stay tends to be of a comparatively short duration.

The foregoing distinction is reinforced when the enter-buy ratios (that is, the proportion of people entering a shop who actually make purchases) of the various establishments are examined (Table 2). The enter-buy ratio of convenience retailers was 0.80 and that of comparison outlets 0.29, though this ranged from 0.09 for soft furnishings to 0.67 for the Body Shop. Interestingly, the highest enter-buy ratios of all were recorded for the service trades (0.90). These visits, admittedly, were few in number but, with the exception of the travel agency, they almost always resulted in a sales transaction. However, as few but fetishists feel compelled to browse in a cobblers, insurance brokers or dry cleaners, this finding pretty much accords with expectations.

Although the analysis of shop visits indicates sharp contrasts in the behaviour associated with the various categories of outlet, it must be emphasised that the vast majority of visits involved a combination of shop types (Table 3). Only 16 per cent of the observed shopping trips were confined to convenience retailers, a further 7 per cent were devoted solely to purveyors of comparison goods and less than 3 per cent were dedicated to the acquisition of retail services. Even when purchasing activities alone are examined, the majority of trips involved purchases in a combination of shop types. Thus although convenience shopping remains very much the 'engine' of the Abbeycentre, the classic convenience-comparison dichotomy – beloved by town planners in particular – is less clear cut than commonly supposed. Indeed, when the evidence of widespread window shopping is also borne in mind, it appears that consumers take the opportunity afforded by routine shopping activities to gather information about and, moreover, consummate the buying process for comparison type merchandise.

Shopper Circulation

By modern UK standards (for example, Metrocentre, Meadowhall) the Abbeycentre must be considered a relatively small out-of-town shopping complex. Yet the observation exercise demonstrated that, even in this 180,000 sq. ft. district centre, the circulation patterns of shoppers were decidedly circumscribed. Only 11 per cent of the groups under scrutiny circulated throughout the entire shopping centre -that is, in each of the eight 'natural' subdivisions of the mall[1] – and approximately one-third confined their movements to less than half the available circulation space. The degree of confinement is all the more pronounced when shop entering and purchasing behaviour is considered. Two-thirds of the shopper groups entered outlets, and more than 90 per cent of the purchases were made, in three or fewer sections of the mall (Figure 2).

In addition to revealing the relatively limited 'ranges' of the observed shopper groups, the survey highlighted marked variations in pedestrian flow and behaviour patterns. As might be anticipated, the most heavily trafficked spot (the section of mall visited by the greatest number of shopper groups) was the 'crossroads' where the main east-west and

TABLE 3
SHOP TYPES ENTERED AND PURCHASING BEHAVIOUR

Shop Types	Enter		Purchase	
	N	%	N	%
Convenience outlets only	34	15.7	76	35.0
Comparison outlets only	14	6.5	14	6.5
Service outlets only	6	2.8	10	4.6
Convenience and comparison outlets	99	45.6	53	24.4
Convenience and service outlets	6	2.8	15	6.9
Comparison and service outlets	13	6.0	16	7.4
Convenience, comparison and service outlets	45	20.7	24	11.1
No purchase	–	–	9	4.1
Total	217	100.0	217	100.0

FIGURE 2

ABBEYCENTRE: SHOPPER CIRCULATION AND BEHAVIOUR

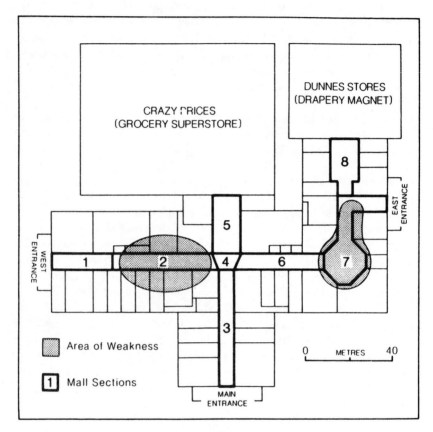

TABLE 4

SHOPPER CIRCULATION BEHAVIOUR

Mall-Sections[1]	Pass-Ratio[2]	Pass-Enter Ratio[3]	Pass-Buy Ratio[4]
Mall section 1	.55	.76	.51
Mall section 2	.63	.42	.20
Mall section 3	.61	.75	.53
Mall section 4	.89	N/A	N/A
Mall section 5	.58	.98	.88
Mall section 6	.73	.61	.47
Mall section 7	.73	.54	.17
Mall section 8	.53	.98	.62

Notes: 1. For an illustration of the mall sub-divisions, see Figure 2.
2. The proportion of shopping groups passing through this section of mall.
3. Shop entrants as a proportion of passers-by.
4. Purchasers as a proportion of passers-by.

north-south malls intersect. More surprisingly perhaps, the culs-de-sac in front of Dunnes Stores and Crazy Prices ranked among the least popular areas of the centre, with a circulation or 'pass' ratio (the proportion of shoppers who passed through that section of mall) of only 0.53 and 0.59 respectively. However, as the vast majority of these shoppers not only entered but made purchases in the outlets therein, these particular sections of mall must be considered the 'killing grounds' of the Abbeycentre.

If the magnet store courtyards were characterised by a low pass ratio but enjoyed a correspondingly high pass-enter ratio, the reverse is the

FIGURE 3

ABBEYCENTRE OBSERVATION STUDY: COMPATIBILITY TABLES

ALL RETAILERS

	Similar Shop Type	Dissimilar Shop Type
Spatially Proximate	138.9	102.2
Spatially Separate	115.8	82.7

CONVENIENCE RETAILERS

	Similar Shop Type	Dissimilar Shop Type
Spatially Proximate	273.8	93.0
Spatially Separate	169.5	73.9

COMPARISON RETAILERS

	Similar Shop Type	Dissimilar Shop Type
Spatially Proximate	126.8	94.2
Spatially Separate	105.5	86.0

RETAIL SERVICES

	Similar Shop Type	Dissimilar Shop Type
Spatially Proximate	44.6	146.3
Spatially Separate	29.8	109.2

case for mall sections seven and two (Figure 2). Here, very high volumes of pedestrian traffic were not being translated into either shop visits or sales. This is indicative of shortcomings in the existing tenant mix and, as rent reviews were imminent, it provided an opportunity to undertake the necessary remedial action. The LQ Shop in mall section two was subsequently replaced by Burton menswear and Olympus Sport superseded Centre Man. In section seven, the vacant unit was let to Adams childrenswear and an optician substituted for Playtime.

The observation study not only exposed areas of overall underperformance in the Abbeycentre but it also provided insights into the detailed patterns of customer movement from shop to shop. Clearly, an enormous number of outlet to outlet combinations exist, many of which are null. Not a single shopper, for example, visited both Tie Rack and Body Shop in the course of their visit, even though the outlets are directly across the mall from each other. By contrast, almost 40 per cent of the customers of Crazy Prices also paid a visit to the newsagent-stationers and over 70 per cent of shoppers in Square One took the opportunity to drop into Dunnes Stores, the adjacent drapery anchor.

However, when all the customer linkages between all the outlets are collapsed into a single compatibility table (where an index of 100 represents a neutral relationship), one overwhelming conclusion is apparent. By far the strongest links occur when similar types of outlet, such as outfitters or food shops, are found in close proximity.[2] In fact, the extent of customer interchange among compatible, propinquitous establishments is *half as much again* as that between dissimilar, geographically dispersed outlets. Further, it is substantially greater than that between similar, spatially separated shops and contrasting outlet types in close proximity (Figure 3).

Although this finding is a striking confirmation of the 'match' as opposed to 'mix' school of tenant placement, it does not hold for every trade type. As Figure 3 indicates, convenience outlets and comparison goods retailers appear to benefit substantially from propinquity. Service establishments, on the other hand, do not possess a positive compatibility index. If anything, they seem to enjoy a greater degree of customer interchange when located adjacent to dissimilar shop types.

Somewhat surprisingly perhaps, Figure 3 also suggests that convenience retailers benefit more from proximity than their comparison goods counterparts. As noted earlier, comparison goods are usually held to involve extensive shopping around, while convenience goods are routine, low involvement purchases. Thus, in theory at least, spatial proximity should have a greater influence on the former than the latter. This counter-intuitive finding, however, is largely due to the crudeness of the classificatory procedure which brackets (say) Chelsea Girl and Radio Rentals within the same broad 'comparison' category. Indeed, more detailed analysis reveals that the highest compatibility index of all is recorded by clusters of clothing retailers. Similarly, the astonishing compatability index of the Abbeycentre's convenience outlets is largely attributable to the fact that this component of the tenant mix comprises non-competitive convenience retailers (that is, a butchers and green-grocers as compared to two butchers).

Irrespective of the taxonomic fineries, the fact of the matter is that, with the exception of the service trades, similar types of retail outlet experience higher levels of customer interchange when located close to one another than when spatially separated. In terms of tenant placement in the Abbeycentre, therefore, this truism indicates: first, that Exhibit, the ladies outfitter adjacent to Crazy Prices, would benefit from relocation to the fashion agglomeration beside Dunnes Stores; second, that either the off-licence or the greengrocers should be moved to the unit vacated by Exhibit; and, third, an attempt should be made to break up the service 'ghetto' athwart the main entrance. The Abbeycentre, admittedly, is a highly successful shopping complex and doubtless each of the forgoing outlets achieves a satisfactory return. However, insofar as the interchange of customers can be considered a surrogate for sales potential, the suggested adjustments could enhance the functioning of the centre in general and the relocated establishments in particular. It must be acknowledged, however, that tenant mix manipulation is less readily achieved in practice than in the conclusions of a research exercise.

DISCUSSION

Although it produced some pertinent and actionable findings and represents an attempt to address hitherto neglected research issues, the results of the Abbeycentre study should be treated with due caution. Care must always be taken when generalising from the conclusions of a single research exercise. A similar observation survey undertaken at a different time of year or in another centre with an alternative mix of tenants may well have given rise to a constrasting set of results. What is more, although the Abbeycentre is a fairly typical out-of-centre district centre, one cannot be certain that the same findings would emerge from analyses of the manifold variations on the shopping centre theme (festival malls, mega-centres, etc.).

Despite the undoubted limitations of the Abbeycentre exercise and notwithstanding the need for additional research on the nature of shopper behaviour and tenant placement within planned centres, it is nevertheless possible to draw some general lessons from the above observation study. Although hardly an earth-shattering revelation, the findings highlighted the key, customer-generating role of the magnet stores and secondary attractors. The location of these outlets relative to each other and the points of entry are thus crucial. By the same token, however, the survey demonstrated that, even in a modestly-sized district centre, the vast majority of shopper groups confined their movements to a comparatively small part of the mall. Indeed, as only 14 per cent of the observed groups visited both magnet stores (bearing in mind that the bulk of shopping expeditions involved a combination of merchandise categories) the rule would appear to be: keep the magnets apart but not too far apart.

Closely related to shoppers' reluctance to exert themselves was the dramatic evidence of the advantages that accrue from placing compatible outlets in close proximity. Whether it be convenience outlets, fashion retailers or purveyors of household goods, the Abbeycentre observation study clearly demonstrates that the volume of customer interchange is vastly increased when a 'match' rather than a 'mix' approach to tenant placement is adopted. The principal exception to the compatibility rule, however, is the retail service sector and, in this respect, the results of the survey run counter to the shopping centre saw which maintains that service outlets should be placed in the side malls close to the entrances. The logic behind this long-standing rule of thumb is that visits to these types of establishment tend to be purposeful and hurried, and customer convenience is maximised by a peripheral, side mall location. The Abbeycentre study, however, revealed very little evidence of this type of behaviour and, if anything, the findings indicate that the formation of service ghettos in side malls is inimical to the functioning of shopping centres. Accordingly, a 'mix' approach to service placement would appear to be best practice, though as a substantial number of the groups under observation visited both the Abbeycentre's (widely separated) restaurants, catering services should arguably be exempt from this conclusion. In fact, the advent of the much-vaunted food court, albeit in danger of degenerating into a shopping centre cliché, would seem to corroborate this conclusion concerning catering services.

If the service placement dictum was debunked somewhat by the observation survey, the same cannot be said for another of the golden rules of shopping centre design – that culs-de-sac should be avoided if possible. There is no doubt that the courtyards in front of Crazy Prices and Dunnes Stores enjoyed much lower pedestrian flows than the other sections of mall. By the same token, however, the outlets in these areas proved more than capable of converting passers by into purchasers. One can infer, therefore, that if culs–de-sac cannot be avoided steps should be taken to ensure that very strong tenants, ideally the anchor stores, are located therein.

Besides tenant placement considerations, the observation survey also highlighted the importance of non-shopping behaviour within shopping centres. Almost 20 per cent of shoppers' time in the complex was expended in the malls rather than the retail outlets. A great deal of this time, moreover, was devoted to renewing acquaintances, entertaining accompanying children and simply watching the world go by. In the past, these forms of non-transactional behaviour have been anathema to shopping centre management and steps have often been taken to reduce 'loitering' activities. Shopping centre seating, for example, has traditionally been designed to be sufficiently uncomfortable to deter all but the most fleshy or masochistic of individuals. The Abbeycentre survey, however, indicates that non-transactional behaviour forms an integral part of the shopping 'experience' and it should arguably be encouraged rather than merely tolerated by shopping centre management. Where possible indeed, it should enhanced through imaginative shopping centre design.

CONCLUSION

While few would deny its influence upon the functioning and performance of planned shopping developments, tenant mix in some respects remains the 'dark continent' of shopping centre design. This article represents an attempt to address an important mix-related issue, that of tenant placement. In the week-long observation survey of the behaviour of 250 shopping groups undertaken in the Abbeycentre, a substantial district centre in the northern suburbs of Belfast, it was revealed that the typical two-person shopping group spent approximately 50 minutes in the centre, entered five shops and made purchases in three. The study also highlighted significant weaknesses in the existing tenant mix and the relative locations of the centre's occupants. More importantly perhaps, it demonstrated the key customer generating role of the magnet stores and secondary attractors; quantified the advantages that accrue from adopting a 'match' rather than a 'mix' approach to tenant placement; reinforced the rule of thumb concerning culs-de-sac; and, drew attention to the important, if occasionally overlooked, social and recreational side of the shopping centre 'experience'. Interesting though it was, however, the Abbeycentre observation study represents a small step towards greater understanding of tenant placement issues and intra-centre

shopper behaviour. Additional research in a wider range of shopping
centre environments is vitally necessary.

NOTES

1. Although subjectively defined, these 'natural' subdivisions were quite clear-cut in
   practice. In the western mall, for example, a substantial number of shopper groups
   turned around and retraced their steps when they reached Boots the Chemist. Similarly, it was not unusual to observe shoppers pausing and looking down a side mall,
   as if weighing up the need to venture into it, before moving on elsewhere.
2. For the purposes of this study, 'close proximity' was defined as the two outlets on
   either side of the target retailer and, where appropriate, the equivalent outlets on the
   opposite side of the mall.

REFERENCES

Abratt, R., J. L. C. Fourie and L. F. Pitt, 1985, 'Tenant mix: the key to a Successful Shop-
ping Centre', *Quarterly Review of Marketing*, Vol. 10, No. 3.
Alt, M. B., 1980, 'Consumer Behaviour and Museum Exhibits', in Market Research
Society, *Research in the 1980s*, Brighton: MRS Conference Proceedings.
Beddington N., 1982, *Design for Shopping Centres*, London: Butterworth Scientific.
Bellenger, D. N. and P. K. Korgoankar, 1980, 'Profiling the Recreational Shopper', *Jour-
nal of Retailing*, Vol. 56, No. 3.
Brown, S. (1989a) *Retail Warehouse Parks*, London: Longman.
Brown, S. (1989b), 'Shopper Movement in a Planned Shopping Centre: Movement,
Memory and Methodology', paper presented at ESOMAR conference, Edinburgh.
Capital and Counties, 1969, *Shopping for Pleasure: a Survey of Shopping Centres in North
America*, London: Capital and Counties Property Company.
Capital and Counties, 1970, *Design for Shopping*, London: Capital and Counties Property
Company.
Casazza, J. A. and F. H. Spink, 1985, *Shopping Centre Development Handbook*, Washing-
ton: Urban Land Institute, second edition.
Darlow, C., 1972, *Enclosed Shopping Centres*, London: Architectural Press.
Davies, R. L., 1984, *Retail and Commercial Planning*, London: Croom Helm.
Davis, D., 1966, *A History of Shopping*, London: Routledge and Kegan Paul.
Dawson, J. A., 1983, *Shopping Centre Development*, London: Longman.
East, R., 1990, *Changing Consumer Behaviour*, London: Cassell.
Finn, A., 1989, 'Consumer Acceptance of Unobtrusive Observation in a Shopping
Centre', in P. Bloom *et al.*, (eds.) *Enhancing Knowledge Development in Marketing*,
Chicago: American Marketing Association.
Gardner, C. and J. Sheppard, 1989, *Consuming Passion: the Rise of Retail Culture*,
London: Unwin Hyman.
Gayler, H. J., 1984, *Retail Innovation in Britain: the Problems of Out-of-Town Shopping
Centre Development*, Norwich: Geobooks.
Goddard and Smith Research, 1990, *The Shopping Centre Business*, London: Freeman.
Greenbury, S., 1974, 'Shopping Centres: Are They What the Public Wants?' *Shop
Property*, October.
Guy, C., 1987, 'The Assessment of Retail Impact', *The Planner* Vol. 73, No. 12.
Gruen, V., 1973, *Centres for the Urban Environment: Survival of the Cities*, New York:
Van Nostrand Reinhold.
Howard, E., 1989, *Prospects for Out-of-Town Retailing: the Metro Experience*, London:
Longman.

Jones, C. S., 1970, *Regional Shopping Centres: Their Location, Planning and Design*, London: Business Books.

Lewis, P., 1987, 'Creating That Magical Mix', *Shop Property*, June.

Maitland, B., 1985, *Shopping Malls: Planning and Design*, London: Construction Press.

Market Research Society, 1989, *Code of Conduct*, London: MRS.

Martin, P. G., 1982, *Shopping Centre Management*, London: E. & F. N. Spon.

McColl, S., 1989, 'Shopping Centres: Back to Retail Basics', paper presented at ICSC Conference, Vienna.

McKenna, T., 1985, 'Shopping Centre Management', in Healey and Baker, *Retail Report 1985*, London: Healey and Baker.

Morgan, P., and A. Walker, 1988, *Retail Development*, London: Estates Gazette.

NEDO, 1971, *The Future Pattern of Shopping*, London: National Economic Development Office.

Northen, I. and M. Haskoll, 1977, *Shopping Centres: a Developer's Guide to Planning and Design*, Reading: Centre for Advanced Land Use Studies.

Orchard-Lislie, P. D., 1980, 'Translating the Ideas into Buildings – A Presentation of Current Town Centre Developments', in URPI, *Town Centres of the Future*, Reading: Unit for Retail Planning Information.

Peters, J., 1990, 'Managing Shopping Centre Retailer Mix: Some Considerations for Retailers', *International Journal of Retail and Distribution Management*, Vol. 18, No. 1.

Rogers, D. S., 1990, *Developments in US Retailing*, London: Longman.

Schiller, R., 1985, 'Land Use Controls on UK Shopping Centres', in J. A. Dawson and J. D. Lord (eds.), *Shopping Centre Development: Policies and Prospects*, London: Croom Helm.

Scott, N. K., 1989, *Shopping Centre Design*, London: Van Nostrand Reinhold.

Sim, L. L. and C. R. Way, 1989, 'Tenant Placement in a Singapore Shopping Centre' *International Journal of Retailing*, Vol. 4, No. 3.

Tindale, W., 1980, 'Restictive User Clauses and Tenant Mix', *Shop Property*, March.

Walsh, S., 1989, 'Shopping Centres: Building on Glitz', in Retail Week, *The Retail Decade*, Special Supplement, 15 December.

Webb, E. J., *et al.*, 1966, *Unobtrusive Measures: Nonreactive Research in the Social Sciences*, Chicago: Rand McNally and Co.

This chapter first appeared in *The Service Industries Journal*, Vol.12, No.3 (1992).

10

Elements of a Franchise: The Experiences of Established Firms

JIM FORWARD and CHRISTINA FULOP

Only a small amount of research has been published which directly addresses the alternative operational methods which have been employed by British franchisors. Similarly, the experiences of well-established firms which have chosen to introduce franchising as a method of expansion have received little attention. In this study, representatives of 13 such firms were interviewed. Their responses have been used to illustrate how franchisors' decisions as regards franchisee selection, the establishment of outlets, the setting of fees, the length of franchise contract, and continuing support, differ according to circumstances.

INTRODUCTION

The last 20 years have seen an increase in the use of business format franchising [B.F.A., 1991]. However, there still exists only a small amount of in-depth research into the subject. Probably the most significant difference between franchising and a 'normal' vertically integrated business is that franchisees are involved, rather than company-employed managers [Ralston, 1989].

Hence the British studies that have been carried out have tended to concentrate on the characteristics of franchisees and/or on the nature of the relationship between the franchisor and franchisees [e.g. Stanworth, 1989, 1991; Hough, 1986]. Another issue that has been addressed is the relative independence of franchisees when compared to other small business men or women [e.g. Stanworth, Curran and Hough, 1984; Stanworth, 1989, 1991]. There has been a greater amount of research conducted in North America, generally focusing on co-operation and conflict within franchise relationships [e.g. Sibley and Mitchie, 1982] or on franchising in comparison to fully vertically integrated methods of business [e.g. Rubin, 1978].

Whilst these all represent important areas of research it appears that there has been little effort to investigate the operational alternatives available to companies which take the decision to franchise. The majority of studies touch upon the subject but few have been exclusively dedicated to it. One exception has been the work by Baron and Schmidt [1991]. These authors reported on the experiences of four franchisees and five franchisors as regards the franchise agreement, selection of franchisees, finance and insurance, location of premises, shopfitting, quality of products, advertising and point-of-sale promotions, initial franchisee training, the specific skill requirements of franchisees, and the franchisor's ability to monitor the network and acquire feedback.

This article aims to add to the insight which the work of Baron and Schmidt [1991] has provided by discussing in-depth five main operational issues of a franchise system. The number of issues considered has been deliberately restricted as it is believed that franchising is more heterogenous than might be first thought [Hunt, 1972; Stanworth, 1991]. Whilst successful franchisors follow the same basic principles when developing a business format franchise operation, they actually employ a variety of different methods. An in-depth analysis provides information on the various alternative approaches which franchisors have taken as regards specific operational aspects. The areas which are discussed are franchisee selection, the establishment of outlets, franchise fees, the length of the franchise contract, and the nature of the support provided by the franchisor.

The 13 sample firms in the study were all relatively well established before they entered into franchising. The sample was selected on this basis because it was felt that the development of franchising in the United Kingdom has witnessed a growing acceptance of this business method by large established firms [Churchill, 1991]. Franchising is no longer driven only by small businesses wishing to grow rapidly; large firms are also increasingly using franchising as a method of expansion. Just as there has been little research directed solely at the operational aspects of franchising, there has been virtually none aimed at understanding the experiences of firms which fall into this category. If the future is to witness an increasing number of established firms turning to franchising [Grant, 1985; Brandenberg, 1989] then a better understanding of the different methods which can be employed is likely to be beneficial.

DEFINING FRANCHISING

The term franchising has been applied to a variety of business formats [Hackett, 1977]. To some this is explained by the view that the franchise arrangement has evolved over time. For example, the licence-style arrangements between fuel suppliers and individuals who operated filling stations, which primarily came into existence at the start of this century, are considered to be an early type of franchise arrangement [e.g. Hall and Dixon, 1988]. Alternatively, it is felt that these arrangements were not (and are not) a type of franchise. Rather, the term has been misapplied [Mendelsohn, 1992] and hence confusion has arisen and consequently a precise definition of franchising remains elusive.

One initiative taken to combat this problem has been the introduction of the term 'business format franchise' [Mendelsohn, 1992]. The firms in this study were generally operating under this arrangement, which involves more than the *franchisor* simply granting permission for the *franchisee* to sell the former's branded products or services. The franchisor should also provide a proven method of operating, support and advice on the setting up of the franchisee's business and ongoing support to the franchisee. Invariably, the latter has to pay both an initial fee and some type of ongoing fee to the franchisor. Franchisees invest money in their business, which is legally independent from the franchisor's operation. Hence to some degree the franchisee is his or her 'own boss' [Mathewson and Winter, 1985; Weinrauch, 1986; Stanworth, 1989].

METHODOLOGY

The study took as its population the franchise operations of well-established firms which had decided to introduce franchising as a method of expanding their business operations. The research covered several business sectors, including: retailing; services; fast food; convenience stores; filling stations; and wholesaling. Given this variety, it was felt not to be practical to demand that all the firms approached should have been established for the same specified number of years, nor should they be of a certain size. Judgement was used to decide which firms should be approached and which should not. It became apparent during the interviews that three of the franchise operations had recently gone through a change in ownership, resulting in the severing of formal ties with the 'large firm'. None the less, an attempt was made to concentrate on the large firm related aspects.

Letters were sent to 18 firms requesting an interview. Interviews were arranged with 13 firms. The final sample covered a range of business sectors, including retailing, services and wholesaling. Semi-structured questionnaires were used in the interviews. The questionnaires were constructed on the basis of knowledge gained from franchising literature and discussions with people in the franchising industry. There were three questionnaires, all similar, but tailored so as to be suitable for questioning firms that had either developed their own operations through franchising, or firms that had bought a franchise business and then developed it, or, firms that had purchased a 'master franchise' [Justis and Judd, 1986]. This last arrangement is typified by an overseas company granting the right to a domestic company to develop the system in the latter's country.

The interview was either with the Managing Director, or the Franchise Director, or the Franchise Manager (hereafter the 'franchisor-interviewee'). The interviews lasted between one hour and two hours.

It is always valuable to understand the limitations of a study. In this instance the final sample was weighted towards firms that had made a relative success of franchising. Although attempts were made to speak to firms that had 'failed' with their ventures into franchising, no interviews were obtained. This was usually because there was either no one left in the organisation qualified to talk about the firm's venture into franchising or the firm refused to be interviewed. However, the majority of firms interviewed had experienced problems at some stage during their history in franchising.

FRANCHISEE RECRUITMENT AND SELECTION

Identifying and Attracting Franchisees

As already mentioned, the fact that a firm is dealing with franchisees rather than company managers is probably the most significant difference between a franchised network and a company-owned (CO) network (i.e. a network where the outlets are owned by the company and operated by employed managers). Several of the franchisor-interviewees attributed the poor performance of specific outlets to the franchisee that ran them. Although it is unlikely that the selection 'of some bad apples' will be totally eliminated, most of the firms found that their selection procedures and criteria evolved over time. Stanworth [1991: 177] also points out that whilst the existence of a selection procedure 'weeds out many unsuitable candidates', the process is not perfect. None the less, the franchisors in our study continually endeavoured to improve:

> The sort of candidate that we were looking for changed because of the experience we gained.

The most vulnerable period is understandably when the first franchisees are being selected:

> Looking back, we took on franchisees in the early days that would not get through our selection procedure now.

At this stage there is no past experience on which to base one's decisions:

> At that stage we did not know who would make a good franchisee – we do now.

And the firm may be too eager to get the business going:

> They were too keen and too greedy – they just wanted to get the money rolling in.

In fact, it was not uncommon for the first franchise contracts signed to be terminated at a later stage.

The media used to advertise for franchisees were: national papers; local papers; trade journals; national exhibitions, and specially arranged promotional exhibitions. Trade journals tended to be used by those firms looking for direct previous experience.

In some cases the mix of media used changed over time. This tended to be for one or more of three reasons. A few firms decided that exhibitions were 'too hard work'. However, on the other hand, some firms felt that their exhibition activities were very productive:

> The enquiries received at exhibitions tend to be more serious – usually they have already read our brochure.

Secondly, as a firm's network expanded across the country it sometimes switched emphasis away from national advertising towards local advertising. This was because it was wanting 'to fill up the holes'. Thirdly, as awareness of the business was deemed to be increasing, some firms no longer felt the need to advertise in order to generate enquiries.

Not all of the firms had advertised for franchisees. Those that had not, relied on an adequate number of enquiries being received. One firm retained the services of a Public Relations firm. PR placings were considered to be an excellent way of attracting enquiries. Franchisees were found from various sources: the 'general public'; company outlet managers; company head office staff; and existing licensees. At least two of the firms had taken on franchisees who were also franchisees of another system. Two firms had awarded franchises to established companies as well as individuals.

There was some caution over the awarding of franchises to company employees:

> This was another lesson – do not normally take managers.

This view was usually due to doubts about managers' commercial ability and their genuine desire to operate their own business. On the other hand, another firm was keen to use managers:

> We have a lot of field management who really will not be promoted but have a lot of experience. We do not want to lose them to the competition, so we offer some of them franchises.

Two of the four franchisees in the study by Baron and Schmidt [1991] were previously employed as managers by their respective franchisors. Baron and Schmidt [1991] appear to credit this situation to the franchisor's positive desire to acquire franchisees with past business experience. Although this was evident in the research, the above quote also indicates that franchisors in our sample are aware of the benefit which competitors might obtain if they were to entice the franchisor's managers into their own organisation. Hence, both 'push and pull' factors influence the decision to award franchises to managers.

Selection Procedure and Criteria

Many of the franchisor-interviewees were very proud of their selection procedure, the stages of which were similar across the firms. First, the prospective franchisee had to fill out an application form. If the applicant seemed potentially acceptable then there was usually an initial informal meeting between the prospective franchisee and the franchisor. This was followed by other meetings, sometimes with more than one member of the franchisor's staff. Often the franchisor met the applicant's spouse or partner. There were visits to existing sites. There was an assessment of the potential franchisee's abilities, suitability, commitment and resources.

Varying degrees of sophistication in the selection procedure were evident in the sample of firms. Many of the firms used tests of some sort and a few had a written-down list of criteria that they were looking for in a franchisee. Specific pass/fail criteria were rare. More commonly, the assessors expressed their subjective view on the applicant's performance and suitability. Other firms had much less sophisticated methods of selection. This type of approach is perhaps akin to that commented on by Sanghavi [1990], who expressed little confidence in the ability of franchisors' selection procedures to distinguish applicants who would become successful franchisees from those who would not. However, the present study did not detect franchisee success as being obviously linked to the degree of sophistication of the methods of selection employed.

Two of the firms in our study will only recruit franchisees with direct previous experience of their particular business. This was because they felt their businesses were too technically complicated to take on non-experienced people. There was no evidence of firms deliberately not taking on people with direct experience, for example:

> We are looking for the right person, whether they have been in this business or any other business.

This view is contrary to that communicated by franchisors in research by Stanworth [1991: 187]:

> Prior experience in the operational line of the franchise was often seen as undesirable. Franchisor executives tended to prefer people from outside their industry with no preconceived ideas or bad habits which might interfere with the franchisor's training programme or contaminate other franchisees.

Four of the franchisor-interviewees stressed that they were looking for people with a general business background. They thought that this was a necessary attribute because although they could teach the franchisees about their particular operation it was not their place to teach them how to run a business in general:

> Somebody who is going to run their own business has got to have some experience of some sort.

Baron and Schmidt [1991] also report that in their sample 'All the (four) franchisees interviewed had previous business experience, often in related retail businesses.' In addition, they mention that the training provided by the franchisors in their study tended to concentrate on the specific skills associated with the 'special system'. The acquisition of general business skills was deemed to be primarily the concern of the franchisee. In the present research, two of the franchisors who now look for past business experience had previously not done so. They had found that franchisees with no business experience had underperformed compared to franchisees in the network who had a business background. This confirms the findings of a study of American fast-food franchisees by Ozanne and Hunt [1971] which also indicated that franchisees with past experience tended to out perform those without.

On the other hand, other franchisors did not specifically look for a business background on the grounds that the high level of support they provided to the franchisees rendered it unnecessary:

The fact that somebody has never been involved in running a business . . . really does not matter, because we will provide them with backup, information, and expertise.

From the above, it is apparent that not all franchisors consider it their job only to teach franchisees about the 'special system' [Baron and Schmidt, 1991]. Some franchisors also provide assistance with, and training in, general business procedures.

Sales and marketing knowledge was another attribute looked for by some franchisors. Here again the feeling was that a franchisee could be taught about the products or services, but they could not be taught how to sell. A couple of the franchisors who looked for sales and marketing experience would take on people without that experience if they appeared to possess a natural selling ability. However, for the majority of franchisors sales and marketing experience was not an issue.

All of the franchisor-interviewees considered personality to be important. This was because the franchisee has to interact with both customers and the franchisor. Personality questionnaires were used by a few of the firms. Usually the results were 'only a small part of the decision to take somebody on or not'. One firm did have a 'pass mark' that the prospective franchisees had to obtain.

The need for a franchisee to have both commitment to the business and to have belief in the product was mentioned by several of the franchisor-interviewees. One franchisor felt that commitment was the one most important factor in the success of a franchisee.

ESTABLISHING OUTLETS

The firms which were adding a franchised network to an existing CO network already had a great deal of experience in identifying appropriate sites, while those that were converting existing sites had a ready-made supply of suitable premises. The franchises that usually involved a franchisee starting their business at home (and possibly moving to a dedicated outlet as they expanded) had their 'sites' predetermined.

Other companies did not have previous experience on which to select sites. The master franchisees (the domestic companies that had been granted the right to develop the system in the UK) received some help from the master franchisors (the overseas company that granted the right to develop the system). However, the master franchisees soon seemed to decide that the criteria given by master franchisors were not particularly relevant to the UK. As a result, they have evolved their own site selection criteria (such as pedestrian counts and traffic flow) over time.

Most selection procedures appear to be 'franchisee-driven'. Here the franchisee is selected first and then an appropriate site is found. Nevertheless, this order of events can cause problems:

> At times it was frustrating because it often took a long time to find a site for an accepted franchisee. There was always the danger that the franchisee might lose interest.

Sometimes there were attempts to find sites first and then recruit a franchisee, but this approach did not always work smoothly. The prime reason seemed to be the difficulty of finding a high calibre franchisee in a specific region:

> We would have liked to pick our areas of operation according to our original plans, but in the end we were stopped from doing this because of the difficulties of finding good franchisees.

Another franchisor-interviewee expressed reservations about a 'site-driven' policy:

> The problem of finding a site and then a franchisee is that you may find a site and then not be able to find a franchisee. Therefore, you let the property go. If this keeps happening the property agents get fed up with you.

The 'site-driven' approach seemed to be most prevalent amongst the firms with a relatively well-developed franchise system and with a CO network. This was due to a number of reasons. Firstly, these firms normally had a property department with a great deal of experience in identifying suitable locations. Secondly, they tended to have a 'stockpile' of sites which could become either franchised or CO sites. The problem of not having a suitable franchisee would be solved by opening the site as a CO outlet. Thirdly, because the businesses had been successfully established over a period of years, many enquiries were received. The sheer volume of franchisee applications meant that suitable franchisees could usually be found for the selected premises. Fourthly, because these franchise systems, along with the CO network, were mature it was often a case of 'filling in the gaps'. In this situation it was impractical to have a 'franchisee-driven' policy as so many applicants would be disappointed because there was already an outlet in their area.

This last reason points to the unwillingness of many prospective franchisees to relocate. This is not necessarily a criticism of franchisees, nor relevant to the needs of franchisors. One of the advantages of franchising is taken to be that of having a local person operating the outlet. If a franchisee had to relocate the franchisor would not gain this benefit and arguably the chance of the franchisee making a success of the outlet may diminish.

As would be expected, the process of finding a site is rarely clear cut. Some of the firms relied on both a 'franchisee-driven' and a 'site-driven' approach to finding sites. Sometimes prospective franchisees would come to the firms either having possession of their own properties, or having particular premises in mind.

Whose Responsibility to Find the Premises?

Obviously, where a firm uses a 'site-driven' policy exclusively, the franchisor finds the site. When the franchisee is selected first, there is a question as to whose responsibility it is to find the site.

In our sample firms the premises were usually found jointly between the franchisee and the franchisor. In these instances the franchisee is usually, but not always, provided with a list of relevant criteria. Where this was not the practice, franchisors accepted the main responsibility for finding the sites. This was normally because the firm had a well-established property department, with the necessary experience in finding sites for CO outlets. Baron and Schmidt [1991] report that of the five franchisors in their study 'most . . . stated categorically that they unilaterally choose the location'. However, although the authors comment that 'normally the franchiser will have established expertise over a number of years . . .', it remains unclear as to exactly why the franchisors employed such a policy. The probability that the franchisors have employees with a great deal of experience in identifying locations may be one explanation, as might the other possible reasons for a 'site-driven' approach – as discussed above.

At the other end of the scale, in our study there were firms that gave the bulk of the responsibility to the prospective franchisee. Here, the franchisor stepped in to assess the site after it had been chosen by the franchisee. Requiring the prospective franchisee to find the site was a significant element of the franchisee selection procedure for one of the firms. They felt that by insisting that the applicant find the site it enabled them to make a better judgement on the applicant's ability and commitment. It was also believed that the hard work involved helped the applicant to become aware of how much they really wanted to run their own business.

None the less, all the franchisor-interviewees indicated that the final decision to take a particular outlet was a mutual one between franchisee and franchisor. This is true regardless of whether the franchisee or the franchisor has taken the major role in originally identifying the location under consideration.

Who Takes the Lease?

Of the 12 firms in the sample which operated out of dedicated outlets (that is, there was one solely home-based franchise), seven took the head lease (or held the freehold) on the properties and sub-leased back to the franchisee. The main reason seemed to be the security that it afforded. The franchisors felt that they were in the dominant position if a franchise was terminated by either party. On the other hand, it is notable that one franchisor has made a decision not to take on the head lease any longer because of the expense involved and the time consuming process of managing the lease, if there is an unwanted flat tied to the store, for example. Such a policy is understandable given that one of the advantages of having franchisees is that they take over a great deal of the responsibility (such as management of the property) for operating the outlet [Stanworth, 1991]. In only one instance did a franchisor say that they have to take the head lease because the franchisee 'cannot supply a sound enough covenant'.

Six of the 12 firms insisted that the franchisee take the lease (note that one firm took the lease in some instances, whereas the franchisee took it in others). The reasoning behind these decisions lay in two of the fundamental advantages of franchising: that of reducing the invested capital of the franchisor, and motivating the franchisee by having them have a significant financial interest in the business.

Multi-Unit Franchisees

Franchisor-interviewees were asked their views on having a franchisee operating more than one site. The responses were of a mixed variety. None of the firms rejected the idea outright, but there were numerous reservations. Concerns revolved around: whether the franchisee could afford it; the distance between the outlets; whether the franchisee had mastered the operational aspects of the business; that the original outlet may suffer as the franchisee put their effort into the new outlet(s); and the dilution of the day-to-day involvement of the franchisee and all the associated benefits. There was no mention of concern over individual franchisees with more than one unit becoming too powerful.

Attempts to mitigate potential problems included an extremely thorough assessment of the proposed venture and the demand that the franchisee elect a different 'nominated principal' for each outlet. The latter would be expected to go through the franchisee training programme. Occasionally, they also had a share in the outlet ownership and were required to pass through the franchisee selection procedure.

It is notable that those firms which expressed reservations over multi-unit ownership have had direct experience of some of the associated problems. None the less, these franchisors were aware that successful franchisees can become frustrated if they are not able to expand past one outlet.

There were two cases where multi-ownership is actively encouraged. This was because it was felt that it was easier to generate growth from within than recruiting new franchisees:

> It is easier to grow the system through the expertise that exists in it, than actually bringing in new franchisees every time you want to open a store.

and

> We want the calibre of person who is capable of running a business that is larger than one store.

One firm is in the process of establishing an equity-ownership scheme for the franchisees' managers, in the hope that those managers will progress on to become franchisees.

THE SETTING OF FEES

There are four basic payments that a franchisee might make to a franchisor. These payments are in recognition of the support that the franchisor provides either during the set-up stage of the outlet or on an ongoing basis. They are also related to the benefits, in terms of consumer awareness, that the franchisee receives because they belong to a branded chain of outlets. There is usually an 'initial or licence fee' that theoretically covers the cost to the franchisor of opening the franchisee's outlet. The franchisee will also pay a 'management service fee' which is based on a percentage of turnover and may also pay a further percentage towards a marketing fund. Alternatively this may be included in the management service fee. Lastly, the franchisor may derive income solely from placing a mark up on goods supplied to franchisees, or may combine this source of income with a management fee.

Initial Fees

All the firms charge initial fees. One firm did not when converting existing licence arrangements to franchise arrangements but did to new franchisees. A couple of the firms did indeed base the fee on costs incurred and felt it was a fair reflection of actual costs:

> It does not cost us that amount to put somebody into business, in terms of external expenditure, but with internal allocation of resources, it probably does – it's a fair charge.

Other franchisor-interviewees were of the opinion that the initial fee did not cover the costs incurred by them. None the less, these firms seemed to be willing to charge at below cost because they anticipated a healthy revenue when the franchisee was up and running, although another explicitly sought to compensate for the shortfall by charging a slightly higher management service fee than they would have done if start-up costs were covered by the initial fee.

Although there was limited evidence of firms having a 'profit element' in their initial fees it would not be unreasonable to assume that a well established business may include a charge for 'joining the club'.

There were other factors involved in the setting of initial fees. One franchisor-interviewee stated that because different franchised outlets cost different amounts to set up, the initial fee had to be 'averaged out'. In other words, the initial fee was based on the estimated cost of opening the planned number of outlets, divided by that number of outlets. In practice this may be a common method of setting the fee, seeing that all franchisees are normally charged basically the same fee. It was notable that only one of the franchisor-interviewees mentioned that experience with the pilot operation was the main basis for fees.

Most of the firms see the need to be competitive. They realise that they are in competition not only with firms selling franchises in their own area of business, but with virtually all firms selling franchises. On the other hand, several of the franchisor-interviewees felt that when they started franchising there were very few other examples which provided a valuable comparison:

> The difficulty was that when we started franchising, it was restricted to a very narrow band of business activities. We were doing something completely different, so there was no valid comparison to be made.

Other influences determining the initial fee included that charged by a master franchisor to the franchisees in their country. There was a divergence in that two master franchisees charged basically the same fee to

British franchisees as the master franchisor charged franchisees in their country, whilst one master franchisee had rejected the master franchisor's fee level as being irrelevant to the UK and had calculated its own. One of the master franchisees had the initial fee charged to a domestic franchisee stipulated in the contract between them and the master franchisor.

Four of the franchisor-interviewees asserted that their initial fees were under revision. For example:

> I believe that we need to ease the need for the franchisee to pay as much as they do.

One of the franchisor-interviewees admitted that the initial fee was probably largely based on 'what had been charged in the past' and did not really take into account present costs.

Ongoing Fees

The range of management service fees, or 'ongoing fees', varied from two per cent to a maximum of ten per cent. The main influences which determined the ongoing fee were the cost of support given to the franchisee; the need to provide an acceptable income for the franchisee; the desire to provide an acceptable income for the franchisor; the gross margin on the product/sales volume relationship; and the need to be competitive with other franchise systems. Despite the difficulty of establishing relevant comparisons, most of the franchisor-interviewees were acutely aware that they were in direct competition with other franchise systems and hence had to take competitors' ongoing fees into account. One franchisor-interviewee clearly stated that the fee was 'based on what we could get'.

Other factors affecting ongoing fees included the income generated by CO sites and what master franchisors charged. With regard to the latter, the percentage charged by the master franchisee (i.e. to domestic franchisees) was virtually the same as that charged by the master franchisor in their country (e.g. to American franchisees). In two cases it appears that the fee level was never challenged, whereas in another the British master franchisee established their own fee level, that happened to be basically the same as the master franchisor's.

There was also evidence of a staged charging of fees. Here the percentage payable by the franchisee was low in the first year, rising in the second, and reaching its final level in the third year. This was based on a recognition that the first years of the franchised operation would be hard for the franchisee. By charging lower rates in the first and second year the franchisor sought to help the franchisees establish themselves.

Resentment was encountered by some of the franchisor-interviewees over the ongoing fees charged to very successful franchisees. This was attributed to fact that it was the successful franchisee who least needed the help and support, but who was inevitably paying more than those who were not achieving comparable results. This resentment may be exacerbated in some cases because the successful franchisee believes that he or she could do as well, if not better, free of the restrictions associated with being part of a franchised network. Finally, because of their higher turnover, the amount of money paid out in fees in absolute terms is likely to appear unacceptably high to some successful franchisees. One of the franchisor-interviewees has attempted to minimise these problems by reducing the ongoing fee percentage after a franchisee has reached a certain level of sales.

Marketing Levy and Marking-Up

A separate marketing fee was levied by several of the firms. In some instances, the marketing fund could only be spent after consultation with – but not necessarily approval by – the franchisees. Two franchisors had some difficulty in getting the franchisees to agree to pay a marketing levy. This was attributed by one franchisor-interviewee to the short-term outlook of some franchisees who do not see the point of activities like advertising because they receive no immediate return.

One firm derives most of its income from marking-up goods sold to the franchisee. It also charges a management service fee but this is relatively low when compared to the fees of the other sample companies. Whilst some of the other firms also acquired part of their income from marking-up goods, this particular franchisor was the only one to utilise this method as the main means of obtaining ongoing payments from the franchisees.

LENGTH OF CONTRACT

The minimum length franchise contract between the franchisor and a franchisee was five years. The maximum was 20 years, although there was one 21-year contract with an option to opt out every seven years. The most frequent length was 10 years. The franchisor-interviewees were asked if franchisees had to pay a fee for renewal of the contract. One firm had formerly charged a renewal fee, but it has now ceased to do so after finding it almost impossible to get prospective franchisees to sign a contract containing this clause. There were instances where refurbishment was linked to renewal, that is, a clause stating that a franchisee wishing to renew had to refurbish their premises. However, it did not seem to be a clause which was strictly enforced, since re-furbishment tended to be linked to necessity rather than the contract and hence occurred at various times.

Those firms with the longer contract term were inclined to stress that they were seeking a long-term partnership with franchisees and the length of the contract was a reflection of this policy. Two of the firms had extended the length of the contract over recent years. One franchisor-interviewee explained why:

> . . . because there are always concerns that people will not renew their contracts, no matter how good a franchisor or franchisee you are.

By extending the length of the contract these concerns were not eliminated, but at least they became less frequent.

ONGOING SUPPORT

The support given to franchisees can encompass several aspects of the business: field staff to sort out problems and provide guidance; ongoing training of franchisees and their staff; 'central services' – marketing, purchasing, and so on; product development; development of the manual; systems development, and so on. In theory one of the advantages of franchising is that franchisees need less support than company managers. This is because the franchisee takes on more of the responsibility of running the business – accounts, wages, staff problems, and so forth [Stanworth, 1991]. Whilst this was borne out by some of the interviews, in practice many of the sample firms had found that this was not the case.

In the majority of the companies with both substantial CO and franchised networks the *type* of support received by both kinds of outlets was virtually identical. In terms of *amount* of support, however, franchised outlets tend to receive more than the CO sites since franchisees have to be taught aspects of running a business which are irrelevant to company managers.

Although only two franchisor-interviewees believed that they were 'making savings' because franchisees needed less support than company managers, there was some evidence that the amount of support given declined after a franchisee had become established. On the other hand, there was just as much evidence that most franchisors continue to support intensively even well established franchisees. One franchisor-interviewee lamented that the amount of support bore little relationship to the degree of success of franchisees:

> When the franchisees are doing well they tend to go off on their own little sidelines. We have to provide a lot of support in order to keep them on the rails. When they are doing badly we have to be there to help them along.

In the final analysis, the reason for the high level of support is that most of the franchisors recognise its importance in the success of their system. For some, the need for support is a lesson learned:

> The company lost its ability to . . . support the system, which is absolutely vital. That is why some of the stores did not succeed when they really should have done.

A number of the firms already had head office service departments in place supporting their CO networks, before the decision to go into franchising was taken. 'Central services' were then extended to cover the franchise network as it developed. Although the norm was to have a small team at the head office responsible for liaising with the service departments, frequently the franchisees communicated with the service departments directly.

Some of the firms had staff out in the field to support franchisees, whilst others used head office based staff. This tended to be a function of size – the larger franchise systems were supported by field staff and the smaller ones from head office. Of the eight with both CO and franchised networks, four had field staff dedicated to looking after franchised units alone, three operated field staff that looked after both franchised and CO outlets, and one had a mixture of these two approaches. Of the four with dedicated staff, three had always operated like this. One had moved over from originally having staff support both types of outlet.

One of the firms with field staff supporting both CO and franchised outlets wanted to move over to the 'dedicated' approach. This franchisor-interviewee expressed the opinion that if he were to start up another franchise system he would insist on having dedicated staff, while another franchisor-interviewee maintained that without a dedicated franchise team the interests of the franchisee might be neglected. On the other hand, another franchisor-interviewee had changed from having a dedicated team to having a combined approach in order to assure franchisees that they were not foregoing the operational experience of the area managers servicing the CO outlets.

The structure of support was also related to the stage of development of the franchise system. In two cases, franchisees had been supported by dedicated staff when the network was small. As the network grew the

support staff were no longer capable of servicing it. As a result, the outlets were transferred to the CO operations division. Unfortunately, this
has led to doubts over how well the CO operations division can cope
with two large networks that require differing approaches.

Throughout the interviews there was considerable discussion and
emphasis on how franchisees must be treated differently to company
managers. The assertion that whilst company managers can be 'told' to
do something franchisees have to be 'persuaded' was confirmed by the
franchisor-interviewees comments. None the less, one franchisor-
interviewee believed that franchisees desire more assertiveness from the
franchisor than is commonly assumed:

> I think that franchisees actually like a little more authority and
> guidance. You may have to do it in a slightly different way, but the
> fundamentals of what you find wrong in a franchise branch are
> basically the same as in a CO branch.

Support is very much an issue among both practitioners and researchers
in franchising. Sceptics may ask what is the reason for franchising if a
franchisor finds it necessary to provide a high level of support. Propo-
nents would probably answer that it is not a question of making savings,
rather it is one of gained benefits. Several of the franchisors have learnt
the importance of support through bad experiences.

CONCLUSIONS

It is apparent from our study that the decision to franchise a business
brings with it a task that entails much detailed planning and decision
making. Although the increased application of business format franchising continues [Hough, 1986; B.F.A., 1991], only a small amount of
research has been published which addresses the operational details of a
franchise system. Whilst general guidelines may exist there is scope to
employ a variety of operating methods. Prospective and present franchisors must consider methods of attracting franchisee applicants, the form
which their selection procedure is to take and the type of person who
would make a successful franchisee. They must decide whether it is best
to find franchisees before locations, or vice versa, or employ a combination of these two approaches. If the former option is chosen, should
the franchisee or the franchisor have the main responsibility for identifying a suitable location? Other property matters include who should take
the head lease and the relative advantages and disadvantages related to
having multi-unit franchisees within the network.

The relative mix of initial fees, ongoing fees, marking-up, and marketing levy is also an important element of a franchise system. In setting

these, our sample of franchisors took into account costs, expected demand for the franchises, the fee levels of competitor franchises, the need to provide both the franchisor and the franchisee with an acceptable income, product margins, the performance of company-owned and pilot franchise outlets, fees charged by master franchisors, and the business life-cycle of franchisees. In addition, attention was paid to the length of contract and conditions of renewal.

Options also exist when a franchisor is considering how to support the franchise network. On the question of support structure, should this be solely provided by head office or by field staff as well? When field staff were utilised they were sometimes responsible for both franchised and company-owned outlets and sometimes only for the former. On the nature of the support, content and style can vary. Whereas some franchisors adopted a low-key approach, others were more authoritative.

This study has shown that a franchisor's chosen methods of operation are related to individual circumstances. For example, all of the above aspects will be affected by the nature of the companies' involvement in franchising – that is, adding franchised outlets to a CO network, converting existing outlets, buying a franchised business, taking a master franchise, or starting a franchised business from scratch. In addition, how long the franchisor has been established will have an influence. For example, a franchisor with an experienced property department will be more likely to take on a higher proportion of the responsibility for finding outlets than one without.

Perhaps the final comment should be that the franchisor owes it not just to itself to develop the system with competence, but also owes a responsibility to the franchisees which are investing their wealth and efforts. Franchising is not an 'easy option'. If franchisors are to increase the likelihood of success for themselves and their franchisees, the suitability of the various alternative operating methods open to them requires serious investigation. It is apparent that it is not enough to rely on knowledge obtained whilst operating in the market using a different type of business format. As one franchisor-interviewee remarked, franchising is a 'business within a business'. No company, therefore, regardless of how many years it has been operating in a particular market, should underestimate the need to make a concerted effort to learn and understand the complexities of franchising and the franchise relationship.

ACKNOWLEDGEMENTS

The authors would like thank the National Westminster Bank for their support of the NatWest Centre for Franchise Research at City University Business School. In addition, our gratitude is extended to the firms and individuals who participated in the research for their generosity in giving their time and their candid responses. The firms were: Alfred Marks; Alphagraphics [UK]; Autela Components; Circle K [UK]; Co-operative Wholesale Society; Kalamazoo Ink; Pentos Retailing Group; Rainbow International [UK]; Recognition Express [UK]; Shell [UK]; Spud-U-Like; Stained Glass Overlay [UK]; and Swinton Insurance.

REFERENCES

Baron, S. and R. Schmidt, 1991 'Operational Aspects of Retail Franchises', *International Journal of Retail & Distribution Management*, Vol. 19, No. 2, pp. 13–19.
B.F.A., 1991, *The NatWest – British Franchise Association Franchise Survey*, Henley-on-Thames: British Franchise Association.
Brandenberg, M., 1989, 'Franchising into the Nineties', *Accountancy*, Vol. 103, No.1146, pp. 143–5.
Churchill, D., 1991, 'Expansion Routes', *Financial Times – Survey*, 4/5 May.
Grant, C., 1985, *Business Format Franchising: A System for Growth*, London: Economist Intelligence Unit.
Hackett, D. W., 1977, *Franchising: The State of the Art*, American Marketing Association, Monograph Series, No. 9.
Hall, P. and R. Dixon, 1988, *Franchising*, London: Pitman.
Hough, J., 1986, *Power and Authority and their Consequences in Franchise Organisations: A Study of the Relationship Between Franchisors and Franchisees*, Doctor of Philosophy thesis, Faculty of Management Studies, Polytechnic of Central London.
Hunt, S. D., 1972, 'The Socio-Economic Consequences of the Franchise System of Distribution', *Journal of Marketing*, Vol. 36, pp. 32–38.
Justis, R. and R. Judd, 1986, 'Master Franchising: A New Look', *Journal of Small Business Management*, Vol. 24, No. 3, July, pp. 16–21.
Mathewson, G. and R. Winter, 1985, 'The Economics of Franchise Contracts, *Journal of Law and Economics*, No. 28, pp. 503–26.
Mendelsohn, M., 1992, *The Guide to Franchising*, London: Cassell
Ozanne, U. B. and S. D. Hunt, 1971, *The Economic Effects of Franchising*, Washington DC: Select Committee on Small Business, US Senate.
Ralston, J., 1989, 'Franchisees Who Think Big', *Venture*, March, pp. 55–7.
Rubin, P., 1978, 'The Theory of the Firm and the Structure of the Franchise Contract', *Journal of Law and Economics*, Vol. 21, pp. 223–33.
Sanghavi, N., 1990, *Retail Franchising in the 1990's*, London: Longman.
Sibley, S. D. and D. A. Mitchie, 1982, 'An Exploratory Investigation of Cooperation in a Franchise Channel', *Journal of Retailing*, Vol. 58, No. 4, pp. 23–45.
Stanworth, J., 1989, 'Socio-Economic Factors in the Franchise Method of Distribution', Paper presented at 5th International conference on Distribution, Milan 1989.
Stanworth, J., 1991, 'Franchising and the Franchise Relationship', *International Journal of Retail, Distribution and Consumer Research*, Vol. 1, No. 2, pp. 175–99.
Stanworth, J., J. Curran, and J. Hough, 1984, 'The Franchised Small Business: Formal and Operational Dimensions of Independence', *In: Success and Failure in Small Business*, edited by Lewis, Stanworth and Gibb, Aldershot: Gower.
Weinrauch, J. D., 1986, 'Franchising an Established Business', *Journal of Small Business Management*, Vol. 24, No. 3, pp. 1–7.

This chapter first appeared in *The Service Industries Journal*, Vol.13, No.4 (1993).

11
Retail Buying in the United Kingdom

DAVID SWINDLEY

Retail buying in the United Kingdom has undergone considerable change in the last 20 years. Faced with a lack of satisfactory published material concerning what retail buyers actually do, the author carried out a survey of buyers in multiple food and apparel retailers. This paper discusses the main changes to have taken place in retail buying in recent years, describes what buyers do, their interface with other functional departments in the business, the characteristics needed by successful buyers, and how buyers are appraised. Finally, it is concluded that the perceived status of buyers does not always reflect their impact on the marketing activity and success of their companies.

INTRODUCTION

It was once said that the three most important factors of success in retailing are location, location and location, but I would like to add a fourth – buying. It occupies a central role in a retail company, providing that essential link between the supplier and 'goods inward' function, and the customer and 'goods outward'. It is also one of the most challenging jobs in the industry and potentially one of the most rewarding. One retail buyer has described it as 'the best job in the world' [Waters, 1989].

Until recently there were no adequate textbooks and precious little literature on the subject. What did exist was mainly American, where retail buying differs from the United Kingdom in several important respects. First, manufacturers have retained more of the balance of power in the United States than in the United Kingdom and there is consequently a lower penetration of own label merchandise. Second, buying is more decentralised in the United States, partly due to greater geographical distances. Buying offices are widely used there, whereas they are rare in the United Kingdom.

Third, American books often tend to describe the department store pattern of retailing and pay too little regard to buying for large multiple chains, such as those which dominate many sectors of UK retailing.

The existing textbooks are not very good at describing what retail buyers actually do. To understand the role of buyers in its entirety would require reading most retailing textbooks cover to cover, since their influence covers the complete range of retailing activities, including merchandising, marketing, stock control, financial planning, personnel and so on.

This article discusses the nature of the buyers' job in UK retailing and raises some of the main issues currently facing them. Smith and Bard [1989] likened the task to that of a person buying on behalf of a family and having to take account of their tastes regardless of their own feelings about the goods, and without necessarily actually using them him/herself. This is a good analogy, except for matters of scale – some British retailers claim to have 20 million different customers in any one year, hence the scale of the task is totally different.

The article also refers to a study of UK retail buying carried out by the author in the autumn/spring of 1989/90 among grocery and apparel buyers. First, a secondary data search was carried out augmented by information gathered from practitioners who had addressed retail students or assisted higher education staff and students with project work. This material was collated and used as the basis of ten semi-structured pilot interviews conducted with buyers. A postal questionnaire was then drawn up and piloted. The final questionnaire was mailed to 150 buyers in 50 large multiple retail companies, selected because of their size and dominance of the UK market. Sixty-three usable replies were received from buyers in 30 companies. These companies, although relatively few in number, represented a very high proportion of food and apparel sales in the United Kingdom.

CHANGES AND ISSUES IN UK RETAIL BUYING

In the last 20 years, most large retailers have moved towards centralised buying structures supported by centralised stock replenishment and allocation. Whilst benefiting from the increased buying power this brings, and the opportunity to apply a systems approach and create a uniform retail image, the role of the store manager in merchandising is often reduced to receiving consignments of goods from a central warehouse and displaying them according to instructions sent out from head office. Store personnel often feel that buyers are insensitive to local needs, and if a range performs badly, there is a tendency for the buyer to blame a poor sales effort and the stores to blame poor buying.

In addition, most UK multiples have separated their buying functions from store operations and selling activities, leaving those who buy located in head offices physically separated from the public on whose behalf they buy. Consequently, they rely heavily on non-personal forms of communication with the customer – for example, suppliers, operations management and market researchers. The exceptions are a small number of traditional department stores and independents for whom the term 'buyer' still refers to an individual who is responsible for buying and selling in a particular department.

Another increasingly important means of communication is the computer. The impact of electronic point of sale (EPOS) on the buying function has been considerable. Buyers can now find out very quickly exactly what is selling, where, and in what quantities. This information properly used is a forceful weapon against suppliers. It has also made certain traditional forms of control, such as 'Open to Buy', redundant, since re-order quantities can be speedily adjusted to take account of *actual* sales rather than projected sales.

However, EPOS cannot say what customers would like to buy that is not currently available nor what they buy in competitors' stores, hence many buyers have to rely on market research suppliers, many of whom also supply the same data to competitors. The same data interpreted in the same way by several competing companies could lead to the same target group of customers being pursued with similar merchandise offerings, leading to the frequently heard charge that British retailers are too alike and that they are boring. Beyond the use of syndicated data, such as retail audits and consumer panel data, there is little widespread evidence of buyers using direct questioning techniques, for instance, to evaluate new ranges.

The buying task has become more and more complex in the last ten years as retailers get larger, product ranges expand, competition intensifies and consumer requirements become more sophisticated and diverse, but as McGoldrick has pointed out [1990], many of the tasks once ascribed to buyers are being taken over by specialist departments, which reduces the buyer's workload but increases the number of other departments with which they must work. The research reported here discovered 30 different departmental titles with which buyers liaised, the most important of which are listed in Table 3.

In Britain, approximately one-quarter of all product-based retail sales were accounted for by own-label goods in 1986 [Euromonitor, 1986], the highest proportion in the Western world. The proportion of sales accounted for by own label can be as high as 100 per cent in fashion clothing and 50–60 per cent in grocery retailing and many retailers make extensive use of exclusive labels.

The implication of own label for the buyer's role is a change of emphasis from negotiating the best deal for 'off the shelf' products to a range of marketing and buying tasks such as sales forecasting, range design, product quality and new product launches. The added complication of fluctuating demand and the greater risks of excess stock and markdowns or unsatisfied demand in fashion markets make the fashion own-label buyer's role even more challenging.

Finally, as consumers become more and more aware of ethical and environmental issues, buyers are faced with pressure to behave in a socially responsible way. This has two aspects. First, strict rules apply in most companies over the acceptance of gifts and incentives from suppliers, even at Christmas. Buyers must be seen to be of the highest integrity.

Second, buyers must react to public, governmental and public pressure for more social and environmental responsibility on a global scale [Swindley, 1990]. One major international fashion retailer has already implemented a policy decision to source only from vendors who provide adequate pay and conditions for their Third World workforce. Perhaps the next major trend, fuelled by organisations such as 'New Consumer' (whose leading report in spring 1990 was entitled 'People Friendly Clothing') will be attending to fair trading standards in developing countries, which will impose a duty on buyers to ensure that products are only obtained from sources which allow a reasonable standard of life for their employees.

THE RESPONSIBILITIES OF RETAIL BUYERS

A former Director of Buying and Merchandising for a major multiple once defined the buyer's role in the following terms:

> Marketing defines, creates and communicates the proposition. Buying implements and maintains the proposition. Merchandising organises and presents the proposition. Operations is part of the proposition and delivers it!
> [Street, 1986]

This statement will now be examined in the light of the survey findings.

THE SURVEY

Sixty-three middle-ranking buyers completed the questionnaire, of whom 38 bought groceries and 25 apparel (clothing and footwear). Exploratory research had suggested that involvement in own labels was the main factor determining breadth of the buyer's role, so respondents were asked whether they bought for own labels, where merchandise was sourced and the extent of buying centrally or at store level. Almost three-quarters of buyers bought *both* own labels *and* brands. Together with the 18 per cent who bought only own labels, this meant that 92 per cent were involved in own label purchasing. Fifty five per cent claimed that at least half of their purchases by value were for own label. The centralisation of buying was illustrated by the fact that 80 per cent stated that no buying took place at store level within their companies. The main sources of goods were directly from the manufacturer (95 per cent of the sample). and 81 per cent through agents, but only 29 per cent bought from raw materials suppliers and 22 per cent through wholesalers. Having established the broad parameters of the buyer's job, the research then ex-amined in detail the range of activities in which buyers might be involved and the extent to which they were solely the buyer's responsibility or shared with other departments (see Table 1).

The three main responsibilities were as follows.

First, the selection, feasibility and monitoring of products was a prime task. Most buyers were involved in product and packaging decisions, new product launches and quality control. However, buyers had more control over deciding on specific products rather than on which product areas were to be carried, the broader issues more often being decided in conjunction with another department, such as Marketing.

Second, the selection and appraisal of, and negotiation with, suppliers was almost exclusively the buyers' job and the buyers' most time-consuming activity. Fifty-five per cent claimed to spend at least half their time dealing with suppliers; only 5 per cent claimed to spend less than a quarter of their time thus.

Third, pricing decisions were seen by the buyers as being firmly in their court. All claimed that no pricing decisions at all were made without their involvement and 82 per cent said it was solely a buying responsibility. Buyers also had a role in the authorisation of markdowns.

Other areas of involvement included sales promotional activity (initia-tion rather than implementation), market monitoring and sales forecast-ing, space allocation, planning and display, and budgeting and Direct Product Profitability (DPP). On the other hand, buyers had low involve-ment in physical distribution, strategic planning, implementing advertis-ing activity, and activities where specialist functions had taken over the responsibility, in replenishment buying, for example.

The survey excluded mail order retailing, which accounted for 5.5 per cent of all non-food sales in 1987 [McGoldrick, 1990]. Its inclusion would have necessitated exploring activities such as catalogue production, liaising with photographers, layout, copywriting and estimating likely

TABLE 1
RESPONSIBILITIES OF RETAIL BUYERS

(percentages)	Buyers' sole responsibility	Shared responsibility	Not buyers' responsibility
Proposing which product areas are to be carried	72	19	9
Deciding which product areas are to be carried	44	43	13
Selecting products within a product area	86	14	0
Product design	19	67	14
Specifying product formulations	18	67	16
Assessing the feasibility of products	58	40	2
Specifying product packaging	19	73	8
Quality control	13	62	25
New product launches	41	57	2
Monitoring product performance	60	40	0
Monitoring stock availability	32	55	13
Allocating stock to stores	33	25	42
Physical distribution	7	19	74
Liaising with stores	36	61	3
Space allocation and planning	7	64	29
In-store display	6	60	34
Direct product profitability	55	31	15
Selecting suppliers	86	13	1
Supplier appraisal	71	28	1
Negotiating with suppliers	89	11	0
Progress-chasing with suppliers	58	36	6
Replenishment buying/ repeat orders	31	34	35
Market monitoring	34	58	8
Identifying market gaps	48	48	4
Sales forecasting	47	45	8
Initiating sales promotional activity	53	42	5
Implementing sales promotional activity	29	50	21
Initiating advertising activity	19	53	28
Implementing advertising activity	5	36	60
Pricing	82	18	0
Authorising markdowns	45	34	21
Budgetting for product purchasing	50	36	14
Strategic planning	7	40	53
Training junior buyers	50	44	7

product returns. In addition to the prompted questioning techniques used in the survey, buyers' attitudes were explored using a five-point attitude scale. In accordance with common practice, mean scores were allocated on the following basis:

Strongly agree	+2
Agree	+1
Neither agree nor disagree	0
Disagree	−1
Strongly disagree	−2

A positive mean score indicates a measure of agreement and a negative score disagreement.

Two of the attitude dimensions related to the buyers' perceived importance of the buying function.

TABLE 2

THE IMPORTANCE OF THE BUYING FUNCTION

Statement	% Agree	% Disagree	Mean Score
The main influence on what my company sells is the buyer	71	21	−0.72
Buying is acknowledge to be the most important function in my company	26	39	−0.05

Although the first statement above was firmly endorsed, buyers also recognised that there were other important influences on what was bought, such as marketing policy and desired image.

In a 1989 study (Woodard [1989]), nine fashion buyers were asked if they bought to reflect their company's image or actually created or imposed an image on their companies through their buying. Eight out of nine said they attempted to reflect the company's desired image, hence this must be a guiding influence on what buyers buy. The second statement suggests either that buyers do not believe they are perceived to be the most important function in their companies, or they are not aware of the esteem in which they are held.

THE INTERFACE WITH OTHER DEPARTMENTS

The literature on organisational buying suggests the existence of 'Decision-Making Units' or 'Buying Centres' [e.g., Webster and Wind, 1972]. The buying centre is 'that set of individuals who are responsible for

TABLE 3
DEPARTMENTS WITH WHICH BUYERS LIAISE

(Rank Order)
Merchandising
Marketing

Product Management
Physical Distribution
Retail/Store Operations
Inventory Management

Packaging/Design
Technologists
Market Research/Analysts
Finance/Accounts
Advertising

Space Allocation/Planning
Promotions/Publicity
Board/Top Management
Corporate Planning
Personnel/Training

the purchase of a particular product'. It includes all the different groups of people, including non-purchasing personnel, who are involved in the purchase.

The nature of the buying centre in retailing was explored by asking for the names of the departments with which respondents liaised in the course of the activities listed in Table 1. Table 3 shows those departments in rank order.

The main interfaces were with Merchandising and Marketing. In fact, they received more mentions than all the other departments put together. Not all retailers include some of the more specialist listed departments in their organisational structure, partly because some cater for certain activities in larger, all embracing departments (e.g., advertising, market research, promotions, etc. may be included under 'Marketing'). Mintel [1987] found that in nine out of 30 retailing organisations' buyers dealt with negotiations, but final authority rested with a committee or senior buyer. These results are consistent with the new findings.

Clearly, the concept of the buying centre has some validity in retailing and some key departments – merchandising, marketing, technologists, etc. – are included within it. The author is aware of no research which has attempted to identify the composition of retail buying centres nor the various roles within it, for example, using Webster and Wind's [1972] classification, to identify the 'initiators', 'gatekeepers', 'influencers', 'users', 'deciders' and 'buyers'. Perhaps this research is a first step in that direction. What is certain, though, is that 'buyers' can be located outside the buying departments, for example, merchandisers who have the responsibility for routine reordering and replenishment in some large multiples.

THE CHARACTERISTICS OF A GOOD BUYER

Diamond and Pintel [1985] identified ten desirable personal qualities for an effective retail buyer:

Enthusiasm   Objective Reasoning
Education   Dedication
Analytical Excellence   Leadership
Ability to Articulate   Appearance
Product Knowledge   Flexibility

In this research the views of buyers themselves were sought using an open-ended question; 'What are the most important characteristics of a retail buyer?'

The responses are shown in Table 4. They suggested three broad types of characteristic. First were personal qualities such as determination, open-mindedness, common sense and self-confidence. These were considered more important than the second group, knowledge (of products, markets, competition etc.). The most important group, though, was communication and other skills. Negotiation skills were ranked the most important factor overall, communication skills were fourth, and skills relating to numeracy, analytical ability and good planning and organisation were also thought extremely important.

These findings have implications for buyer training and development in that most of these skills can be taught to individuals who have the right mix of personal qualities. Responses to the attitude statement 'Good buyers are born not made' (Table 5) also suggest that buyers believe that the necessary skills can be acquired and that the innate qualities of individuals are less important than training and experience.

HOW UK BUYERS ARE APPRAISED

Buyers were asked what were the main criteria on which they were appraised. With such an array of skills, personal qualities and knowledge required to be an effective buyer, there would appear to be plenty of scope for incorporating these into an appraisal scheme. Responses are given in Table 6. It was noticeable that three main criteria featured

TABLE 4

THE MOST IMPORTANT CHARACTERISTICS OF A RETAIL BUYER

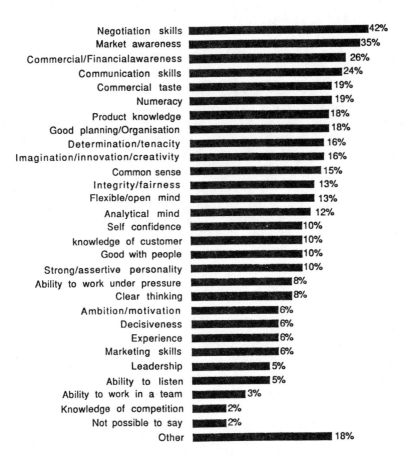

TABLE 5

Statement	% Agree	% Disagree	Mean Score
Good buyers are born not made	19	61	−0.45
Expected profit contribution is the most important decision criteria in my buying	52	21	+0.42
Buyers must be ruthless if they are to succeed	26	49	−0.32

strongly in the responses: sales turnover, profit and the ability to meet set targets or budgets. Profit was measured in a variety of ways – margin, gross profit, or increases in profit, but clearly the 'bottom line' was all important in a buyer's activities. Few mentioned factors such as creativity, open-mindedness or knowledge in their replies.

Responses to the second attitude scale in Table 5 also confirmed the importance of profit contribution for retail buyers. A final statement was put to buyers which asked if they had to be ruthless in order to be successful (Table 5). Although one-quarter agreed with the statement, the majority rejected the idea that a buyer must be ruthless. Most buyers perhaps feel that ruthlessness may occasionally be required in some circumstances but in the longer term could damage supplier relationships and hence their company's interests.

CONCLUSION

Buyers are in a powerful and influential position within a retail company. They have the biggest influence on the products stocked and pricing and contribute to promotional and merchandising activity courtesy of their role as product procurers and managers of supplier relations. The continuing growth of own labels in the United Kingdom has involved buyers in product development in both a marketing and a technical sense, and some buyers have even created new markets through the imaginative use of own label.

This demanding role needs individuals with a wide range of talents, including imagination and creative and commercial flair, a flexible open mind, numeracy and analytical skills and the ability to communicate effectively – a far cry from the stereotypical buyer of 30 years ago whose reputation was for saying 'no' in an unpleasant manner.

Despite the calibre of these individuals, the pivotal role of buying is regarded as one of implementing a marketing proposition developed elsewhere in the business. Buyers themselves do not see themselves as strategists or marketeers despite their obvious involvement in the crucial marketing activities of their businesses.

TABLE 6

THE MAIN CRITERIA ON WHICH BUYERS ARE APPRAISED

	Total Sample (%)
Sales turnover	51
Profit – unspecified	44
Meeting set targets/achieving budget	33
% Margin	17
Gross profit	14
Increasing profit	11
Managing/motivating staff	8
Successful new product development	6
Training staff	6
Quality (control)	5
No waste/unnecessary markdowns	5
Stockturn	3
Market share	2
Terms negotiated	2
Creativity/flair	2
Promotional activity	2
Other activity	14

REFERENCES

Anon., 1990, 'People Friendly Clothing', *New Consumer*, No. 3 (Spring), Newcastle upon Tyne: New Consumer.

Baron, J. S., B. J. Davies and D. G. Swindley (eds), 1991, *Macmillan Dictionary of Retailing*, London: Macmillan.

Diamond, J. and G. Pintel, 1985, *Retail-Buying*, Englewood Cliffs, New Jersey: Prentice Hall.

Euromonitor, 1986, *The Own Brands Report*, London: Euromonitor.

McGoldrick, P. J., 1990, *Retail Marketing*, Maidenhead: McGraw Hill.

Mintel, 1987, *Retail Practices*, Mintel Retail Intelligence, Vol. 5, 3.25–3.28.

Smith D. V. L. and M. Bard, 1989, 'Everything You Always Wanted to Know About Industrial Buying But Were Afraid To Ask – In Case It Made The Research Too Expensive', *Journal of the Market Research Society*, Vol. 31, No 3 (July).

Swindley, D. G., 1990, 'UK Retailers and Global Responsibility', *Service Industries Journal*, Vol. 10, No. 3 (July).

Waters, M., 1990, Presentation to students at Manchester Polytechnic, March, unpublished.

Webster, F. E. Jr. and Y. Wind, 1972, *Organisational Buying Behaviour*, Englefield Cliffs, New Jersey: Prentice Hall.

Woodard, T. M., 1989, *A study of the influences affecting fashion buying decisions*, BSc. (Hons.) Dissertation, Department of Retail Marketing, Manchester Polytechnic, unpublished.

This chapter first appeared in *The Service Industries Journal*, Vol.12, No.4 (1992).

12

A Comparison between Dutch and German Retail Price Setting

RENÉ G.J. DEN HERTOG and A. ROY THURIK

This article examines the differences between Dutch and German retail price setting. The study is based on an econometric approach in the sense that the estimates of the coefficients of a one-equation model explaining retail profit margins are compared. Extensive datasets are used for both the Dutch and German case, allowing a general comparison between the two countries to be made. An ex post *interpretation of the differences in coefficients found is given.*

INTRODUCTION

In the literature the general topic of retail price setting has not received extensive attention. In the marketing literature the interest in retailing is growing [Berry, Gresham and Millikin, 1990], but so far attention to the narrower topic of pricing in retailing has focused mainly on specific products, shops or consumer segments or upon specific promotional situations.[1] In the industrial organization literature there is also a lack of studies attempting to explain retail behaviour. Particularly in the area of price setting, theoretical and empirical studies tend to concern manufacturing [Cubbin, 1988; Schmalensee, 1989].

The limited orientation towards retailing may be the result of the considerable differences between retailing and manufacturing.[2] Straightforward differences are product and market. The 'product' of retailing is a 'bundle of services' with several dimensions, such as price level, proximity, accessibility, assortment width and depth [Hall, Knapp and Winsten, 1961]. Retailing does not offer a clearly defined product. The market of retail services is inherently imperfectly competitive and in this market conditions of (spatial) oligopoly may arise [Hall, 1949].

The lack of studies attempting to compare the retail price setting of different countries is even greater. We know of only two studies: Den Hertog, Potjes and Thurik [1994] and Nooteboom, Thurik and Vollebregt [1988].[3] The lack of appropriate data usually hampers studies with an international dimension. Nooteboom, Thurik and Vollebregt [1988] deal, for instance, with only one year and a limited number of shop types. In the present study we shall try to fill the gap in studies of retail price setting from an international perspective by comparing the Dutch and German situation. For the two countries, data are used for the same period, 1981–86, and the same 21 shop types. The shop types cover almost completely the entire spectrum of shop types across retailing. This allows a comparison between the retail trade of the two countries as a whole.

Instead of presenting anecdotal evidence on possible differences in retail price setting between the Netherlands and Germany, we shall start with an empirical analysis of the retail price setting of both countries in order to determine the differences. Once the differences have been identified, we will give a more specific explanation of them. We shall follow an econometric approach in the sense that the analysis of the differences in retail price setting will be based on the estimates of the coefficients of a one-equation model, which explains retail profit margins for the Netherlands and Germany separately. The equation is the full average cost pricing model presented in Nooteboom [1985]. The model explains the average percentage gross margin as an average percentage profit mark-up on average percentage operating costs excluding a reward for shopkeepers' labour.[4] The mark-up is composed of four elements that represent a scale effect, a shop type effect, a life cycle effect and a business cycle effect. The model has also been used to analyse structural changes in retailing such as increasing scale, concentration and declining share of independents and their causes [Nooteboom, 1986], and to explain differences in profit between small and large scale manufacturing [Thurik and Van der Hoeven, 1989].

The structure of the current study is as follows: the second section presents the model; the data are described in the third; and the fourth discusses the results.

MODELLING RETAIL PROFIT MARGINS

According to Nooteboom [1985:647], his model explains differences in retail profit margins between different shop types as well as the development in time per type of shop. His model has been used in various studies.[5] In the mark-up model the average percentage gross margin, M, is modelled as an additive function of the percentage operating costs, K,[6] a constant term and four variables that account for a scale effect, a shop type effect, a life cycle effect and a business cycle effect. Both the margin and the costs are expressed as a percentage of sales.

According to Nooteboom, the percentage profit mark-up is inversely related to the sales size of a shop, because a higher sales size allows a lower percentage of sales to achieve a given minimum reward for the shopkeeper. This scale effect is accounted for by ratio of the consumer price index, P, to the sales size, Q. The shop type effect implies that a more varied range of products and a higher service level require a higher percentage profit mark-up to achieve a given return on investment. Nooteboom [1985] uses income elasticity of products and services offered to determine the importance of the shop type effect. Nooteboom, Kleijweg and Thurik [1988] have, however, shown that the stock level, that is defined as the stock as a percentage of sales, V/Q, appears to be a better indicator than the income elasticity. The underlying idea is that a high stock level often accompanies a deeper and wider range of products and hence a higher service level. A deeper and wider range of products also means more uncertainty, for which the retailer requires a compensating premium.

The underlying idea of the life cycle effect is that the margin depends on the phase of the life cycle of the shop type: during the penetration phase there is a bonus on novelty, during the phase of saturation this bonus disappears; and during the phase of decline the profit mark-up shrinks due to heavy competition of new types of trade. The mark-up model of Nooteboom [1985] contains the change in market share of the shop type to account for the life cycle effect. In the current study this variable had to be dropped because no data are available. The growth of consumer spending (in volume), CCS, accounts for the dependence of the profit margins on the economic situation, that is, the business cycle effect. Price competition is assumed to become more intense in a contracting market because retailers attempt to sustain sales volume.

In the current study, the mark-up relationship is

$$M_{it}=a_0+a_1 K_{it}+a_2 P_t/Q_{it}+a_3 V_{it}/Q_{it}+a_4 CCS_{it}+u_{it},$$

for shop type i and year t, where u is the error. If percentage gross margins are indeed a percentage profit mark-up on the percentage operating costs, the coefficients a_0 and a_1 should be zero and one, respectively. However, in Nooteboom, Kleijweg and Thurik [1988] a_0 was found to be significantly different from zero. From the discussion above, we know that the coefficients a_2, a_3 and a_4 should be positive. It can be shown that the coefficient a_2 represents a net profit level which is independent of the characteristics of the shop type. Nooteboom [1985] and Nooteboom, Kleijweg and Thurik [1988] report estimates for a_2 close to the legal minimum wage for employees.

The above approach is classified by industrial economists as belonging to the behaviourial theories. These theories represent the view that optimising behaviour is not the key issue in a world of uncertainties, irrationalities and misty simultaneous and collective decision making [Waterson, 1984].

DATA

Both the Dutch and German data are used for the period 1981-86 (6 years) for 21 shop types, yielding a total of 126 observations. For the profit margins, the operating costs, sales and stock level the data are the average values for the shop types. For Germany our main data-source is Sundhoff and Klein-Blenkers [1982-87]. The German price index used to compute P/Q is taken from the International Financial Statistics of the IMF (yearbook 1987). The data on the growth of consumer spending are based on data of the National Accounts of the OECD.

For the Netherlands, the data-source is an ongoing panel of independent, mainly small Dutch retailers called 'Bedrijfssignaleringssysteem' (firm signalling system), which is operated by the Research Institute for Small and Medium-Sized Business (EIM) in Zoetermeer, the Netherlands. The data on the Dutch price index and the growth of consumer spending were gathered by the Central Bureau of Statistics (CBS) in Voorburg, the Netherlands. The data were elaborated by the EIM.

The 21 shop types are presented in Table 1. One can see that they practically span the entire spectrum of shop types retailing in Germany and the Netherlands. Food shop types are underrepresented.

TABLE 1
A SURVEY OF THE SHOP TYPES

Groceries	Lighting and electric
Tobacco shop	Floor-covering and wallpaper
Clothes shop: men and children	Chemist's shop
Clothes shop: women and children	Photographer's shop
Clothes shop: men, women and children	Jeweller's shop
Clothes shop: mixed assortment	Cycle shop
Bed-clothes	Sports shop
Shoe shop	Bookshop
Furniture store	Florist's shop
House and kitchen utensils	Toys
Iron tools	

Note: For all shop types data are available for the period 1981–86 for both the Netherlands and Germany.

TABLE 2
ESTIMATION RESULTS

	Constant	K	P/Q	V/Q	CCS
Netherlands	2.466*	1.078*	13.208*	0.031*	0.150*
	(0.751)	(0.027)	(2.603)	(0.015)	(0.025)
Germany	1.693*	0.969*	20.802*	0.040*	-0.041
	(0.855)	(0.029)	(2.679)	(0.009)	(0.065)
F-test	0.720	11.751*	3.994*	0.350	8.966*

Note: Standard errors are in parentheses. To test for differences in the coefficients between the
two countries, an F-test is used. * denotes significance at the 5 per cent level.

EMPIRICAL RESULTS

Dutch and German data are available for the same set of shop types and the
same period. This allows us to use the method of Seemingly Unrelated
Regressions (SUR). SUR accounts for the correlation between the residuals of
the two countries [Judge *et al.*, 1985]. This method has two important advantages. First, SUR provides more efficient estimates of the coefficients.
Secondly, an F test of the hypothesis that there is no difference in the coefficient between the two countries can be calculated for each explanatory variable. The results are presented in Table 2.

The results indicate no significant differences in the intercept and the coefficient of the stock level between the Netherlands and Germany.[7] For both
countries the intercept is positive and significantly different from zero. Since
the intercept determines the direct relation between sales size and net profits,
the results suggest that an increase of scale has a direct positive effect on net
profits in the Netherlands as well as in Germany. The service level, represented by the stock level, has a significant, positive effect on both Dutch and
German retail profit margins. The customers of both countries seem to be prepared to pay not only the higher operating costs resulting from a higher stock
level but also a bonus for more service.[8]

The F tests indicate significant differences between the coefficients of the
costs, K, the inverse of deflated sales, P/Q, and the growth of consumer
spending, CCS, for the Netherlands and those for Germany. These differences
can be explained by the difference in firm size between the two countries. The
average shop is smaller in the Netherlands than in Germany. Ravesloot and
Vogelesang [1989] report average sales of 291 and 552 thousand ECU in 1986
for Dutch and German firms, respectively. Average sales calculated from our
data show the same difference. The difference in firm size may be a result of
the Dutch government's restrictive policy with respect to hypermarkets and
other large scale stores in peripheral areas.

The difference between the coefficients of the costs, 1.08 for the Netherlands and 0.97 for Germany, may be the result of the difference in firm size. The way in which retailers pass on their operating costs reflects the amount of risk they are prepared to take.[9] The owners of small firms have less financial resources to take care of financial problems resulting from unexpected increases in costs or unexpected lower sales volumes. Moreover, these owners usually need to generate a family income. For both reasons, they do not want to take much risk and pass on even more than 100 per cent of their costs to their customers.

The difference in firm size is also consistent with the different coefficients of the inverse of sales. As mentioned in the second section, the coefficient of this variable reflects a net profit level independent of the shop type characteristics. It is comprehensible that this basic profit level is lower for a country of which retailing's average firm size is lower. Given the definition of the variables, we find a basic profit level of about 13,200 Dutch guilders for the Netherlands and 20,800 DM for Germany at 1976 prices.[10] These estimated values are close to the minimum wages of both countries.

It is also interesting to see that the small Dutch firms are more sensitive to changes in economic conditions than the large German firms. In contracting markets small firms may find it more difficult to sustain their sales volume, and therefore they need to reduce their profit margins more than large firms. In growing markets small firms seem to be able to exploit the market opportunities better, ie., the prices of small firms can increase more than the prices of large firms.

CONCLUSIONS

Comparing the retail price setting of the Netherlands and Germany, one does not expect many differences a priori. The two countries have a common border and their economic differences are small. Remaining differences are eliminated by the continuing integration within the European Union. We have, however, found differences in the effect of operating costs and growth of consumer spending on retail profit margins and different basic rewards. We argue that it is the variations in average firm size that may cause these disparities in retail price setting between the Netherlands and Germany. It is not unrealistic to assume that the difference in firm size may also cause variations in other marketing practices between the two countries, and may also explain differences in marketing practices between other European countries. Studies of retail marketing with an international dimension need to account for the differences in firm size between the countries that are studied.

No formal mathematical model lies at the basis of our endeavour in the sense that the model employed is explicitly derived from a set of behaviourial assumptions or that departures from equilibrium are explicitly modelled. No long-run equilibrium is thoroughly discussed. We employ a reduced type model which has been used successfully in earlier studies. We stress comparing and contrasting the empirical results for two different countries, in preference to the one-country study where the modelling is often governed too strictly by typical data opportunities. Empirical evidence becomes convincing when it is valid for different environments, particularly if the model employed is not explicitly derived from formal mathematical modelling.

ACKNOWLEDGEMENTS

We wish to thank the Institut für Händelsforschung of the University of Cologne and EIM Small Business Research and Consultancy for the provision of the data, and Herman van Schaik for the elaboration of the data.

REFERENCES

Berry, L.L., L.G. Gresham and N.L. Millikin, 1990, 'Marketing in Retailing: A Research Agenda', *International Review of Retail, Distribution and Consumer Research*, Vol. 1, pp. 5-16.

Bode, B., J. Koerts and A.R. Thurik, 1986, 'On Storekeepers' Pricing Behaviour', *Journal of Retailing*, Vol. 62, No. 1, pp. 98-110.

Cubbin, J.S., 1988, *Market Structure and Performance: The Empirical Research*, Chur: Harwood Academic Publishers.

Den Hertog, R.G.J., J.C.A. Potjes and A.R. Thurik, 1994, 'Retail Profit Margins in Japan and Germany', *Weltwirtschaftliches Archiv*, Vol. 130, pp. 375–90.

Den Hertog, R.G.J. and A.R. Thurik, 1992, 'Expectations and Retail Profit Margins', *International Review of Retail, Distribution and Consumer Research*, Vol. 2, No. 3, pp. 263-82.

French, N.D. and R.A. Lynn, 1971, 'Consumer Income and Response to Price Changes: A Shopping Simulation', *Journal of Retailing*, Vol. 47, No. 4, pp. 21-31.

Hall, M., 1949, *Distributive Trading*, New York: Hutchinson.

Hall, M., J. Knapp and C. Winsten, 1961, *Distribution in Great Britain and North America*, London: Oxford University Press.

Judge, G.G., W.E. Griffiths, R.C. Hill, H. Lütkepohl and T.C. Lee, 1988, *Introduction to the Theory and Practice of Econometrics*, 2nd edition, New York: John Wiley and Sons.

McElroy, B.F. and D.A. Aaker, 1975, 'Unit Pricing Six Years after Introduction', *Journal of Retailing*, Vol. 55, No. 3, pp. 44-57.

Nooteboom, B., 1985, 'A Mark-up Model of Retail Margins', *Applied Economics*, Vol. 17, No. 4, pp. 647-67.

Nooteboom, B., 1986, 'Costs, Margins and Competition: Causes of Structural Change in Retailing', *International Journal of Research in Marketing*, Vol. 3, No. 4, pp. 233-42.

Nooteboom, B., A.J.M. Kleijweg and A.R. Thurik, 1988, 'Normal Costs and Demand Effects in Price Setting: A Study of Retailing', *European Economic Review*, Vol. 32, No. 3, pp. 999-1011.

Nooteboom, B. and A.R. Thurik, 1985, 'Retail Margins during Recession and Growth', *Economics Letters*, Vol. 17, pp. 281-4.

Nooteboom, B., A.R. Thurik and S. Vollebregt, 1986, 'An International Comparison in the

General Food Trade: Cases of Structural Change', *International Journal of Research in Marketing*, Vol. 3, No. 4, pp. 241-7.

Nooteboom, B., A.R. Thurik and S. Vollebregt, 1988, 'Do Retail Margins Differ between European Countries? A Comparative Study', in E. Kaynak (ed.), *Transnational Retailing*, Berlin/New York: Walter de Gruyter.

Ravesloot, T.K. and W.J.P. Vogelesang, 1989, *Facts and Figures on Retailing in the Netherlands, Europe and the United States*, Zoetermeer: Research Institute for Small and Medium-Sized Business.

Schmalensee, R., 1989, 'Inter-industry Studies of Structure and Performance', in R. Schmalensee and R.D. Willig (eds.), *Handbook of Industrial Organization*, Amsterdam: Elsevier Science Publishers.

Sundhoff, E. and F. Klein-Blenkers, 1982-87, *Mitteilungen des Instituts für Händelsforschung an der Universität zu Köln*, Cologne: University of Cologne.

Tellis, G.J., 1987, 'Consumer Purchasing Strategies and the Information in Retail Prices', *Journal of Retailing*, Vol. 63, No. 3, pp. 279-97.

Thurik, A.R. and W.H.M. van der Hoeven, 1989, 'Manufacturing Margins: Differences between Small and Large Firms', *Economics Letters*, Vol. 29, pp. 353-9.

Walter, R.G. and H.J. Rinne, 1986, 'An Empirical Investigation into the Impact of Price Promotions on Retail Store Performance', *Journal of Retailing*, Vol. 62, No. 3, pp. 237-66.

Waterson, M., 1984, *Economic Theory of the Industry*, Cambridge: Cambridge University Press.

Wilkes, R.E., 1972, 'Consumer Usage of Base Price Information', *Journal of Retailing*, Vol. 48, No. 4, pp. 72-85.

Woodside, A.G. and J.T. Sims, 1974, 'Retailing Experiment in Pricing a New Product', *Journal of Retailing*, Vol. 50, No. 3, pp. 56-65.

NOTES

1. Leafing through the main journal in this area, *The Journal of Retailing*, we come across French and Lynn [1971], Wilkes [1972], Woodside and Sims [1974], McElroy and Aaker [1979], Bode, Koerts and Thurik [1986], Walters and Rinne [1986], Tellis [1987], etc.

2. The limited orientation towards retailing is not justified by its limited economic significance. In the European Community (EC-12) the retail trade employs well over 11 million people in about 3.5 million establishments representing a market of approximately 1,000 billion ECU [Ravesloot and Vogelesang, 1989].

3. Den Hertog, Potjes and Thurik [1994] compare Japanese and German retail price setting. In Nooteboom, Thurik and Vollebregt [1988] a comparative study of the retail margins of different European countries is presented. In an earlier study, Nooteboom, Thurik and Vollebregt [1986] made an international comparison of the general food trade between various countries.

4. The margin is defined as the difference between sales and purchase value of sales as a per centage of sales.

5. The model has been used to study the relevance of expectations for retail price setting [Den Hertog and Thurik, 1992], to analyse the Dutch retail margins during recession and growth [Nooteboom and Thurik, 1985], and to examine the influence of normal costs and demand effects on the Dutch retail price setting [Nooteboom, Kleijweg and Thurik, 1988].

6. The operating costs exclude a reward for shopkeepers' labour because this reward is treated as a part of the residual net profit.

7. In the current study we use a 5 per cent significance level.

8. The variable K accounts for the effect of the higher costs of the service level on the profit margins.

9. Den Hertog, Potjes and Thurik [1992] have compared German and Japanese retail pricing setting, and found similar results. The cautious Japanese shopkeeper tends to pass on more of his operating costs than his German colleague.

10. One US dollar was equal to about 2.5 Dutch guilders and about 2.4 DM in 1976.

13

Shopping Motives

by

Francis Buttle and Marilyn Coates

Retailers' revenue is a function of two factors – store traffic and average purchases per customer. Retailers who are adept at activating motives for shopping should be able to generate more traffic. This paper explores the motives for making shopping trips and reveals that the simple buying of products is far from being the sole motive. Shopping meets a variety of needs, only some of which involve spending money. Suggestions are offered on how to convert those non-spending trips into revenue-earning opportunities.

INTRODUCTION

An often repeated joke about New Zealand tells of the air hostess for a European airline whose 'plane is landing at Auckland airport. She announces: 'Will passengers please extinguish their cigarettes, fasten their seat belts and set their watches back 20 years.'

In the context of an argument which has been raging in New Zealand for the last couple of years, the joke is highly relevant. The argument concerns Saturday trading. Until 1976, trading hours for most outlets were restricted by law from 9.00 a.m. to 5.30 p.m., Monday to Friday, with one late night permitted per week. However, 1976 saw the introduction of the Shop Trading Hours Act which extended trading hours from 7.00 a.m. to 9.00 p.m. Monday to Friday. The government was convinced of consumer demand for longer hours and fought opposition from the Retailers Federation and the Shop Employees Union.

Some retailers, particularly those located in tourist areas, began to defy even this relatively liberal law and opened on Saturdays. Another tale which would appeal to the cynical reader tells of the American who flew into New Zealand one Saturday morning and caught the next flight out because the country was closed. However, circumstances have now changed. Legislation was introduced in July 1980 which permits trading on Saturdays from 7.00 a.m. to 9.00 p.m. That American tourist now flies in (and out) on Sundays.

Whilst researching the views of retailers to Saturday trading in early 1980, the attitude generally encountered was antagonistic. The research team was told that it would cause inflation, that it was a threat to the traditional weekend of sport and family activities, that it would change the nation's social life, that staff would have to be paid double time, that the revenue from five days' trading would be spread over six, that services such as banks and post offices would not be open to cope with the financial needs of retailer or shopper, that it would deplete the country's energy stocks, that it would depersonalise shopping, and that because banks were not open there would be an increased incidence of robberies. However, the one remark which finally persuaded us to conduct this research into why people make shopping trips was made by the chief executive of a department store group which had consistently refused to open for even one late night per week. He said: 'If a man really wants to buy a shirt, he'll take time off work, travel into town, and damn well make the sacrifices necessary to buy one.' That approach to business is enough to make any marketing man who believes in adapting the product offering to suit the needs of customers shake in his boots. Surely there is more to shopping than simply purchasing.

PREVIOUS RESEARCH

The only pertinent previous study located by the authors was undertaken by Edward Tauber [1972]. He concluded that:

> People's motives for shopping are a function of many variables, some of which are unrelated to the actual buying of products. It is maintained that an understanding of shopping motives require the consideration of satisfactions which shopping activities provide, as well as the utility obtained from the merchandise that may be purchased. If needs other than those associated with particular products motivate people to go to a store, the retailer should incorporate this information into his marketing strategy. [Tauber, 1972: 46-49].

Tauber's research hypothesised eleven motives for shopping behaviour. He divided them into personal and social motives:

1. *Personal motives*
    1.1 *Role playing.* Food shopping, for example, is an integral part of the housewife's role.
    1.2 *Diversion.* Shopping can be an opportunity for diversion from the daily routine of life and thus represents a form of recreation.
    1.3 *Learning about new trends.* Many people are interested in keeping informed about the latest trends in fashion, styling or product innovations. While such learning may take place with or without a purchase, a certain segment of shoppers for each product category is more prone to buying new items. Stores which are trend conscious may appeal to these innovators.
    1.4 *Physical activity.* Shopping can provide people with a considerable amount of exercise.

      1.5   *Self gratification.* For example, a person may go into a store in search of diversion when he or she is bored or in search of social contact when he or she feels lonely.

      1.6   *Sensory stimulation.* Retail institutions provide many potential sensory benefits for shoppers. Customers browse through a store looking at the merchandise and at each other; they enjoy handling the merchandise.

2.   *Social motives*

      2.1   *Social experiences outside the home.* Some shopping trips may result in direct encounters with friends; on others the social contact may be more indirect, as exemplified by the pastime of 'people-watching'.

      2.2   *Communication with others having similar interests.* Stores that offer hobby-related goods serve as a focal point for people with similar interests to interact. People like to talk to others with similar interests and sales personnel are frequently sought to provide special information concerning the activity.

      2.3   *Peer-group attraction.* The patronage of a store sometimes reflects a desire to be with one's peer group or a reference group to which one aspires to belong; for instance, record stores are common hangouts for teenagers.

      2.4   *Status and authority.* Many shopping experiences provide the opportunity for an individual to command attention and respect. In few other activities can an individual expect to be 'waited on' without having to pay for this service..

      2.5   *Pleasure of bargaining.* For many shoppers, bargaining is a degrading activity; haggling implies that one is 'cheap'. Others, however, appear to enjoy the process believing that, with bargaining, goods can be reduced to a more reasonable price.

RESEARCH OBJECTIVES AND METHOD

The main aim was simply to satisfy the authors' curiosity about shopping motives with a view to converting the recalcitrant department store executive to a pro-Saturday trading stance. Formally, the research tested whether the motives hypothesised by Tauber were significant in a different continent a decade later.

This study is exploratory and does not pretend to be definitive. Twenty in-depth interviews were conducted in February 1981 with a convenience sample of women. All were city dwellers aged between 19 and 55 years. Half were married, six single and four separated, widowed or living with a partner. Thirteen were in paid employment, two were students and five were full-time housewives. Eight were mothers.

All interviews were conducted in the interviewees' homes and followed an unstructured pattern. The interviewer carried a prompt sheet which listed open-ended questions devised to probe four areas: shopping activities in general, the interviewee's last shopping trip, other shopping trips and the shopping behaviour of others. This last topic was included in case there were shopping motives which were embarrassing or socially unacceptable. The interviewee was able to attribute these motives to others. The interviews were tape-recorded for later analysis.

FINDINGS

There were many ways in which the declared motives could have been categorised for ease of understanding. Different analysts agreed that the final eight-part categorisation was a fair representation of the tapes' contents.

Interestingly, when describing their shopping behaviour most of the women drew on experiences with one type of merchandise to describe their behaviour. Clothing was most common. The sample did not like, or did not want to identify, food purchasing as a form of shopping; scant reference was therefore made to this form of ritual shopping in the interviews although the interviewees did, when probed, accept that their most common shopping endeavours concerned groceries.

The comments reproduced below are extracted verbatim from the tapes.

Declared Motives for Shopping

To Kill Time

Shopping is simply a way of passing time: 'It's nice to have a chance to spend time looking at things.' Women may have time to kill on their way to or from work or during their lunch breaks: 'If I go into work early I will look around the shops to pass the time.' 'Shopping in my lunch-hour keeps me busy – I go practically every day.' Waiting time may be used for shopping: 'If I'm waiting to meet somebody I'll have a look around.' 'To fill in time on the way to my dance class I'll look at any shops I care to on the way.'

Women may go into town for no other reason than . . . 'I just went into town because I had a bit of free time.' 'I go most Friday nights because it's something to do – I go into town to fill in time – haven't got much else to do so I muck around looking in shops.' Some members of the sample did not regard shopping as a way of filling time: 'I'd rather do something at home because my time is so busy.' 'If I've got nothing else to do I'd rather go for a run or swim.' 'With three small kids I couldn't think of anything worse than going to town.'

Exercise/Relaxation/Stimulation

Closely allied to the 'time-killing' motive is the use of shopping as a source of pleasure: 'I like walking around for the actual walk – it depends on the time – if I'm not rushed then it's a leisurely time.' 'I will take a walk for the sake of it after meeting a friend for lunch – glancing in the shops.' 'If I have a day off work I'll shop in the city – wander around the shops.' Most women found that the more relaxed the shopping occasion, the more enjoyable it was: 'Christmas shopping (without the kids) is more lazing around – I enjoy it more – taking it more quietly.' 'I would like to come back to days when shopping was more friendly – (the shop assistants).' 'When you're just looking it's more relaxed – not standing to lose anything. It's *fun* just to look and do silly things.' 'Often we go into town at the weekend for something and I'll wander past shops and peer in – it's more relaxing because there is no rush.' Many find shopping both stimulating and exciting: 'There are a lot of things to look at, watching people is good.' 'I like watching people's faces.' 'I enjoy it more (at Christmas) because I'm not doing that shopping all the time.'

This is a direct contrast to grocery shopping which many see as an unavoidable, boring necessity: 'I hate grocery shopping because it's the same each week . . . I enjoy shopping for clothes because you're not doing it each week.' 'Supermarket shopping is a chore – I make myself go because it's a necessary part of life.' 'I may put my grocery shopping off until the next day because I can't be bothered going.' When shopping is not part of the daily routine, it is much more enjoyable: 'There's always something happening in town – it's a change from being inside the house all the time.' One woman recalled her sheer enjoyment of shopping when she was a teenager: 'When I was 15 we'd go to Queen Street and wander up and down then go home – never had any money to spend but we'd look at people.'

A Reflection of Temperament

When and why some women shop is attributable to the moods they experience. Some feel that when depressed or miserable a little spending is a great tonic: 'From time to time I go out just to buy something – I feel like buying something possibly because something happened at work – it could be depression – I may feel like buying something to lift up my spirits – need to treat myself – usually I buy something small.' 'I think if you're a little depressed or perhaps had an argument with your husband you tend to go out and buy something – maybe you've been thinking about it and you think, right, I'm going to spend that money now.' 'I feel like doing something or being out on the town.' Others simply enjoy spending money: 'I like spending and enjoy going out to buy.' 'I enjoy buying sports gear so I often go into a sports shop and end up buying something.' 'I like to see something in my shopping bag – it makes me feel good – I must like spending money.'

Anticipation of a particular purchase can add spice to the shopping trip: 'I enjoy shopping more if I know I'm going to buy things than just looking, because I can't afford most things.' 'I prefer to go shopping with a purpose rather than just admiring things.' 'If I'm looking for something specific and I can't find it I get very frustrated.' 'When I want to buy something in particular I don't enjoy it because I just like buying things spontaneously – when I've got to look for something special I can never find it (it's the wrong colour or size) – it seems such a waste coming home with nothing.' Some shoppers delight in the sensory satisfactions derived from shopping: 'I might go into a shop (for example, a delicatessen) with no intention to buy and don't, but I like to look at the way things are packaged and laid out.' 'I like to see an effective window display – if it's a good impact I often go in.' 'Some shops are nice to go into because they have background music and a certain atmosphere about them – this is because of the way the goods are laid out, the decorations, noise and smell.'

Information Acquisition

Many women said they shopped simply to find out what was available in the shops – a sort of curiosity motive where pleasure is often obtained from exposure to new merchandise: 'Just looking on Friday night to see what is around, especially clothes.' 'Generally looking to see what stocks the shops have.' 'See which shops have a good range of what.' 'I worked in town so every day I drifted around to see what was in the shops.' 'Looked to see what shops had – it's very pleasing because you think gosh, I never knew they had that.' 'Occasionally I go down to the local shops to see what's there.' Usually, this curiosity was restricted to only one type of merchandise, most often clothing: 'I try and buy clothes at the beginning of each season so I go down to the local shops at lunchtime to see what's available.' 'Back-pay is coming up so I'm investigating the clothes scene, having a reconnoitre – seeing what's available before I buy. If you're doing a good reconnoitre you usually go into most shops.'

Such exposure to the merchandise available in the shops often made subsequent purchasing decisions easier. Shopping is undoubtedly a source of information: 'When you come to live in a place you automatically sus out the best places to shop and where to go.' 'I knew the shops off by heart because I was in town every day at lunchtime, so I knew which shops to go to.' 'You know some shops have something you want – you know where to go and buy, because you have looked around before.' Another dimension of this, particularly for those who could be conceived of as opinion leaders, was to keep up to date with trends: 'Looking at books in a shop is quite a good way of keeping up with the latest.' 'I like to see what the new ones (clothes) are and their prices.' 'Looking to see general trends.' 'There's new lines coming in all the time.' 'Looking to get ideas, for equipment around the home.' 'I like to look at clothes and pick up ideas, if I can't afford to buy them I make them.' 'I get ideas from clothes in stores – ideas to make them.'

Subordinate Activity

Shopping is often part of some grander trip where the shopping element is subordinate to some more significant purpose: 'If I have got time when I go to the bank I look in nearby shops.' 'I window-shop for dresses when I go into town to post the mail or go to the library – usually go to the library on a Friday afternoon so I'll make a day of it to potter around.' 'Quite often go into the Post Office in town and have a look around as I'm wandering along.' 'I may go into any shop that I come across in my day's activities.' 'I combine a lot of my shopping with going to the library.' 'I often have to go into the bank so I always allow myself an hour or two to look around the shops.' 'If I'm in a department store I will do the rounds of everything (all departments).' 'I will occasionally meet a friend for lunch and while walking home I may go into a shop that attracts me, such as a book or gardening shop.' One member of the sample did not approve of mixing shopping with her other affairs: 'If I'm going somewhere, such as to the pictures, I don't muck around much (looking in shops).'

Shopping as a Social Event

For some people, shopping is sometimes part of a social calendar. For them, shopping is an enjoyable, pleasurable event and the presence of others simply enhances their delight: 'Like on a Friday night if you go shopping you never leave town without having a few drinks, it's part of your social life – for women I think it is.' 'I like shopping at places where you can not only shop but can go and have a drink and a meal, meet friends for lunch, such as Parnell and Parapa – I really enjoy that.' 'I often go into town to meet somebody . . . I get bored easily by shops so with someone else I tend to stay around – it's a lot slower but more fun – I go into a lot of shops I wouldn't normally go into – get a closer look.' 'In Hastings on holiday I'll meet somebody for lunch in town because it's a special treat – here I see my friends all the time.' 'I didn't want to buy anything but I was prepared to go with her because we had a meal afterwards – it was basically a shopping trip and a meal afterwards.' 'I like it when my husband comes and helps me with the groceries, because I feel that we are doing something together.' 'Jogging about the shops isn't much fun unless you've got some company and it's a fun thing.' 'I went into Wellington with a friend of mine a couple of times – we just wandered around, had a cup of coffee – looked at things – I enjoyed it – it was a sociable occasion.' 'Sometimes I wander around with girls from the office – I don't generally buy anything – they don't spend either usually because it's a sociable occasion – not a spending occasion – we chat about things, look at things.' 'When I really want to do a lot of buying I don't like to be with other people – I like to get my business done – not dawdle around. But when I just want to look more then I like being with other people.'

Comparison Shopping

Some women deliberately choose to shop now with a view to purchasing later. Shopping is part of the evaluation stage of the buying process for deliberative purchases such as clothing or high fidelity units. For the woman who buys her clothing once a season this form of shopping may be extended over a period of several weeks and shopping trips: 'Looking is part of definite buying.' 'At the moment I'm not looking because I can't buy yet.' 'It may take me three months to get one dress I want – so I look indiscriminately – intermittently I'll go into town until I find exactly what I want.' 'I am watching out for some material I want.' 'I work out what I need while I'm looking and then buy it.' 'Usually when looking at materials I have something in mind that I need.' 'With shoes I usually go around all the shops to see what there is first – comparing prices, colours, size, qualities and then buy later – it's easy to get around the shops in Palmerston North.' 'I never buy then, I always go home and think about it first.' 'If I'm intending to buy something I generally take a couple of days to look around – compare prices, assess things and then buy.' 'Sometimes I'll have a really good look around on Friday – decide what I've seen, what I will buy and then buy it on Tuesday.'

Other shoppers are more impulsive: 'I wander around the shops and perhaps I might see something I like – if I liked it I'd buy it – often just go into a shop – that's how I buy . . . my son wants me to go home when we've got everything but I'd rather have a wee look around – I just might see something.' 'I was always looking for clothes . . . I love buying clothes – always have the intention if I see something I'll buy it!' 'Generally I'm just looking at clothes shops because I like clothes – if I really fancy something then I intend to buy it.' 'Always looking so that if I see something I like I can put it on layby – have always got my cheque book.' 'Just looking in the shops – no intention to buy but I keep it in mind – I just decide to go into some shops and compare items and prices and keep it in mind.' 'Sometimes gone to look in a particular shop (such as a second-hand one) with no intention to buy, but you just want to have a look – hoping you'll find a real bargain or find something interesting.' 'If I'm in C & C I might look in another department because I have an account there.' 'In a store that has a children's department I always go to that department just to have a look.'

Shopping as a Special Occasion

Shopping is often used to enhance a special occasion or may, from time to time, be a special event in its own right: 'Shopping is part of the holiday fun.' 'A day to be shopping if it's grotty.' Of course, not everyone agrees . . . 'I only go shopping if there's some reputed shop in that area – otherwise I can't be bothered.' Holiday shopping is often particularly enjoyable: 'In Australia, with my daughter, I just shop, shop, shop because it's a different aspect.' 'Everything is bigger, brighter and better.' 'You see things you never see at home.' 'I enjoy looking at what I think is different merchandise – I think it's just the different layout of the shop that appeals.' 'Other places have different things – I go into art shops – not to buy but to see what types of things are produced up there.' 'I usually go into different types of shops than normal – it's just an interest thing.' 'When people visited us up North we'd take them somewhere to look specifically at craft shops that the area specialises in.' 'It's fascinating seeing some things.' Holiday shopping is often enjoyed because it can be done at a leisurely pace: 'When you're on holiday you're not exposed to any time factor, so you can make your own time for shopping – spend the whole day if you want to.' 'It's more relaxed – usually you're on a holiday feeling.' 'Can spend hours browsing – not in a hurry to go anywhere.' 'Likely to drift in and out of shops.' 'I browse, I look – I love poking around in craft shops.' Other special shopping occasions are when a new store opens or when a trip is made to a new shopping area.

SUMMARY AND CONCLUSIONS

Shopping behaviour is not necessarily caused by the need to acquire products. There are many other motives for making that shopping trip. Whilst Tauber's eleven categories of motive have been couched in sociological or psychological language, we decided that rather than translate verbatim statements of the interviewees into such terminology we would keep strictly to the language they used to describe their behaviour. Consequently, the eight reasons for shopping are:

1. To kill time.
2. To relax, exercise and be stimulated.
3. A reflection of temperament.
4. To acquire information.
5. To take advantage of proximity to the shops when a trip has been made for some other purpose.
6. To enjoy shopping as a social event.
7. To compare alternatives.
8. To enhance, or actually be, a special occasion.

All of the quotations extracted from the tapes can be fitted into Tauber's classification. However, three of Tauber's hypothesised motives did not emerge in any of our interviews. These were communication with others with a similar interest, opportunity to command attention and respect, and to obtain pleasure from bargaining.

A dimension of this last motive is price and product comparison, a common activity for our sample. New Zealanders believe they live in an egalitarian society without rigidly defined class barriers, so it is perhaps not surprising that shoppers do not regard shopping as a way to enhance a need for authority. Whilst not one member of our sample mentioned the enjoyment of talking to others with similar interests, it is clear that many took pleasure in shopping for interest items such as books or sports gear.

What is the significance of these findings for retailers? Clearly, they must realise that shoppers have many reasons for making these shopping trips; retailers could learn to motivate shopping by satisfying non-purchase needs and then apply merchandising techniques to persuade shoppers to buy. There is, therefore, a two-stage process involved: first, attract shoppers to the store or trading area; second, persuade them to part with their money.

A thorough discussion of merchandising techniques is available elsewhere [Buttle, forthcoming] so we shall now offer some ideas to retailers to attract shoppers. Through satisfying non-purchase needs, retailers can, co-operatively or individually, obtain a competitive advantage that product-orientated retailers could not easily emulate:

1. Set aside an area for the display of new products so that those who want to keep up to date with current trends can do so.
2. Run demonstrations, events, competitions, fashion shows, tastings, etc.
3. Provide refreshment facilities for snacks, drinks and meals.
4. Provide children's play areas.
5. Install seating for 'people-watchers'.
6. Locate specialist retailers and services in a trading area with general stores.
7. Display inter-store price comparisons to appeal to the 'professional' shopper.
8. Show films or tape slides.
9. Devise 'scenic walks', 'historic walks' and 'interest walks' (past retail outlets, of course).
10. Construct external and internal displays to appeal to the senses. Use mobiles and bright colours. Disperse cooking, baking and roasting odours into the most heavily populated pedestrian areas.
11. Allow customers the opportunity to touch – especially important for clothing and fruit/vegetable lines.
12. Employ expert staff to deal with knowledgeable customers. This is already being done by sports and motor accessory dealers.
13. Run community interest events and meetings.
14. Build related-item displays which show how new lines fit into existing life-styles. This is especially important for fashion items.
15. Extract maximum promotional mileage from special shopping events such as mother's day and Easter. Invent others such as 'handyman day' when all retailers carrying home-improvement lines run specials.
16. Build open-air relaxation areas with trees, shrubs, tables, flowers, etc., so that lunch becomes a sensory delight.
17. Promote cut-price lunches to offices and factories with plenty of potential for lunch-time shopping. Do this on pay-day.

18. Advertise in or around banks, post offices, libraries, pubs, coffee bars, cinemas to attract those in town on some non-shopping errand.
19. Use souvenirs, curios and craft displays to appeal to holiday makers. Promote round-the-town trips for tourists to become acquainted with the shopping facilities available. Promote through hotels, motels and camp sites.
20. Display non-food lines in grocery areas to reduce the tedium of grocery shopping. Also, run other in-store attractions and on-the-spot prizes for lucky shoppers.

POSTSCRIPT

The primary objective for the research, which was to satisfy the curiosity of the authors, was achieved. More significantly, however, the department store executive whom we were trying to convince of the benefits of Saturday trading agreed that there was good evidence to support our contention that there was more to shopping than simply making purchases. He agreed to a trial period of weekend trading and took on a merchandising specialist to create the in-store environment necessary to produce sales from the traffic he expected to generate from activating non-purchase motives in his customers.

REFERENCES

Tauber, E. M. 1972, 'Why do people shop?', *Journal of Marketing*, Vol. 36, October.
Buttle, F. A., forthcoming, 'Merchandising', *European Journal of Marketing*.

This chapter first appeared in *The Service Industries Journal*, Vol.4, No.1 (1984).

14
Shopping Motives Constructionist Perspective

FRANCIS BUTTLE

Some twenty years ago the Journal of Marketing *published an article by Edward Tauber entitled 'Why do people Shop?', which hypothesised that shopping trips were not always related to the purchase of goods, and that a number of other social and personal motives account for shopping behaviour. This article is an updated replication of Tauber's study but was conducted under an explicitly different set of metatheoretical assumptions from those implicit in Tauber's 1972 piece. Tauber's basic findings are corroborated but significantly developed in this replication, which is grounded on constructionist rather than positivistic assumptions. Accordingly, motives are defined not as internalised states but as descriptive or ascriptive accounts of some contextualised act, expressed in terms of prefigurative or practical logical force.*

Three key findings distinguish this article from the earlier one. First, people account for their shopping behaviour in terms of logical force. Shopping trips are made both as a result of prefigurative causes and for practical reasons. Second, motives for shopping are not personal attributes or general orientations. People account for their shopping behaviour in a number of ways which are incompatible with the notion of a general orientation towards shopping. Finally, motives for shopping are contextualised. People contextualise the shopping experience before offering motivational accounts. Since shopping is contextualised in different ways shopping motives are also contextualised. The context markers which are cited most often are life-script, life-style, episode (product class), relationships, gender and location. Motives can therefore be thought of as structured in some way around the realities of lived experience, rather than being abstract internalised potentialities.

In 1972, the *Journal of Marketing* carried an article by Edward Tauber entitled 'Why do People Shop?'

Twenty years after publication, this article is still cited in contemporary texts of consumer or buying behaviour as a seminal piece of work which offers insight into shopping motives [Engel, Blackwell and Miniard 1986; Assael 1984]. The article 'hypothesises that peoples' motives for shopping are a function of many variables, some of which are unrelated to the actual buying of products'. Tauber hypothesises six personal motives for shopping (role playing, diversion, learning about new trends, self-gratification, physical activity and sensory stimulation), and five social motives (social experiences outside the home, communiation with others having a similar interest, peer group attraction, status and authority, and pleasure of bargaining).

The world of the 1990s is not the same as the world of 1972. There have been many demographic, social and retailing changes. This modified replication of Tauber's work was originally prompted by the question: what is the descriptive or explanatory power of Tauber's hypotheses in contemporary American society? It certainly seemed possible that these changes could have impacted upon opportunities to shop, the role of shopping in community and personal life and the character of the 'shopping experience'.

America has changed. The population is growing. Its people are also ageing, divorcing, and establishing more households. The American of the 1990s is much more likely to live outside the nuclear family context than the American of the 1960s. Simultaneously, retailing is changing: there are fewer, but larger stores per unit of population; retail power is concentrated in fewer hands; America has been malled; downtown has lost much of its attraction. The forecast to the year 2000 for both population and retailing is more of the same. A fuller statistical account of these historical changes and forecasts is available in an earlier unpublished working paper [Buttle, 1989].

RESEARCH METHOD

Tauber's Assumptions and Method

The research method chosen for this replication differs considerably from Tauber's original. Since his article neither articulated his assumptions nor fully explained his method, he was telephone interviewed at his Arizona home.

To Tauber's knowledge, no one had updated or repeated his shopping motives inquiry.[1] Although he had saved none of the original data, he was able to recall details of the research design, sampling method, interview protocol, data-recording method and analytical procedures.

He moderated two focus group interviews to confirm his suspicion that people made shopping trips for reasons other than buying merchandise. Thirty personal interviews were then conducted in which specific motives were sought. A convenience sample of adult residents of Binghampton, NY, comprised his interviewees. No quota controls were applied. The sampling unit was the individual.

Tauber employed no interview protocol. His general procedure was to ask his sample to describe their behaviour whilst last visiting Binghampton shopping mall. From these behavioural descriptions he extracted the 11 hypothetical shopping motives. He neither recorded on tape, nor took notes during the interviews. He simply interviewed each sample member and, during the course of the interview 'translated' the self-reported behaviours into motives. Data analysis was therefore contiguous with data collection.

Although Tauber's article does not make them explicit, a number of ontological and epistemological assumptions appear to ground his research.

Ontological Assumptions

People have motives. These motives are internalised and may be subconscious, so people may not be aware of why they stop. A finite array of independent personal and social motives account for shopping and other behaviour. Tauber wrote: 'Considerable progress has been achieved in identifying *the* behavioral dimensions of buying . . . Less is known about *the* determinants of consuming and shopping . . .' (emphases added). In opting for the internalisation explanation, Tauber failed to acknowledge the role of culture or social organisation in defining roles. He claims, for example, that 'grocery shopping is a customary activity of the housewife', without noting that social custom may have determined personal practice. It was because motives were thought to be internalised that Tauber resorted to depth interviews.

Epistemological Assumptions

According to Tauber, the principal task of consumer researchers is to establish universal laws of consumer behaviour. The aim is 'grand theory' in the tradition of the natural sciences. In this endeavour, quantitative research is preferable to qualitative research. Tauber wrote: 'A unified theory of shopper behaviour does not presently exist. This exploratory study has sought to advance the development of such a theory.' Furthermore, 'future research should attempt to quantify the relative importance of these motives'.

Constructionist Assumptions and Method

This replication proceeds from the assumption that people live in a social world which is co-created in interaction with others. From the constructionist perspective, persons can be thought of as both products and producers of their social world. Any one person stands at a particular map-reference with respect to a multiplicity of social systems. For example, a career-oriented married woman may find herself variably enmeshed in a working-class family history, a middle-class marriage between professionals, an organisation which affords freedom of expression, and a dominant culture in which the individual is privileged more than the community, to cite but a few systems. Each of these systems may construe shopping in different ways, so it is quite conceivable that shopping has paradoxical meanings for the woman. Potential for disorder is the norm, since these systems may inhibit, proscribe, afford or compel certain actions.

A constructionist investigation such as this proceeds from three basic premises. First, social reality is real for those who live within it. Second, objects in the social world are less notable for their tangible character than for the meanings they have for people. Third, meanings are expressed in social action, such as talk. In the words of Pearce and Cronen [1980: 305]: 'Communication is the link between the particular social world persons inhibit and the human condition of being variably enmeshed in multiple systems each with its own logic of meaning and action.' To access those logics and locate individuals within or amongst them, a new approach to doing research is necessary, one which privileges meanings.

A constructionist critique of Tauber's work would be based on the grounds that motives are evident in the talk and social practices of individuals in a community. Motives are not internalised and hidden, but acted and expressed.

The research design for this replication is consistent with the constructionist perspective.[2]

Research Objective

The research objective was to produce a (new?) understanding of the place of shopping in contemporary American life, grounded in a constructionist perspective. This exploratory research focuses on the meanings that shopping has for people and the relationships between shopping and other dimensions of a social life.

Sampling Plan and Data Collection

It is a fundamental constructionist assumption that meanings are the product of social relationships in which communication is the primary productive process. Therefore, each sampling unit consists of at least two persons who live in each other's communication. In all cases, the sampling unit consisted of adult members of households. A sample of ten families from the Amherst area, in Massachusetts, was interviewed in their homes.

In constructionist research, as in qualitative research generally, sampling is usually non-random. Random sampling is necessary only if inferences are to be made about the larger population from which the sample is drawn. Constructionist researchers attempt to make intelligible to system outsiders the social reality which is 'common-sense' to native system insiders. Social constructionists model persons as self-monitoring rule developers, not mechanical law followers. Household members co-create their own rules (i.e., logics of meaning and action) which are potentially dissimilar to the rules of other households. Since system members co-create their own rules of meaning and action, inferential statistics are not employed. Sampling is therefore purposive and no inferences are drawn about the larger population. Social constructionists opt for depth, rather than breadth.

Interviews were conducted until no new meanings were being generated. The indication that a wide – if not full – array of meanings has been accessed was to be that no further meanings were generated in two successive interviews, the ninth and tenth.

DATA COLLECTION

Data were collected in a series of personal interviews with adult members of each household. In each intervention, two adult members were co-interviewed simultaneously. Interviews were recorded on cassette tape. Three forms of questions were asked – lineal questions, circular questions and reflexive questions [Thom 1988].[3] Lineal questions which are based upon a linear, cause-and-effect logic are investigative; for example, when you arrived at the Mall, what was the first thing you did? Circular questions are grounded in systemic or cybernetic thinking and are exploratory; for example, why do you think your husband bought the paint and brushes at Aubuchon? Reflexive questions acknowledge that the interviewer becomes a part of the system which is co-creating meanings with the interviewees. Reflexive questions are facilitative in the sense that they are formulated so as to bring about new ways of thinking; for example, 'if you couldn't do your grocery shopping on a Thursday evening, what would you do?' The interview protocol used both Tauber's original work and Pearce and Cronen's [1980] *Coordinated Management of Meaning* (CMM) to help frame some of the questions.

The interviews were conducted as follows: (1) The interviewer identified the 'system in focus' before commencing more detailed questioning. (2) Questions were specific, neutral and open-ended. (3) Responses were confirmed. (4) Questions focused on particular episodes and progressed in small steps. (5) Opening questions were lineal and factual. Later questions became circular and reflexive, as they focused on relationships between people in the system and the role of shopping in those relationships. (6) The interviewer attempted to identify context markers for the meaning of shopping, and the prefigurative and practical forces which account for shopping action.

Prefigurative logical force is 'synonymous with the general usage of 'I did that because of . . . ', whereas practical logical force is synonymous with 'I did that in order to . . .'. In the former case action is explained as driven by external events or conditions, whereas the latter models people as purposive agents [Pearce and Cronen, 1980 : 164]. This conception of logical force is critical to the question of motivation. Both types of logical force permit persons to account for their action, and enable observers to infer causes and reasons.

DATA ANALYSIS

Taped interviews equivalent to more than 100 pages of single-spaced transcripts were content-analysed. Content analysis focused on the following three questions.

> What are the key symbols or terms used in talk about shopping? In this paper I have reported those which are repeated, recurrent patterns in the talk of participants in these interviews; those which are widely intelligible; those which are more fully elaborated; and those which appear to be subject to cultural or local systemic rules [see Ortner, 1973; Carbaugh, 1987].

> Do people account for their shopping trips in terms of prefigurative or practical force?

> Are there context-specific variances in the meanings attributed to, and motives which account for, shopping?

Implicit in these issues is a reworking of the construct 'motive'. In general use, motive is thought of as 'a consideration or emotion that excites to action' [Chambers, 1983]. The term has also been appropriated by psychologists and has taken on language-game specific sets of meanings.

In this article I take a different view of motive, one which does not privilege the Cartesian view of personhood. In other words, I attempt to escape the notion that we are all autonomous individuals; rather, we are persons enmeshed in multiple systems which are co-created, maintained and modified in concert with others. Such a perspective disempowers the concept of mind, and its corollory that motives are mental states. Instead, consistent with the observations made earlier that motives are not internalised and hidden, but acted and expressed, I offer the following constructionist definition of motive.

> Motives are *accounts* of some *contextualised act*, expressed in terms of *prefigurative or practical logical force*.

By this definition, motives are descriptions or ascriptions; these de/ascriptions are context-specific, although amenable to employment across contexts; and they are expressed as causes or reasons. This reconceptualisation of motive is quite different from that implicit in Tauber's work.

FINDINGS

There are three principle findings:

1. People account for their shopping behaviour in terms of both prefigurative and practical force;
2. Motives for shopping are not personal attributes. This investigation identified multiple motives for shopping. In other words, people are capable of accounting for their shopping behaviour in a number of ways, and at times in ways which are incompatible with the notion of a general orientation towards shopping; and
3. Motives for shopping are contextualised. People contextualise the shopping experience prior to offering motivational accounts. Since shopping is contextualised in different ways shopping motives are also contextualised.

These findings are now discussed in greater detail.

Finding 1: People account for their shopping behaviour both in terms of prefigurative and practical force.

Prefigurative force operates when people account for their action by reference to external conditions being motivational forces. Al and Cindy, for example, explained their joint decision to shop for a truck bus:

> *Al*: We've discussed it a couple of times; casually you know – the truck is getting quite small for the three of us and maybe twice it has been mentioned and then we went down and bought it.
> *Cindy*: And Rachel couldn't be seatbelted either if all three of us were in the vehicle. Rachel couldn't be seatbelted, so it almost made it like we. . . . it necessary until waiting until maybe it was financially better to do so.

The shopping trip to buy the truck did not occur until external events compelled action. The critical moment was Rachel's birth, and the expansion of the household from two to three members.

In Paul and Ellen's household, Paul does most of the shopping, but it was not always this way. Prefigurative force accounts for Paul's more frequent shopping trips these days, as the following opening sequence shows.

> *Interviewer*: First things first – who does most of the shopping in this household?
> *Ellen*: At this point in time, Paul does.
> *I*: Paul does? Has it always been this way?
> *E*: No. The last two years
> *I*: Circumstances have changed?
> *E*: I got ill – he took over and I just let him continue taking over.

Practical force also accounts for shopping acts. Practical force operates when persons account for their actions in terms of agency, or wanting to achieve some future state.

Anne, of Anne and Ed's household, explains that she goes plant and clothes shopping because she wants to achieve aesthetic effects:

> *Anne*: . . . the sense of being able to plant them outdoors and being able to picture what's going to happen in design or whatever . . . there's a lot more to plant shopping that's aesthetic, and probably clothes shopping. There's more of the aesthetic involved in the making yourself look better.

Paul, of Paul and Ellen's household, gives another perspective on practical force:

> *Interviewer*: Now, Paul, how does the shopping trip when you're

on your own differ from when you're with Ellen.

P: I'll poke through lots of things that I don't necessarily want to buy – I just want to find out about.

I: In particular areas? Particular products that you're interested in?

P: Yeah. I like Chinese food. Ellen's not fond of that at all.

Paul makes shopping trips to inform himself about merchandise of particular interest to him. He is motivated to achieve some future state of product knowledge. Clearly, then, both practical force and prefigurative force account for shopping action.

Finding 2: People account for their shopping behaviour in a number of ways, and at times in ways which are incompatible with the notion of a general orientation towards shopping.

Kari and Steve account for their own and each other's shopping by reference to six different motives. Ed and Anne refer only to three motives. The interview with Walt and Diane produced eight shopping motives, which they attributed to themselves, each other, and generalised other persons.

Perhaps more significantly, within each household system the shopping motives of persons were sometimes accounted for in terms which were quite inconsistent. Al and Cindy provide an illustration. Asked about his feelings about shopping, Al said: 'I don't even do my clothes shopping – she bought me a new coat, a pair of pants, some shorts last week. I don't . . . At this point Cindy interjected emphatically: 'He hates it!' Al chuckled and nodded in agreement, saying he'd rather stay at home and watch TV. However, later on in the interview, Al talked enthusiastically and at length about shopping for fishing equipment. He was clearly excited and found shopping for this class of product stimulating and pleasurable.

Early in another interview, Carolyn and Bill described Bill's feelings about shopping. Bill does not shop; he 'hates being indoors'. Carolyn does all of the shopping. Later, however, Bill began to wax lyrical about shopping with his granddaughter. They hold hands, walk at leisure around stores, pick up merchandise, talk about it and sometimes buy it.

The evidence from this research is that people do not have a general orientation towards shopping. Therefore, there is not a single set of motives which account for a person's shopping trips. As intimated in these last few paragraphs, shopping motives are contextualised.

Finding 3: Motives for shopping are contextualised.

People's motives for shopping are manifold. The accounts of the pre-

figurative causes of, and practical reasons for, shopping are highly
varied. Shopping is a contextualised act. Shopping is not merely shopping. Shopping trips are made in a variety of contexts: the motives for
shopping for gifts are not the same as the motives for shopping for groceries; neither is shopping on vacation the same as shopping at home;
neither are the motives for shopping alone as the motives for shopping
in company.

In this section of the article, I offer a taxonomy of context markers
which account for most of the variance in shopping motives. Note that
there are no conclusions about the structure of the taxonomy; there is
no assumption of hierarchical ordering, nor of independence.

Descriptions of practical and prefigurative force varied according to
the following context markers:

> Life-script
> Lifestyle
> Episode
> Relationships
> Gender
> Location

Life-script

Life-script refers to the characteristic 'me-ness' of a person, or, as
defined by Cronen, Pearce and Tomm [1985: 206], ' a person's conception of self in social action'. Although none of the systems
investigated claimed that shopping was a model or central component of
their own life-scripting, many claimed that they knew of others for
whom shopping was a significant scene in which life-scripting was enacted. Indeed, there were references to people who 'live to shop'. Trish,
of Gino and Trish's household, talked of a girlfriend of hers – Marilyn.
Asked whether her shopping habits were simply a reflection of her
wealth, Trish commented:

> I think there was more to it. I think there was an emotional thing
> to it . . . in my experience with women, I don't know many men
> who live to shop . . . Marilyn and other women that I know of live
> to shop because they were depressed or there was something else
> in their life, they don't have much control and they want to be
> happy, so they were, like, obsessed with it.

Whereas some people seem to find their 'sense of value' or 'self worth'
from shopping, others find that shopping is a positive challenge to life-
scripting. Ellen, of Paul and Ellen's household, explained her loathing

of shopping thus: 'It's just me!' Anne, from the Ed and Anne house-hold, explained that they would rather be 'doing some sort of outdoor activity' or, Ed added, 'playing with the kids'. They made these observations which indicate that shopping is antithetical to their life-script:

> *Ed*: . . . in other things the emphasis is on nature or, you know, something that is in a way – I think – has more meaning than consumer goods.
> *Anne*: Yeah, I feel kind of empty in the malls.
> *Ed*: It's kind of an artificial environment.

For this household, shopping was a 'distasteful chore'. Shopping has the potential to supply a series of interactive episodes in which life-scripting is defined. Taken as a whole, these episodes may enable 'a recognition of "this is me" or "this is something I would do"' [Pearce and Cronen, 1980: 136]. For Ellen, Ed and Anne, the contrary is true. Shopping supplies a series of episodes which produces a 'this is *not* me' life-scripting. Life-scripting connects to motives by providing an overarching context within which the causes of, and reasons for, individual shopping episodes maybe accounted for. Life-scripting enables people to claim: 'I am the sort of person who shops because. . . . ' Life-scripting supplies a kernel of permanence to the interactive self.

Lifestyle

Lifestyle does not have the permanence of life-script. Lifestyle can be defined as a 'pattern of living the world as expressed in the person's activities, interests and opinions' [Kotler, 1988: 182–3]. Lifestyle describes how a person interacts with his or her environment, rather than a characteristic 'me-ness'. Whereas lifestyles change as, say, a person becomes more affluent, life-scripts tend to be less malleable.

The evidence of this research is that shopping fits into lifestyle in a number of ways. Shopping may be an activity or interest which is an integral component of lifestyle. Equally, opinions about shopping may be thought of as an expression of lifestyle.

Paul and Ellen are retired. Paul is a former woodwork teacher in high school. He loves to potter, or as he puts it, to 'poke around' in stores. It's part of the retirement lifestyle for this couple. This exchange between Paul and Ellen tells the story:

> *Ellen*: You've done a lot more shopping since you retired.
> *Paul*: Well, yeah, because I've had more time. There's no doubt about it.

Cindy and Al are strapped for cash and time. Cindy is a student mother.

Al is a working father. They live in a rented apartment and are saving hard for their own home. Generally, they are careful, frugal shoppers who, like many other people, are prone to making what they think of retrospectively as bad errors of judgement in shopping. They told a story about buying bulk meat at what they thought was a low price:

> *Cindy*: . . . I was pregnant and it was almost my due time and I was very concerned about having everything here. I just wanted to be able to come home with the baby and food on hand and not to have to shop a lot . . .
>
> *Al*: We realised that we needed the meat and . . .
>
> *Cindy*: plus my freezer was empty.

The meat purchase turned out to be unsatisfactory. Careful, price-conscious shopping is part of their lifestyle. Furthermore, they shop ethically. Cindy said: 'I don't buy disposable diapers and even when we go on vacation I don't want to use them.' Shopping fits into their lifestyle by providing an opportunity to demonstrate their values, and by supplying a much-needed source of cheap entertainment. In Cindy's words:

> When we have more money again, I'll probably be able to go out clothes shopping again; and that will be the fun shopping, and grocery shopping will be back to its mundane weekly thing. . . . Right now I enjoy grocery shopping.

Betty and David are empty-nesters whose children live away from home. They are better off financially now than when the children were at home. As their lifestyle has changed due to family circumstances, so has the place of shopping.

> *Betty*: . . . we went through a whole period where after being poor we started buying too much and it sort of went against what we decided as a couple when we were first married we wanted to do – you know, we wanted to have things pretty simple and it really got out of hand there. And about five years ago we made a conscious decision to go back to what we had originally decided to do when we were first married.
>
> *Interviewer*: So shopping is really – in a sense – a denial of the sorts of values which you try to live up to now? You started off with those values?
>
> *Betty*: Yeah.

Lifestyle, therefore, is a context marker against which motives vary. Paul is motivated to shop as a means of meeting other people; otherwise he would lead a more isolated, homebound life. Betty and David have adjusted their shopping to fit their lifestyle values. Cindy shops not only because it enables an enactment of lifestyle choices, but because it supplies entertainment. She described shopping for a big-ticket item as 'important' and 'exciting'. Indeed, in keeping with such high emotion, Cindy reported that she and Al *'fell in love* with it [a truck] when we saw it'.

Episode

Shopping is episodic. Episodes are sequences of acts which are viewed by actors as distinct wholes. Typically, episodes were defined by respondents along product class dimensions. All of the systems researched discriminated between different sorts of shopping. The three most common categories of episode are shopping for groceries and household items, clothing and gifts. Grocery and household shopping is generally thought of as a pleasureless chore which has to be done (prefigurative force). Ellen explained her feelings about grocery shopping with venom in her voice:

> . . . I did for so many years – but then I reached a point it was like saturation – I was just sick of doing it. I said to him [Paul], I could easily live like Jackie Onassis and go to a different restaurant every night of the week – I was just so sick of trying to plan inexpensive meals for every night of the week for so many years – and I think all of this comes into place – not wanting to look at another coupon and all this kind of . . . Stuff the comparison.

Not all the interviewees agree. Paul (Ellen's husband), Gino of Gino and Trish's household and Cindy, of Cindy and Al's household, all said that they enjoyed grocery shopping. Paul enjoys poking around in deli sections; Gino is developing an interest in food; Cindy is so busy at home with her family and at school with her studies that her fortnightly grocery shopping is a welcome break.

Clothes shopping is more attractive to most people. It is an opportunity for self-expression, fantasy, a break from the normal routine of shopping, and perhaps a little self-indulgence. Trish described her clothes shopping with great glee:

> . . . sometimes window shopping is just enjoyable – you know – dreaming . . . going into a fancy store and trying on things that cost $300 and you know you can't . . . but you do it anyway because you're all alone and nobody knows – that's enjoyable to me. Not necessarily buying something.

Again, there are exceptions: Al, Walt and Bill rarely do any of their own clothes shopping, let alone shop for clothes for other members of their households.

Episodes of gift shopping are described in the most favourable terms. Putting time and effort into buying something which will delight a loved one seems to produce the greatest satisfaction.[4] Practical logical force seems to be at its strongest. Persons make gift shopping trips in order to achieve some purpose: they want to say I like you, I love you, I am sorry, I am proud of you. Walt and Diane, and especially Diane, obtain great pleasure from showing how much they care for others.

Shopping episodes are context markers because they are perceived as being distinctively variable. Not all shopping episodes are the same. Neither do similar episodes have similar meanings for different shoppers. Whereas one person may be motivated to shop for groceries out of a sense of obligation to other household members; another may shop for groceries in order to meet with other people.

Relationships

Motives for shopping also vary at a relational level. This is not just to claim that the motives for shopping alone may differ from the motives for shopping with a significant other, with siblings, friends or as a family group. Consideration must also be given to the persons for whom the shopping trip is undertaken. The motives for 'shopping with' are not the same as those for 'shopping for'.

Anne, of the Anne and Ed household, commented:

> With Ed, actually when we shop together there's usually tension so I don't enjoy it because of that – we always see things differently . . . we generally don't see eye to eye. We argue the whole time we are shopping.

When different persons are involved the feelings are different. Anne:

> . . . I would say that I enjoy it more – shopping with a sibling. I don't enjoy shopping with a friend because of the tension involved but with a sibling I can enjoy it.

Cindy commented favourably about shopping with a friend, that it was more like an 'outing'.

> I picked up my friend Beth, coz she's home pretty much all day with her child too, so its kind of like an outing and we went in and grabbed a cart . . .

Ellen, who is mother to four grown boys, endorses the problems of shopping with family members:

I could not bring myself to take off even half the kids when I went shopping. That just boggled my mind. It just doesn't make any sense. I saw too many people getting mad at the kids and screaming and everything else, so I waited until they went to bed. He'd (nodding at Paul) babysit and I'd do the grocery shopping.

Notwithstanding the problems of shopping with four young children (oldest 10 years, youngest 6 months), Ed and Anne do take their children on occasional shopping trips. This is a positive attempt to socialise their offspring. As Ed comments: 'I think shopping is part of life . . . so that's sort of an opportunity to share that experience . . .'. He also finds that shopping with children serves to bind the family together; it is an activity which all the family can share.

Clearly, shopping with others can be a pleasure or pain. If painful, it seems reasonable to assume a powerful prefigurative force compelling action. If pleasurable practical force would appear more significant.

The issue of the shopper's relationship to others not necessarily present also accounts for some of the variance in shopping motives. Shopping for gifts for other loved ones is generally spoken of as a pleasurable experience, although the crowds at festival times such as Christmas are thought to diminish the pleasure somewhat. Bill, of Carolyn and Bill's household, was amongst the more extreme interviewees in his distaste of shopping, but he found enormous satisfaction both in shopping with, and in shopping for, his granddaughter. It was not a pleasure he was able to explain articulately – even to himself – but his bright and animated talk expressed his feelings clearly. Diane, of Walt and Diane's household, works part-time but spends some of her leisure time shopping for others -possibly more than all the others interviewed. She has a close and affectionate family. Shopping for gifts is a way to express that closeness; indeed, it is an enactment which reconstitutes that closeness. She spoke warmly of seeing the pleasure on the faces of family members as they opened her gifts.

Shopping also provides an opportunity for social interaction.

> *Ellen*: . . . I think part of it is because if he [Paul] stops and starts talking to someone, and I really don't want to start talking, I just kind of turn my direction and I just go right on with what else we have to pick up . . . I think this is just me – when I go shopping I don't particularly want to stand in an aisle for half an hour when I know I have another half to three-quarters of an hour's shopping to do . . .
> *Paul*: It's much more so for me.
> *Ellen*: . . . If we go down to the mall and we are just kind of poking

around . . . I'll stand there and chat and everything else, but if I have a specific list, like for food or something like this . . . I just want to get it all done and get out.

Bill and Carolyn noted a lot of youngsters 'hang out' at the mall, meeting at the roller-skating rink, cafés or music store. A lot of university students seem to assemble in town, at bars of cafés. Paul and Ellen also noted that shopping is a solution to being housebound, especially for older people during the long winter months. Equally, it could be an air-conditioned relief from the humid mid-summer heat of their houses.

Relationships, therefore, serve as a context marker against which shopping motives vary. A shopping episode may be used to affirm relationships, socialise children, meet others, demonstrate affection or perform a perceived duty towards others.

Gender

Egalitarian households notwithstanding, only one of the systems investigated, that of Paul and Ellen, featured a male doing most of the shopping, and this only because of Ellen's recent illness. Shopping is still a scene in which the female is dominant. Although none of the females claimed that they thought of shopping as a female activity, a number of males expressed the view that shopping was for women. The following exchange illustrates the point well:

> *Interviewer*: . . . you enjoy shopping for groceries?
> *Cindy*: Right now I enjoy grocery shopping.
> *I*: Al, does that surprise you?
> *Al*: No, it's really not . . . women like to shop more than men. I'll go into a store and I'll go in and get what I want and leave. If I go into a store with her, I'll go get what I want and be ready to go, and she'll say: 'no, I'm shopping.' And want to be there for another hour. She may not buy anything but she wants to shop.

Walt, of Walt and Diane's household, took a similar view, but expressed a sheepish guilt about his opinion.

Shopping, then, is a scene in which sex-role orientations are enacted. In this research men reported shopping, but with less frequency. They could be described as specialist-shoppers. They shop for insurance, fishing equipment, camping gear, yard (outdoor) goods. One motive for shopping appears to be that it enables sex-role orientations to be enacted and reconstituted. It is as if men say: 'one thing which makes men men is that they do not shop.' Women did not make any similar claim.

Location

Shopping motives vary by location. Uproot a family from their home, move them to a different location, and different shopping behaviours are likely to be performed.

Ellen, who had previously expressed a loathing for shopping and a dislike of Paul's custom of 'poking' around in stores, was asked whether shopping on vacation was different from shopping at home. 'Oh yeah'. she said, 'just to poke along and look at what they've got – you're in no rush. We don't have to hurry to get anywhere. . . . When on vacation, who cares? I'm not in any hurry to get anywhere.'

For Anne and Ed with their young family, vacation shopping is quite different – less tense and more fun.

> *Ed*: . . . on vacation we'd all go grocery shopping or something like that.

Interviewer: Do you think of that as an outing for the children, or do children respond as if it is . . .
Ed: Yeah.
Anne: Yeah, that can be fun.

Even cash-strapped Cindy and Al act differently on vacation:

> *Cindy*: When we're on vacation we shop together and that makes it different – you know, like we go grocery shopping together – it's definitely different. It's not the same as grocery shopping when we're home.
> *Interviewer*: Different or not different? Do you like the difference?
> *Cindy*: Yeah, it's part of the vacation – like we buy things we normally wouldn't buy. You know, like cookies or something like that – for camping.

Paul, of Paul and Ellen's household, voiced a similar thought. Paul said: 'Well, part of it you – along when you're on vacation a certain amount of money that you have agreed is mad money – is not accountable money basically.'

Vacations are not the only locational changes which are accompanied by changing shopping behaviour. Walt, Diane and their teenage boys sometimes make day trips to the coast and enjoy visiting the factory outlets. When Diane drives out-of-state to visit her sisters they often go shopping together.

What is going on here? It seems that shopping fits into an everyday pattern of living in a particular way. If the pattern of living changes, the nature of shopping changes. What was once a chore becomes a pleasure.

Once routine, shopping becomes special. Shopping motives under changed locational contexts are more likely to reflect a practical force: the respondents talked of killing time, finding out what's new, enjoying the aesthetics of local crafts and souvenirs, enjoying the vacation atmosphere.

CONCLUSION

Shopping is not just shopping. It is constructed in talk in many varied ways. Neither does this research support the notion that there are a number of shopping motives held in cognitive isolation. The evidence is to the contrary. Shopping motives, expressed as prefigurative causes or practical reasons, are linked to particular shopping contexts. For example, motives for grocery shopping are not the same as those for gift shopping; neither are the motives for shopping on vacation the same as those for shopping at home. Furthermore, people are capable of living quite comfortably within a complex multi-dimensional matrix of apparently incompatible motives. Anne and Ed, whose family values are antithetical to shopping, conduct successful family shopping trips when vacationing. Al, described by his wife Cindy as hating shopping, expresses an innocent enthusiasm for shopping for fishing equipment. Walt, who has not even bought a pair of socks for himself in three years, will spend weeks shopping for an ideal present for his wife. Paul, who disliked grocery shopping whilst a working man, thoroughly enjoys it now retired. This is powerful evidence of there being no such phenomenon as a general orientation towards shopping; rather it supports the contention that shopping motives are structured around context markers. Six context markers, which account for the vast majority of motivational ascriptions or descriptions have been identified: life-script, lifestyle, episode (product class), relationships, gender and location.

NOTES

1. In fact, Buttle and Coates [1984], exploiting the same method as Tauber, produced a classification of shopping motives using the folk terms of their sample.
2. See Buttle [1991] for a review of the implications of social constructionism for consumer researchers.
3. A fourth class of questions – strategic questioning – was inappropriate to this investigation. The aim of strategic questioning is to facilitate change. It is much more likely to be encountered in therapeutic or counselling interviews.
4. Further research could determine the extent to which the time and effort diverted to gift-purchase is a cultural imperative.

REFERENCES

Assael, H. 1984, *Consumer Behavior & Marketing Action*, (2nd edition), Boston, MA: Kent.

Buttle, F. A., 1989, 'Why Do People Shop? A Constructionist Perspective', Unpublished Working Paper, Department of Hotel Restaurant and Travel Administration, university of Massachusetts/Amherst.

Buttle, F. A. 1991, 'Social Constructionist Consumer Research', *Marketing Education Group Annual Conference*, Cardiff, Wales.

Buttle, F. A. and Coates, M., 1984, 'Shopping Motives', *Service Industries Journal*, Vol. 4, No. 1, pp. 71–81.

Carbaugh, D., 1987, 'Communication Rules in Donahue Discourse.' *Research on Language and Social Interaction*, Vol. 21, pp. 31–61.

Chambers 20th Century Dictionary, 1983, Edinburgh: W. & R. Chambers.

Cronen, V. E., Pearce, W. B. and Tomm, K. 1985, 'A Dialectical View of Personal change', in K. J. Gergen and K. E. Davis (eds.), *Social Construction of the Person*, New York: Springer Verlag.

Engel, J. F., Blackwell, R. D. and Miniard, P. W. 1986, *Consumer Behavior*, (5th edition), New York, NY: Dryden Press.

Ortner, S. B., 1973, 'On Key Symbols', *American Anthropologist*, Vol. 75, pp. 1338–46.

Pearce, W. B. and Cronen, V. E., 1980, *Communication, Action and Meaning: The Creation of Social Realities*, New York, NY: Praeger.

Tauber, E. M., 1972, 'Why Do People Shop' *Journal of Marketing*, Vol. 30, October, pp. 46–72.

Thom, K. 1988, 'Interventive Interviewing: Part III. Intending to Ask Lineal, Circular, Strategic or Reflexive Questions?', *Family Process*, Vol. 27, No. 1, pp. 1–15.

This chapter first appeared in *The Service Industries Journal*, Vol.12, No.3 (1992).

Further Reading

Bolen, W.H., 1988, *Contemporary Retailing*, Englewood Cliffs, NJ: Prentice-Hall.

Cowell, D., 1984, *The Marketing of Services*, London: Heinemann.

Crimp, M., 1990, *The Marketing Research Process*, Englewood Cliffs, NJ: Prentice-Hall.

Davidson, W.R., D.J. Sweeney and R.W. Stampfl, 1984, *Retail Management*, New York: John Wiley.

Davies, G.J. and J.M. Brooks, 1989, *Positioning Strategy in Retailing*, London: Paul Chapman.

Foxall, G., 1984, *Marketing in the Service Industries*, London: Frank Cass.

Grönroos, C., 1990, *Service Marketing and Management*, Lexington, MA: Lexington Books.

Guy, C., 1980, *Retail Location and Retail Planning in Britain*, Farnborough: Gower Press.

Jobber, D., 1995, *Principles and Practice of Marketing*, London: McGraw-Hill.

Johnson, G. (ed.), 1987, *Business Strategy and Retailing*, Chichester: John Wiley.

Katz, B., 1987, *How to Manage Customer Service*, Aldershot: Gower.

Knee, D. and D. Walters, 1985, *Strategy in Retailing*, Oxford: Philip Allan.

Lovelock, C.H., 1991, *Services Marketing*, Englewood Cliffs, NJ: Prentice-Hall.

McGoldrich, P.J., 1990, *Retail Marketing*, London: McGraw-Hill.

Palmer, A., 1994, *Principles of Services Marketing*, London: McGraw-Hill.

Piercy, N., 1985, *Marketing Organisation: An Analysis of Information Processing, Power and Politics*, London: Allen and Unwin.

Piper, W.S. and L. M. Capella, 1993, 'Male Grocery Shoppers' Attitudes and Demographics', *International Journal of Retail and Distribution Management*, Vol. 21, No. 5.

Segal, M.N. and R.W. Giacobbe, 1994, 'Market Segmentation and Competitive Analysis for Supermarket Retailing', *International Journal of Retail and Distribution Management*, Vol. 22, No. 1.

Swindley, D.G., 1992, 'The Role of the Buyer in UK Multiple Retailing', *International Journal of Retail and Distribution Management*, Vol. 20, No. 2.

Walters, D., 1989, *Strategic Retailing Management*, London: Prentice Hall.

Walters, D.W. and D. White, *Retail Marketing Management*, Basingstoke: Macmillan.

Zeithaml, V.A., A. Parasuraman and L.L. Berry, 1990, *Delivering Quality Service*, New York: Free Press.

Notes on Contributors

Gary Akehurst is at Portsmouth University Business School, Department of Business and Management, Locksway Road, Southsea, Hants PO3 8JF, UK.

Nicholas Alexander is in the School of Commerce and International Business, University of Ulster, Coleraine, Northern Ireland, BT52 1SA.

Stephen Brown is in the School of Commerce and International Business, University of Ulster, Coleraine, Northern Ireland, BT52 1SA.

Francis Buttle is at Manchester Business School, University of Manchester, Booth Street West, Manchester, M15 6PB, UK.

Donald Cowell is at the University of Central England, Business School, Perry Barr, Birmingham, B42 2SU, UK.

René G.J. Den Hertog is at Erasmus University Rotterdam, Tinbergen Institute, Oostmaaslaan 950-952, 3063 DM Rotterdam, The Netherlands.

Jim Forward is at the City University Business School, Natwest Centre for Franchise Research, London, UK.

Christina Fulop is at the City University Business School, Natwest Centre for Franchise Research, London, UK.

Gordon Greenley is at the University of Birmingham, Birmingham Business School, Edgbaston, Birmingham, B15 2TT, UK.

Graham Hooley is at the University of Bradford, Management Centre, Emm Lane, Bradford, BD9 4JL, West Yorkshire, UK.

Nigel Piercy is at the University of Wales College of Cardiff, Cardiff Business School, Aberconway Building, Colum Drive, Cardiff, CF1 3EU, UK.

David Shipley is at Trinity College, University of Dublin, School of Business Studies, Dublin 2, Eire.

Leigh Sparks is at the Institute for Retail Studies and School of Management, University of Stirling, Stirling, FK9 4LA, UK.

David Swindley is a consultant, formerly of Bournemouth University, Department of Service Industries, Poole, Dorset BH12 5XH, UK.

A. Roy Thurik is at Erasmus University, Centre for Advanced Small Business Economics, Rotterdam and EIM Small Business Research and Consultancy, PO Box 7001, 2701, AA Zoetermeer, The Netherlands.